GUNNERS' GLORY

MAINSTREAM SPORT

GUNNERS' GLORY

14 MILESTONES IN ARSENAL'S HISTORY

GRAHAM WEAVER

MAINSTREAM
PUBLISHING

EDINBURGH AND LONDON

For Amy, Maddie and Joey

First published as *12-0 To The Arsenal* in Great Britain in 1998 by
MAINSTREAM PUBLISHING COMPANY (EDINBURGH) LTD
7 Albany Street
Edinburgh EH1 3UG

ISBN 1 84018 667 4

This edition, 2002

A catalogue record for this book is available from the British Library

Typeset in Janson Text and Stone Print-Roman
Printed and bound in Great Britain by Cox & Wyman Ltd

CONTENTS

ACKNOWLEDGEMENTS

My thanks go to those people that have helped me in the writing of this book. I am especially grateful to Ben Marden; Bob Wilson; Pat Rice; Alan Smith and Richard Stubbs for their time, help and reminiscences; and to Ian Cook for his assistance.

Thank you to Souvenir Press for permission to quote from *Arsenal from the Heart* by Bob Wall; to Andre Deutsch for permission to quote from *The Glory and the Grief* by George Graham; and to Queen Anne Press for permission to quote from *Going Great Guns* by Kenny Sansom. I must also thank Mainstream Publishing for permission to quote from *My Story* by David O'Leary. I am particularly grateful to Camilla James for her help and to Bill Campbell for agreeing to publish the book.

To my fellow Gooners – Steve, Nick, Dave, Alan and Mark who have suffered and celebrated with me over the years – this is for you boys, hope you enjoy it. Thanks also to John Butler for his encouragement and advice and for pointing me in the right direction.

Special thanks to my family. To my Mum and Dad (thanks for taking me to Highbury all those years ago, Dad) and particularly to my wife Heather for her encouragement and understanding.

Finally I would like to thank all those at Arsenal Football Club, past and present, who made all these special moments possible – may there be many more. Come on you reds!

Chapter 1

THE FIRST TRIUMPH

FA Cup final
Arsenal v Huddersfield Town
Saturday, 26 April 1930

As the 'Roaring Twenties' ended and the 1930s began, Association Football in England was still very much a northern game; in its first 40 years no team south of Birmingham had won the league championship, and only Tottenham – in 1901 and 1921 – had won the FA Cup.

The most successful team of the decade had been Huddersfield Town. As well as winning the FA Cup in 1922 and reaching the final on two further occasions, they had achieved a hat trick of league championships between 1924 and 1926, and were runners-up in the following two seasons. In 1925, however, their manager, Herbert Chapman, was lured south by Arsenal – a club that had yet to win a single major honour.

Herbert Chapman was one of the greatest football visionaries of all time and he made revolutionary innovations both on and off the field of play – some of which are still evident at Highbury today: it was Chapman who persuaded the London Electric Railway to change the name of Gillespie Road underground station to Arsenal, and it was also his idea to erect a clock at what is now known as the Clock End at Highbury. Chapman realised the potential that the London club had and he was prepared to move from the most successful team in the country to a small struggling side in order to realise it.

On his arrival in London, Chapman announced that it would

take him five years to build his team, and in April 1930, almost exactly five years later, the still trophyless Arsenal reached the FA Cup final for only the second time in their history. The club was now only 90 minutes away from its first-ever major trophy but, ironically, the team that stood in the way was Chapman's old side, the mighty Huddersfield.

Every Arsenal fan knows that the club went on to dominate the 1930s and become one of the most famous teams in the world, but if Arsenal had lost that one game all those years ago would the team have been broken up, would Chapman have survived a fifth season with no trophies to show and would Arsenal have become the world-renowned club that it is today?

THE PLAYERS

If there was one player who must have been desperate to win an FA Cup-Winners' medal it was goalkeeper Dan Lewis. The Welshman had played in Arsenal's first Cup final in 1927 against his fellow countrymen from Cardiff City. There were only 16 minutes remaining when Lewis dived to meet an innocuous-looking shot, but as he did so the ball squirmed beneath him and, as he tried to retrieve it, he turned the ball over the line with his elbow. It was the only goal of the game. Three years on he was still Arsenal's first-choice goalkeeper but remained desperate to make up for his mistake.

In defence lay the chalk-and-cheese partnership of Eddie Hapgood and team captain Tom Parker. The experience was provided by Parker: signed from Southampton in 1926, he more than made up for his lack of pace with his intelligent positioning and accurate passing from defence. The youth came from Hapgood who had been signed in 1928 at the age of 19 having played just 12 games for non-league Kettering. Despite his inexperience, he soon proved that his speed and fitness made him the perfect partner for the Arsenal skipper.

Until the 1970s when George Armstrong broke his record, Bob John had appeared in Arsenal colours more often than anyone else. John, playing at half-back, was one of the few remaining players that had been at the club before Chapman arrived. He was not the most eye-catching footballer, but he was quietly efficient and dependable and Chapman soon appreciated his importance to the team. John's fellow half-backs were Alf Baker, a fellow veteran of the pre-Chapman era, whose versatility was such that he is the only player in the club's history to have appeared in all 11 positions in first-team games, and Herbie Roberts. Roberts was very much a defensive player, rarely venturing upfield, but he consistently won the ball and fed it to his more skilful team-mates. Also playing at half-back was Bill Seddon, whose strengths were accurately summed up by *The Times* in their Cup-final preview when he was described as 'a stout-hearted worker'.

The Arsenal forward line contained some of the most famous names in the club's history: Joe Hulme, David Jack, Jack Lambert, Alex James and Cliff Bastin. Hulme and Bastin were probably the club's greatest-ever pair of wingers. The former was reputed to be the fastest in the game, while Bastin had sufficient skill to embarrass any defender. Their crosses would invariably be aimed at Lambert, a classically tall and strong English centre-forward, but they would score as many goals as they created. In the 1932–33 season the two wingers scored 53 goals between them, and with 150 league goals in his Arsenal career, Bastin is still the club's all-time leading goalscorer in league games.

The player with the greatest big-match experience was David Jack. He had already won two Cup-Winners' medals with Bolton when he joined Arsenal for the record-breaking transfer fee of £11,500 in 1928. Jack was one of the best-known players in the country, with his ability to constantly feed the ball to his two wingers and his eye for goal being of vital importance to the team. Completing the forward line was the great Alex James. The Scotsman was signed from Preston in 1929 and went on to become one of the greatest players in British football history. On the eve of the Cup final *The Times* summed up his ability: 'He has generally played this season far back . . . roaming all over the place, seeking to rescue the ball from the opposing forwards or his own defence and get it clear away with long and well-directed passes . . . but James can play another way, up in the front, dribbling as no other can with a ball that seems to be fastened to his boot, tricking man after man and making the chance for his neighbour to score.'

THE BACKGROUND

Arsenal began the 1929–30 season in great style winning five of their first six games, including a 2–0 away win to defending champions Sheffield Wednesday – who would go on to retain their title that season. The optimism that this engendered soon foundered as Arsenal proceeded to win only four of their next 20 league games. Arsenal began their FA Cup campaign, therefore, knowing that it represented their only chance of glory that season.

The third-round draw gave Arsenal a home tie against Chelsea who were looking like they would be promoted from the Second Division. With Arsenal in such poor form it looked to be a difficult game and Chapman decided that changes would have to be made. With only three goals having been scored in the five games over the Christmas period Chapman felt that the service to the forwards had not been good enough and so he controversially dropped Alex James.

Fifty-six thousand spectators packed Highbury to see if in-form Chelsea could beat their First Division neighbours, but Chelsea rarely threatened to do so. Arsenal took the lead after 28 minutes when Lambert latched on to a through ball from Hulme and shot past Millington, the Chelsea goalkeeper. Six minutes after half-time Hulme again created a goal when his centre across the goalmouth was driven in by Bastin for Arsenal's second. Shortly afterwards the pitch was turned into a quagmire by a storm of rain and sleet, which made a Chelsea comeback almost impossible. Arsenal's defence stood firm and they eased their way into the fourth round.

In the next round a fortnight later Arsenal met Birmingham City at Highbury with James still missing from the line-up. Dan Lewis was also missing after injuring his knee and he was replaced by the reserve goalkeeper Charlie Preedy. Birmingham were similarly placed in the First Division so Chapman knew that Arsenal had to make the most of their home advantage. At half-time everything was going to plan; despite Birmingham's defensive tactics Arsenal found themselves with a 2–0 lead. After 23 minutes a free-kick on the edge of the Birmingham penalty area was touched to Jack who scored and placed the home side into the lead. Eighteen minutes later Bastin received a long pass from the right, warded off a challenge from a defender and hit the ball against the underside of the bar and into the net. After the break the visitors resorted to all-out attack and completely outplayed their opponents. With 15 minutes left they were back on level terms and by the final whistle the majority of the 43,000 crowd were relieved that Arsenal had escaped with a draw.

Having seen Birmingham dominate the second half to such an extent, Chapman knew that Arsenal would have to play very well to survive the replay. They would obviously have to have all their best players on show and that meant that Alex James would have to be recalled. In the return match James shone as Arsenal gained a hard-fought victory. The only goal of the game came after 50 minutes when Lambert was tripped in the penalty area. Baker hit the resulting spot-kick hard and low into the corner of the net to win the tie.

The fifth round saw Arsenal travel north to Ayresome Park to take on a Middlesbrough team that had already beaten them 2–1 earlier in the season at Highbury. Fortunately, the Gunners produced one of their best performances of the campaign and it was James in particular who caught the eye. James's dribble and pass to Bastin in the first minute almost produced the perfect start, but it was merely a prelude to the opening goal just minutes later. James ran at the Middlesbrough defence and dribbled past two defenders before squaring the ball to Lambert who had only the goalkeeper to beat. A low shot into the corner of the net gave Arsenal the lead. By half-time it was 2–0 after Lambert flicked on a long pass from Parker and Bastin headed into the top left-hand corner. There was no chance of Arsenal losing the lead as they had done in the last round. After the break they were content to sit back in defence, and the returning Lewis in goal was rarely troubled by the Middlesbrough forwards.

The quarter-final draw meant that Arsenal again had to travel to play a team that had already won at Highbury that season. The journey this time was much shorter as they were paired with West Ham for their second London derby of the competition. The strength of both teams lay in their forward line, and a close, high-scoring game was expected in a match that contrasted West Ham's home-grown talent with Arsenal's expensive purchases. In the end only Arsenal's forwards lived up to their reputations as they cruised to a comfortable victory. After just 11 minutes David Jack's header towards goal was handled by a West Ham defender and Baker scored from the penalty. Despite incessant pressure Arsenal did not increase their lead until an hour had been played when Lambert ran strongly through the centre of the Hammers defence and gave the goalkeeper no chance with his shot. Four minutes from time Lambert rounded the goalkeeper to score his second goal and seal an impressive 3–0 win.

On reaching the semi-final stage, Arsenal finally received the luck of the draw. They managed to avoid the big guns of Huddersfield and Sheffield Wednesday – who had won five of the last seven league championships between them – and were drawn against Second-Division Hull City who surprisingly had beaten the First-Division sides of Manchester City and Newcastle in previous rounds.

It looked, on paper, as though Arsenal had secured an easy route to Wembley, but Hull's performances in the Cup so far were such that nothing could be taken for granted. Arsenal were in confident mood, however, as the players kicked off at Elland Road before 48,000 spectators.

It soon became clear that Arsenal were in for no easy match. The forwards were continually frustrated by their opponents offside trap and Hull were quick to break upfield and attack the Arsenal goal. After 15 minutes the favourites were rocked by an opportunist goal: Lewis in the Arsenal goal made a poor clearance and the ball dropped ten yards inside the Arsenal half to Howieson, the Hull forward, who immediately lobbed the ball over the stranded goalkeeper and into the net. On the half hour things got even worse for Arsenal: Howieson's pass found Duncan whose cross shot went into the net off Hapgood.

Half-time came and went with no further score and it looked as though Arsenal were on their way out. Chapman knew that something had to be done to counter Hull's offside ploy so he decided that the thoughtful and intelligent Jack should swap positions with the strong and eager Lambert, in the hope that Jack could time his runs better and beat the trap. As a result, Arsenal were not caught offside once while Jack played forward, and they exerted more and more pressure on the Hull goal. The early second-half goal which Chapman so dearly wanted did not materialise, however, and with just 20 minutes to go it seemed that Arsenal would never score; but then came the vital breakthrough. James found Hulme on the wing who ran half the length of the pitch before sending a low cross into the centre where Jack ran in to control the ball and beat the goalkeeper from close range.

Now Arsenal were right-back in the game and the bombardment around the Hull goal became even fiercer. A powerful shot from Hulme was just tipped over the bar by the Hull goalkeeper Gibson, a free-kick on the edge of the penalty area saw Lambert send his header just wide, then Gibson saved a shot from Bastin at the expense of a corner.

With six minutes remaining Hull's resistance was finally broken when James found Bastin who dribbled the ball to the edge of the penalty box – leaving defenders in his wake – and hit a hard, curling shot into the net. *The Times* reported: 'The ball travelled so fast that the goalkeeper had hardly moved when it entered the net at about the level of his shoulder, and a finer goal than this was is seldom seen.'

The replay took place four days later at Villa Park. Arsenal received a blow when the injured Hulme was unable to play, but his replacement Joey Williams was to be instrumental in creating the winning goal. After quarter of an hour, James swung a long pass out to the right-wing which seemed certain to run out of play, but Williams raced towards the ball and just kept it in before crossing the ball into the centre. Jack was there to meet the cross and drive the ball into the net.

From then on Arsenal had little trouble in keeping their lead as Hull seemed increasingly to be more concerned with kicking lumps out of their opponents than chasing an equalising goal. Eventually their centre-back Arthur Childs was sent off for sending a flying kick at James. Arsenal missed several chances to make sure of victory, but in the end they were comfortable 1–0 winners and were on their way to Wembley for only the second time in their history. Their opponents in the final were to be Huddersfield – who had beaten the league leaders Sheffield Wednesday 2–1 in the other semi-final.

With the players that they had at their disposal, Huddersfield were going to be no push-over in the final. Ray Goodall, a former England captain, was reputed to be the finest right-back in England, while the skipper Tom Wilson had been the stopper at the heart of the team's defence for ten years. Bob Kelly in attack was one of the greatest forwards of his time and if any pair of wingers could match Bastin and Hulme it was Huddersfield's Jackson and Smith.

Much is now made of the fact that English football teams play too many games, but judging from Arsenal's experiences this is not a new phenomenon. Between the replay at Villa Park and the final itself, Arsenal played eight games in just 24 days, losing only once. This included an 8–1 win over Sheffield United, a remarkable 6–6 draw at Leicester and a 2–2 away draw to Cup-final opponents Huddersfield.

Following their epic draw at Leicester just five days before the final, Arsenal travelled to Brighton where they trained for the big day. On the eve of the final they journeyed back up to a private hotel in Hendon for the night. Before retiring for the night, Chapman held a team meeting inside a locked sitting-room where, with Jack sitting at his right hand, he elaborated on the tactics for the game. A diagram of the ground was laid out on the table with figures to represent the 22 players as they discussed the players Wembley roles. Every one of the Arsenal team was ordered to be in bed by 10.30 p.m. and Chapman went round the hotel corridor to check that all the lights were out. The Huddersfield team spent the night at Bushey Hall Hotel and just before having an early lunch on the day of the match, they held a secret conference to discuss match tactics.

The Football Association's ticket arrangements meant that obtaining a Cup-final ticket was even more difficult than it is today. The clubs were allocated only 7,500 tickets each when they could both have sold 50,000, hence there was, as usual, a roaring black-market trade. Extra trains – especially laid on for the occasion – brought people from all over the country into London just so that they could be in the capital on Cup-final day. An estimated 120,000 football fans arrived on 150 special trains with many thousands of them, of course, coming from Huddersfield.

Most pundits agreed that the two teams were well matched and few would venture an opinion on who would emerge victorious. The *Daily Mirror* thought that: 'there never was a more open final. By no purpose of analysis is it possible to pick the probable winners.'

THE MATCH

Having played so many games in the run-up to Wembley, Arsenal were fortunate that only one of their players – goalkeeper Dan Lewis – was ruled out by injury but this was no consolation to Lewis who so desperately wanted to make up for his mistake in the Cup final three years previously. Instead the replacement goalkeeper Charlie Preedy came into the team.

There was already a carnival atmosphere at Wembley even before the teams took to the field. King George V had not been seen in public for 18 months due to illness, so a great cheer went up around the ground when it was announced that he was on his way to the stadium from Windsor. The traditional community singing that followed raised spirits even further.

As the two teams entered the arena they made history by being the first two teams to walk out side by side at a Cup final. The King then received a great ovation as he came out to be presented to the players, and the national anthem was said to have been sung with particular gusto.

The game started with some of the most thrilling football ever seen at a Wembley Cup final. Both teams went forward with skill and pace as the attacks went from one end to the other. Both goals came under threat, but there was no doubt that the most dangerous attacks came from Arsenal. From a free-kick just outside the penalty area, Parker's shot just skimmed over the bar, then Lambert found himself through on goal before Turner, the Huddersfield goalkeeper, came out to smother the ball, next Lambert flicked the ball on to Bastin who looked certain to score but could not control his header. Arsenal came even closer to scoring when Lambert headed against the Huddersfield crossbar followed by Jack shooting wide off the rebound. At the other end, Preedy's nervousness in goal was providing heart-stopping moments in the Arsenal defence, but the Londoners still looked the most likely to score and it was no surprise when, after 17 minutes, they took the lead.

In his book *Arsenal from the Heart*, Bob Wall, who was then Arsenal secretary, recalls that the opening goal came as a result of a conversation on the Wembley-bound coach when Alex James turned to Cliff Bastin and said: 'If we get a free-kick in their half Cliff, I'll push out a quick pass to you. Let me have it back immediately and I'll have a shot at goal.' Wall also reports that 'as Alex was essentially a creator rather than scorer of goals, his suggestion caused some amusement among the rest of the team'. James's team-mates, however, would soon be thankful for his pre-match planning.

After being fouled by Goodall just inside the Huddersfield half, James took the free-kick quickly and played the ball out to Bastin on the wing. Goodall chased the Arsenal winger towards the corner flag before Bastin wrongfooted him by checking his run and pulling the ball back to the edge of the penalty area where James ran in to shoot the ball into the net. It was only James's sixth goal of the season – but what an important one! Alex James thus went down in history as the first player to score for Arsenal in an FA Cup final.

Shortly afterwards came one of the most famous moments in FA Cup history as the giant German airship, the *Graf Zeppelin*, appeared overhead. Flying at just 2,000 feet, the *Daily Express* reported that the airship 'dropped so low that it seemed near enough to touch'. Passengers in the cabins leant out of the windows and waved at the crowd, but not all of the spectators were happy at such an intrusion and there was much booing from those who did not want to be distracted from the game itself. There were also complaints after the match when it was discovered that the pilot had taken part in several air-raids over London in the Great War. Nonetheless, when the airship dipped it's nose to salute the King he raised his hat in return as the *Graf Zeppelin* made its way overhead.

Up until half-time, Arsenal continued to threaten the Huddersfield goal and a drive by Hulme flashed just inches past the post. There were also scares at the other end, however, and there were three occasions before the interval when the ball had to be scrambled away by Arsenal defenders after being dropped by Preedy.

The first 45 minutes had certainly belonged to Arsenal and they deserved their lead at the interval. In the second half, however, the game changed completely with Huddersfield attacking ceaselessly in an attempt to cancel out their opponents' lead. James and Jack were forced back to defend against the repeated onslaught on the Arsenal penalty area, and for much of the half it seemed inconceivable that Huddersfield would not score. Only the massed ranks of Arsenal defenders in their own penalty area kept them at bay, but with so many men back in defence Arsenal could only clear the ball by hitting it far up the field where it would invariably be met by an opposing defender who would set up another Huddersfield raid.

Fortunately for Arsenal Preedy rediscovered his form in the second half, otherwise the Cup would almost certainly have headed north once again. Smith, the Huddersfield winger, repeatedly sent teasing crosses into the area only to see them either flash across the penalty box, intercepted by defenders or hit wide of the goal by one of his forwards. Wilson twice narrowly missed from dead-ball situations while Raw was denied by Preedy. The Huddersfield captain later wrote: 'I remember two thrilling occasions in the second half when I said to myself, "Here's a goal." One was when Preedy made a great save from Raw's head and the other when Jackson made a magnificent shot at the Arsenal goal. Seddon, the Arsenal centre-half, tried to clear it with his head, but as it happened the ball just went over the bar. Those are just two of the narrow escapes that the Arsenal goal had in the second half. If I remember rightly there were eight or nine occasions on which Huddersfield almost produced a goal.'

For 43 minutes of the second half Huddersfield continuously attacked the Arsenal penalty area and yet, with just two minutes remaining, it was Arsenal who scored, putting victory beyond doubt. Yet again a Huddersfield attack was foiled and Alex James sent a long ball downfield. This time, however, the ball fell not to a Huddersfield defender, but to Lambert who raced between the two backs and bore down on goal. The goalkeeper raced off his line to meet him but Lambert managed to stab the ball past him and score

Arsenal's second goal. Lambert turned with his arms outstretched, ready to accept the congratulations of his team-mates, but they were all still down at the other end of the field, so Lambert had to applaud himself as he jogged back down the pitch.

The Huddersfield spirit was finally broken and just two minutes later the referee, Mr Crewe, blew the final whistle – Arsenal had won their first major trophy. The heroes of the hour were Parker and Hapgood, who led the desperate rearguard action in the second half, and Alex James who not only scored one goal and created another – but with his running and tackling which helped his defenders keep the Huddersfield attack at bay – was also instrumental in Arsenal's survival when they were under the cosh.

The majority of the spectators at Wembley that day were supporting Arsenal and as the *Daily Telegraph* reported, 'the victory of the Arsenal was a popular one, and when the captain, Parker, received the cup from the King there was unbounded enthusiasm'. Such enthusiasm was shown by the large turnout of fans the following Monday afternoon when the team was given a civic reception at Islington Town Hall. Later that same day Arsenal were greeted by more of their supporters as they took on Sunderland in their penultimate league fixture of the season. The *Daily Telegraph* reported that: 'The Arsenal were accorded an enthusiastic reception when they appeared on their ground at Highbury to play a league match with Sunderland last evening. There was a brave display of the colours of the club; a huge duck, their mascot, was perched in the centre of the stand; innumerable rattles, cornets and fireworks were employed by way to commemorating Saturday's triumph at Wembley. The team, played on to the field as "conquering heroes", were met by their visitors who greeted each member by a hearty shake of the hand and the kick-off was done to the roar of 35,000 spectators.' Arsenal lost 1–0 and were also beaten by Aston Villa the following Saturday, but few people cared. The important work had been done at Wembley.

In the next eight seasons Arsenal won five league titles and won the FA Cup once more – Huddersfield have yet to win another major trophy. We can only guess at what might have happened if all that Huddersfield pressure had paid off that day and they had won the Cup, but what we can say for sure is that 26 April 1930 was the day that the breakthrough was made for Arsenal Football Club with the likes of Herbert Chapman, Alex James and Jack Lambert setting Arsenal on the road to fame and glory. The club may have been founded nearly 50 years earlier, but as far as being the great club that we know today – with its marble halls, huge support and bulging trophy cabinet – is concerned it was that day in 1930 that saw the beginning of Arsenal as a club to be reckoned with.

FINAL SCORE

Arsenal	2	Huddersfield Town	0

James	17 mins
Lambert	88 mins
Attendance:	92,488

Arsenal: Preedy, Parker, Hapgood, Baker, Seddon, John, Hulme, Jack, Bastin, James, Lambert

Huddersfield: Turner, Goodall, Spence, Naylor, Wilson, Campbell, Jackson, Kelly, Davies, Raw, Smith

Chapter 2

FOR THE TEAM

FA Cup final
Arsenal v Liverpool
Saturday, 29 April 1950

After their FA Cup triumph in 1930 Arsenal had gone on to dominate English football until the onset of the Second World War. They were league champions in 1931, 1933, 1934, 1935 and 1938 and had won the FA Cup again in 1936. By now Arsenal were the biggest and most famous club in the country.

The spectre of war in Europe brought professional football to a halt for seven years as both players and spectators fought and, in many cases, died together. When the war was finally over football began again, but all the clubs were now virtually starting again from scratch with many teams having only a few of the players that had started the foreshortened 1939–40 season.

Initially, Arsenal struggled to recapture their pre-war form and when play finally resumed in 1946 they could only finish 13th in the First Division. It was only when manager Tom Whittaker signed more experienced players like Ronnie Rooke and Joe Mercer, that Arsenal recaptured the glory days of the 1930s by winning the championship in 1948.

Unfortunately, their championship success was short lived. The 1948–49 season saw Arsenal finish a disappointing fifth in the league and their indifferent form continued through the following season. As a new decade began, however, Arsenal embarked on a Cup run that would see them go all the way to Wembley.

The team that reached the Cup final was unusual in that it was one of the teams to reach that stage with the majority of players in their thirties, and yet it was also a typical 'Arsenal team'. Like the great Arsenal sides of the past and of the future they had outstanding individuals such as Joe Mercer and Jimmy Logie, but the emphasis was always on playing for the team. As centre-forward Reg Lewis recalled: 'We were all a team. We would run for each other and work hard and get kicked till you were black and blue. You would run till you dropped to win that game. The team was everything.'

The players had a pride in playing for 'The Arsenal' and a determination to help each other to succeed. With so many of them reaching the end of their careers, this appeared to be their last chance of glory. And so, as they got nearer and nearer to Wembley, the question on everybody's lips was: could this ageing team work together to bring the Cup back to Highbury, or would they fall at the final hurdle?

THE PLAYERS

In goal for Arsenal was one of the survivors from the 1938 championship-winning team, George Swindin, Swindin had been signed from Bradford City in 1936 and in his first years at Highbury he was one of several men who seemed to share the goalkeeping position and in each of the three seasons leading up to the war he had never played for the first team more than 21 times. After the war, however, he was firmly established as the club's number one goalkeeper and was ever present in both the 1948 championship-winning side and during the 1950 Cup run.

In defence was Walley Barnes: Barnes was equally effective in both full-back positions and went on to captain both Arsenal and Wales. He made his Arsenal debut during the first post-war season and amazingly, considering the continuous trouble that he had with his knee ligaments, he was still playing for the Gunners in 1955. His bravery in the face of so many injuries and his excellent defensive play were an example to the rest of the team. Barnes's fellow full-back was Laurie Scott: Scott had first appeared for Arsenal in the wartime competitions and had since then kept his place in the team, playing an important part in Arsenal's strong defence.

Although his versatility was such that he was known to play at centre-forward, Leslie Compton was at the heart of the Arsenal defence from the end of the war until 1951. Even in his late thirties he was a commanding presence at the back and in November 1950 he made his debut for England at the ripe old age of 38. During Arsenal's Cup run he was accompanied in the team by his younger brother Denis. Denis Compton was one of the great English sporting heroes of the generation – not only was he a dashing forward for Arsenal but he was also one of the best batsmen in the world. The pressures of combining his cricket and football careers were starting to catch up with him, however, and the 1949–50 season was to be his last for Arsenal before he retired from the football pitch with knee problems.

Completing the defence was Alex Forbes. Forbes's performances at inside-left for Sheffield United had impressed the Highbury staff and prompted them to pay £12,000 for him in 1948. A goal in his debut match quickly endeared him to the Arsenal supporters and his strong running and fierce tackling made the Scottish international a favourite with the crowd for years to come.

In the first few months of post-war football, while Arsenal were struggling near the foot of the First Division, the club made one of the finest and most important signings in its history. Joe Mercer had been one of England's best attacking wing-halves and had just broken into the national team as war broke out. Now, at the age of 32, he was seen by his club Everton as being past his best. Mercer was on the verge of retiring but Arsenal saw him as the ideal man to anchor their midfield and persuaded him to sign for them. His one condition before signing for the club was that he could continue to live and train in Liverpool as he had his own grocery business in the area. It was agreed that Mercer should train with the Liverpool team and travel down to London on match days. Mercer played as a defensive half-back and went on to become the team captain. He played more than 270 games for Arsenal in his eight years at the club which included the championship victory of 1948, but one major ambition still remained: in his long and successful career Mercer had yet to win a Cup-winners medal and his greatest wish was to finally taste Wembley glory. His popularity was such that fans throughout the country hoped that his wish would come true and for once in their history, Arsenal had the support of the nation behind them.

Arsenal's start to the season had been fairly poor with only two wins from their first seven games. At this stage of the campaign, a Wembley Cup final seemed very unlikely. The Gunners' results started to improve, however, when they brought in two new players to the team. The first was Freddie Cox who was bought from Tottenham in September 1949; Cox was versatile enough to play in several positions, but he usually played at outside right. His debut for the club saw Arsenal beat West Brom 4–1 and they went on to remain unbeaten for a further nine matches. Cox's great strength was in providing the ball for the other new boy in the side, Peter Goring. Goring was signed from part-time Cheltenham and made an immediate impact by scoring on his debut. He went on to score 21 goals in his first season and form an effective forward partnership with Reg Lewis.

Lewis was an outstanding goalscorer who had also scored on his Arsenal debut in 1938. His ability in front of goal was unaffected after the war and he continued to find the back of the net when football resumed. He and Ronnie Rooke had been a lethal forward pairing during Arsenal's championship-winning season and the departure of Rooke and the introduction of Goring did nothing to hamper Lewis's goalscoring talents.

The final member of the team was Jimmy Logie. Like Lewis he had signed for Arsenal before the war, but had managed to shine even after seven years of conflict. His great dribbling ability was good enough to see him compared with the great Alex James and he was instrumental in setting up many of the goals that were scored by Goring and Lewis.

THE BACKGROUND

The nine-match unbeaten run that followed the signing of Freddie Cox may have quashed any thoughts of a relegation struggle, but the nine games which followed produced only one win, ruling out any championship challenge for that season. The beginning of Arsenal's cup campaign in January, therefore, was of great importance to the club. Before the third-round draw, goalkeeper George Swindin predicted that the Gunners would be drawn at home, and sure enough when the balls came out of the bag, Arsenal had what most teams hope for – a home tie against a side from a lower division. Their opponents, however, were not to be taken lightly; Sheffield Wednesday were to be promoted to the First Division along with Tottenham at the end of the season and were, at that time, unbeaten in the last three months.

Cup fever was certainly in evidence at Highbury on 7 January 1950. The *Evening Standard* reported that 40,000 people were queuing outside the ground when the gates were opened with some having waited since 11 o'clock the previous evening, while hundreds of visiting supporters had been brought from Sheffield in special trains and coaches.

For most of the match it looked as though it would be the Wednesday fans who would be going home the happier as the visiting team held firm against the Arsenal attack. As the game entered its final moments there was still no score but, with the referee's watch showing just 13 seconds remaining, Reg Lewis scored a last-gasp goal to send the Gunners through to the next round.

Before the fourth-round draw, George Swindin again predicted that Arsenal would have a home tie, and yet again they ended up with home advantage against a Second-Division side. This time their opponents were Swansea, whose league form suggested that they would not prove to be as troublesome as Sheffield Wednesday. In the event, however, Arsenal struggled yet again to win the match. Swansea battled hard and deserved better than the 2–1 defeat that they suffered courtesy of a goal from Logie and a penalty by Walley Barnes.

Swindin continued to forecast that Arsenal would have a home draw and again he was proved correct, but this time their opponents were First-Division Burnley. Burnley had won at Highbury on the first day of the season so they went into the match with confidence, but goals from Reg Lewis and Denis Compton saw Arsenal progress more easily through this round than they had against lesser opposition previously.

On reaching the quarter-final stage of the competition Arsenal, like all the other seven teams, had a realistic chance of going to Wembley – especially if they could get an all-important home draw in the sixth round. Hopes were raised when Swindin, still in prediction mode, made his most specific pronouncement so far and announced that Arsenal would be drawn at home to Leeds United. Sure enough, Arsenal made it four home draws out of four and their opposition was to be . . . Leeds United. Another home game against Second-Division opponents reinforced the 'lucky Arsenal' tag but, as Arsenal had found in their previous games and indeed throughout their whole history, it was often the lesser teams that gave them the most trouble.

Leeds were certainly no exception and it was the defenders that were Arsenal's heroes that afternoon. Leeds had at least as much of the play as their hosts, but the home defence restricted them to few real goal chances. Leslie Compton in particular was responsible for keeping their attacks at bay, despite suffering a bloody head wound that required stitches during the game. Alex Forbes also had an excellent game and it was he who set up the crucial goal. The *Daily Telegraph* reported that: 'Forbes, outstanding and tireless, lifted the play above the ordinary by one wonderful effort. He beat three men, thus taking the Leeds defenders, including Charles, out of position, and when Roper centred Lewis was able to score the vital goal.'

Reaching the semi-final stage meant that Arsenal would finally have to leave Highbury to play a Cup tie but as it turned out they would not have to journey very far. When they avoided clashes with both Liverpool and Everton and were paired with London rivals Chelsea, it was announced that they would have to make the long trip to . . . Tottenham.

The league table suggested that the two teams would be evenly matched. But in front of a packed White Hart Lane crowd it was Chelsea who seized control of the game after less than half an hour: Roy Bentley – the England centre-forward who just a month later would score the winning goal against Scotland at Hampden Park – gave Chelsea the lead after 20 minutes. The ball was cleared out of defence by Hughes and the flick-on by Williams found Bentley cutting in from the left. Swindin in the Arsenal goal raced out to close the forward down, but Bentley lobbed the ball over the advancing goalkeeper from 15 yards and gave his team the lead. Just five minutes later Arsenal fell even further behind. Again the goal came from a long clearance by Hughes and again it was Bentley who seized on the ball and shot past Swindin to make it 2–0.

In their previous Cup ties, Arsenal had relied on the strength of their defence to a great extent, but now they knew that they had to go forward in an attempt to save their season. As the *Evening Standard* reported: 'Arsenal now flung everything into a bid for recovery. They chased desperately. They went wholeheartedly into every header, every tackle . . . It was exciting. It was dramatic. But it did not look like bringing goals.' The Chelsea defence was holding firm and seemed able to cope with whatever the Arsenal attack could throw at them. If the Gunners had ever needed some of that 'lucky Arsenal' good fortune it was now, and sure enough as the first half entered its final minute, it arrived. Arsenal had won a corner and as Freddie Cox took the kick, the wind caused the ball to swing towards the goal and sneak inside the near post as Medhurst in the Chelsea goal vainly tried to punch it away. It may have involved a huge amount of luck – Cox never claimed that he had meant to go directly for goal – but coming at the time that it did, the goal changed the whole tempo of the game. Chelsea had looked so comfortable and with a 2–0 half-time lead they would have been odds on to reach Wembley but now with only a goal separating the two teams, the Arsenal players knew that they were still in the game and started the second half with renewed determination.

The second half saw almost constant pressure from Arsenal with the Chelsea defence continually scrambling the ball to safety. Wave upon wave of Arsenal attacks went towards the Chelsea goal, yet with only 15 minutes remaining Arsenal were still trailing. As the game entered its last quarter of an hour Arsenal won yet another corner. As Denis Compton prepared to take the corner kick, he waved at his brother Leslie to make his way towards the Chelsea penalty area where his height might cause some uncertainty in the opposing defence. Joe Mercer, the Arsenal captain, shouted at the big defender to stop and waved him back. Fortunately for Arsenal, Leslie decided that they urgently needed a goal and ignored Mercer's instructions. The *Daily Telegraph* reported what happened next: 'Then as if they had rehearsed it all, the Compton brothers staged their Arsenal saving act. Denis from the corner flag sent over the in-swinger which, if it had been a cricket ball would have caught Bradman in two minds. Up leapt a massive figure in a red shirt and Leslie, lynx-eyeing the flight of the ball to a split second, which is the golden gift of the born ball-player, headed down into the corner of the net.' Leslie Compton had put so much into the header that as the ball sped between goalkeeper Medhurst and his right-back Winter into the net he completely lost his balance and fell head over heels. Only the roar of the cheering Arsenal supporters told him that he had scored.

There was no further score in the match and so the two teams had to return to White Hart Lane four days later. The replay was a much less dramatic affair with no goals having been scored after 90 minutes. It was not until extra-time that Arsenal made the breakthrough and, as in the first game, it came in the minute before half-time. After 104 goalless minutes, it was obviously going to take something special to score in this match and Cox's solo run followed by a powerful shot with his weaker left foot certainly came into that category. Chelsea were unable to come back from behind and so Arsenal reached their first FA Cup final in 14 years. Now they had to prepare for the trip to Wembley – their longest journey throughout the competition.

Arsenal's opponents in the final were Liverpool who reached the final after their 2–0 win over Merseyside rivals Everton. This posed a problem for both teams as Joe Mercer trained with the Liverpool team before joining the Arsenal players on match days. Liverpool understandably asked Mercer not to train with the team, but graciously continued to allow him to use the Anfield ground in the afternoons.

Following a week at Brighton, the team that would take the field for Arsenal at Wembley were beaten 3–0 by Wolves on the Saturday before the Cup final, but importantly there were no injuries to report when the team – minus Mercer – met at Highbury on the following Monday. Following a normal day's training on the Tuesday, the Arsenal team spent Wednesday playing golf at the South Herts course. It may have been late April, but the players tee-offs were delayed by snow and after nine holes they were forced into the clubhouse by driving rain. Later that evening Joe Mercer arrived in London.

On the eve of the final the Arsenal players worked on some light training in the morning before resting for the remainder of the day and getting to bed early. The Liverpool camp was concerned with goalkeeper Sidlow's pulled leg muscle, but after a fitness test in a local playing field he was pronounced fit to play by the club's trainer – club manager George Kay being unable to oversee the test as he was in bed with a chill. With all his players fit, Arsenal manager Tom Whittaker had few decisions to make regarding team selection. The only real speculation centred on whether to play Reg Lewis or Doug Lishman up front. Despite his goalscoring record, Lewis sometimes gave the impression of being lazy and lethargic – he himself admitted, 'I didn't see the point of running for balls you would never get. I didn't run about too much, I couldn't see the point of chasing dead balls, and perhaps some people were critical because of that.' – while the younger Lishman had already proved his ability in front of goal. There were reports that Lewis only got the nod at the insistence of Joe Mercer, but the centre-forward later denied this saying: 'Tom Whittaker said "if he doesn't go on the pitch, I don't go on the pitch". There was never any question that I wouldn't play. He had faith in me and I repaid it, thank God.' Whether there was any debate or not Whittaker plumped for the experienced Lewis – a decision that he would be thankful for. That evening, Whittaker was asked what he thought of the Gunners' chances. He replied: 'A Cup final is a match on its own and I'm not prophesying. Everyone is well. We have tried to keep as near ordinary Cup routine as possible so that the players have had a better chance of relaxing.'

Over the years many FA Cup finals have been blessed with hot and sunny weather, but the 1950 Cup final was not one of these. Almost throughout the day the heavens opened and Wembley was soaked. This did nothing to dampen the enthusiasm of the two teams' respective supporters and there was a roaring trade in black-market tickets. In those post-war rationing days, however, it was not just money that was changing hands. The *Evening Standard* reported that in a Euston café a man offered a box of American nylons for a ticket and at a Baker Street coffee stall another man opened a suitcase full of Scotch whisky in the hope of tempting someone to part with one.

With both teams seeming so evenly matched few pundits were able to pick a winner, although Liverpool's Billy Liddell was confident enough to back his own side. With each team having such effective wingmen many expected the match to be won and lost on the flanks. For Arsenal, Whittaker instructed Denis Compton and Freddie Cox to play as wide as possible so as to provide space for Logie to run through, while Liverpool's Liddell and Payne would have to be stopped from providing the through ball to the free-scoring Stubbins. This meant that the Arsenal full-backs, Scott and Barnes, would have to be on their best form.

The Times concluded that: 'Liverpool, more promising in attack, have the advantage of youth which on this rich tiring surface is a great consideration. But Arsenal possess the experience, the iron will-power, a great tradition and a system. They are said to be lucky too and it may well be that the mischievous imp who lives at Wembley will this time join forces with the south. Yet clearly the afternoon is delicately balanced with every prospect of extra-time and the first replay of a final for 38 years.' The Arsenal players were in no doubt that they would be victorious, Tom Whittaker had instilled great self-belief into his team, and as they made their final preparations, they were supremely confident that they would win.

THE MATCH

Neither of the teams took to the field in their familiar red. The colour clash meant that both teams had to change, but as both teams' change strip was white, Arsenal were forced to find another colour scheme. Tom Whittaker decided on the most eye-catching combination that he could think of: gold shirts, white shorts and black and white socks, while goalkeeper George Swindin wore a brilliant crimson jersey on the basis that not only was it the nearest permissible colour to Arsenal's normal kit, but that the brightness of the shirt might distract the Liverpool forwards. Liverpool were dressed in white shirts and black shorts.

Arsenal kicked off the game towards the dressing-rooms, but it was Liverpool who started more strongly forcing three corners in the first ten minutes and winning two free-kicks in dangerous positions. Not that Arsenal were without chances – Forbes twice found himself through on goal but finished weakly and Cox twice beat his marker on the wing and produced a dangerous cross.

As the game passed the quarter-of-an-hour mark, Arsenal were beginning to take a hold of the proceedings. Much of this was due to Alex Forbes shadowing of Liverpool's dangerous left-winger Billy Liddell. In *Arsenal from the Heart* Bob Wall recalls how Tom Whittaker had seen Liddell as Liverpool's greatest threat and that he had decided that Forbes should make sure he was kept quiet: 'Before the match Tom said to Alex, "Liddell is the man who can win the match for Liverpool. It's up to you to see that he doesn't." In the eyes of the Liverpool club and their supporters, Alex took these instructions a bit too literally. He set out to destroy Liddell's chances in their infancy. He thundered into his tackles, cut off the cross balls and never allowed Liddell a moment's respite. I have seldom seen a more devastating wing-half display.'

After 17 minutes Arsenal scored one of the great Cup-final goals of all time. A long clearance out of the Liverpool defence by Hughes found the head of Leslie Compton who flicked the ball sideways to Barnes, as Stubbins sprinted towards him in an effort to close him down, Barnes flicked the ball upfield to Logie who was starting to impose his skill and trickery on the match. Just at that moment Goring in the centre-forward position ran across the defensive line, pulling defenders with him and opening up a huge gap in the middle of Liverpool's defence. Reg Lewis then began to run forward into the space and Logie's perfectly weighted pass found him with just the goalkeeper to beat. Lewis was able to take the ball in his stride and glide it past Sidlow and into the Liverpool goal to put Arsenal ahead. The goal was described in the *Daily Mail* as an 'all-important effort ranking among the Wembley classics'.

After 20 minutes Forbes came close to increasing Arsenal's lead with a shot that went just wide of the post, but the Liverpool spirit had yet to be broken and they soon struck back. As the play switched to the other end a great run and cross by Payne on the Liverpool wing resulted in Swindin pushing the ball against the crossbar and quickly diving upon the rebound as Stubbins bore down on him. Moments later Liddell managed to evade the attentions of Forbes and flash a teasing cross over the Arsenal penalty area which the diving Stubbins missed by a whisker. After these close scares, however, Arsenal's defence regained its composure and the midfield and forwards began to find more space for themselves and enjoy more freedom.

At half-time Tom Whittaker's greatest concern was the form of Denis Compton who had had a distinctly unimpressive first half. Compton was planning to retire from football at the end of the season due to an injured knee, and Whittaker used this to motivate Compton. The manager went to Compton and told him, 'Now, you've got 45 minutes left of your soccer career. I want you to go out there and give it every ounce you possibly can.' A glass of whisky was then produced and a fortified Compton went out for the second half.

Moments after the teams re-emerged for the restart, Arsenal had another scare when Swindin misjudged a cross from Liddell and slipped as it curled towards the goal. Luckily for the goalkeeper he was just able to scramble the ball to safety from the goal-line and keep the Gunners lead intact. After that it was the reinvigorated Compton who held centre stage; the Arsenal winger sent a string of dangerous crosses into the penalty area which had the Liverpool goalkeeper in trouble on more than one occasion. Indeed one cross almost resulted in Spicer, the Liverpool defender, scoring an own goal.

As in the first half the Arsenal team slowly took control of the game, and just like the first half they scored after 17 minutes. Goring on the left played the ball through to Cox near the edge of the penalty area and his first-time flick found Lewis who ran on to the ball and beat the goalkeeper to score his and Arsenal's second goal of the match. There could be no doubt now that Whittaker's decision to keep faith with Lewis had been justified.

As the game entered its last 15 minutes, Liverpool began to throw caution to the wind and they came close to scoring on several occasions. First, a Taylor header hit the bar and Stubbins forced Swindin to make a diving save from the rebound, then Fagan shot wide from close range after Payne headed a Liddell cross down to his feet. Liddell and Payne swapped wings and made numerous openings but Scott, Barnes and Leslie Compton stood firm in the Arsenal defence and kept the Liverpool attacks at bay.

And it was not all one-way traffic as Denis Compton kept the Liverpool defenders on their toes with a succession of shots at goal.

For all their efforts, however, Liverpool were unable to find a route to goal and the final whistle signalled victory for Arsenal with Tom Whittaker dashing onto the field to embrace Joe Mercer. The Merseysiders had certainly battled gamely but, as *The Times* reported: 'Liverpool perhaps had deserved one goal in that final spasm, but at the last, as the flags on the corner posts hung limp and wet and the massed bands of the Brigade of Guards played the National Anthem, the right captain, Mercer of Arsenal, held the coveted trophy which he had received from the King.'

For once in the history of Arsenal Football Club, the sight of their captain climbing the Wembley steps to receive the FA Cup was an almost universally popular one. The majority of the country's football fans were pleased that one of football's gentlemen was finally going to get his hands on a Cup-winners medal at such a late stage in his career. Things did not go entirely to plan, however, for after the King had presented the trophy to Mercer and he had held the Cup aloft to the cheers of the celebrating Arsenal fans, the Queen incorrectly gave him a losers' medal. Fortunately the mistake was discovered and rectified before the captain made his way down the steps.

The two players who received the most attention after the match were Mercer and the goalscoring hero Reg Lewis. At the celebration dinner later that night at the Café Royal Mercer said: 'What a wonderful thing it is to be an Arsenal player! But I am very proud of my Merseyside birth tonight because of the wonderful sportsmanship of all the Liverpool players.' Yet even in his greatest moment of triumph, Mercer's concern for others shone through. A 19-year-old reserve player called Billy Duffy had been taken ill with a chest complaint three months earlier and was now convalescing near Dublin. Mercer took a menu around the tables for autographs for the young player and wrote at the top, 'In our moment of happiness we are thinking of you'. Meanwhile, on his departure from the dinner, Lewis found great difficulty in finding a taxi home due to the late hour. Fortunately a member of the press intervened with a policeman on his behalf and so the Wembley goalscoring hero and his wife made their way home in a police car.

It had certainly been a great day for Arsenal. The club's players, officials and supporters would definitely have expected more Cup triumphs over the coming years, but the FA Cup would not return to Highbury for over two decades. As a result the club had plenty of time in which to dwell on this triumph and remember the major players in that victory. Tom Whittaker's tactics certainly had a great part to play in the win, but in the end it was the performances of three players who lived in the memory – following his half-time pep-talk, Denis Compton had played a major role in what was his penultimate game for Arsenal and he could not have chosen a better way to finish his footballing career; Reg Lewis had silenced all the doubters with his two clinical and ice-cool finishes that had won the Cup for Arsenal and Joe Mercer had finally got his Cup medal.

Mercer's triumph may not have gone down in football folklore in the way that Stanley Matthews' did three years later, but it meant as much to him and the Arsenal supporters. It had been a great performance by the veteran captain, but his role in motivating his team, both by word and deed, had been even more important. It was, without doubt, a team victory, but Reg Lewis summed up what it meant to the team to have such an inspirational captain on such a big occasion: 'It was a keen, hard game, but when you've got players like Alex Forbes and Joe Mercer, you just knew you were going to win. They could have been crippled, they could have been unable to run, but they would have found something from somewhere. Joe was such a good captain.'

It was not, however, a day for individuals. There were eight other heroes playing at Wembley that day and they had won the Cup together. It was a triumph for experience, comradeship and collective spirit. In the end they had done it not for themselves, but for 'the team' and for 'The Arsenal'.

FINAL SCORE

| Arsenal | 2 | Liverpool | 0 |

Lewis	17 mins
Lewis	62 mins
Attendance:	100,000

Arsenal: Swindin, Scott, Barnes, Forbes, L. Compton, Mercer, Cox, Logie, Goring, Lewis, D. Compton

Liverpool: Sidlow, Lambert, Spicer, Taylor, Hughes, Jones, Payne, Baron, Stubbins, Fagan, Liddell

Chapter 3

0.099 OF A GOAL

Football League First Division
Arsenal v Burnley
Friday, 1 May 1953

The 1951–52 season had promised much for Arsenal as they made a strong challenge in both the league and the Cup. Eventually, though, Arsenal fell at the last hurdle in both competitions. Needing to win handsomely at Old Trafford in their last game to take the league title, they were crushed 6–1 as Manchester United were crowned champions, while in the FA Cup final an injury to Walley Barnes after just 40 minutes meant that they had to play the majority of the match with just ten men and were beaten by a single Newcastle goal, scored just six minutes from time.

The double disappointment that they had endured seemed to bind the team even closer together as they embarked on their championship challenge at the start of the following season. It was to be a topsy-turvy campaign, but the team's determination saw them through to the last game which, for the second successive season, Arsenal needed to win to become the champions. What followed was one of the most tense, nail-biting and dramatic games ever to be played at Highbury and a night as memorable as any in the club's history.

THE PLAYERS
1952–53 was a transitional season as far as the Arsenal goalkeeping position was concerned. George Swindin had been the Gunner's top keeper since the war but was now coming to the end of his career.

This meant that a young man, Jack Kelsey, had a chance to force his way into the first team. Kelsey had been brought to Highbury from his native Wales in 1949 to understudy Swindin. His early appearances for Arsenal had not augured well for his future at the club when he conceded eight goals in his first two games, but he did not let that affect his confidence. Both Kelsey and Swindin had important roles to play in Arsenal's championship win – they made 25 and 14 appearances respectively – before Kelsey took over as first choice at the start of the following season. Kelsey went on to give the Gunners a decade of outstanding service and became widely regarded as one of the best goalkeepers of his generation.

With Walley Barnes out for the season following his injury in the FA Cup final, Joe Wade came into the team at left-back. Despite the loss of such a fine player as Barnes, Wade made light of his absence and filled in admirably, missing only two games of the season. Another regular in defence was the Yorkshireman Lionel Smith. Smith had made his debut in an 8–0 win over Grimsby in 1948 and had played at both centre-back and left-back since then. Although never establishing himself as a regular in either position, he made around 30 appearances in each of the next five seasons and would play six times for England. Completing the back line was Welshman Ray Daniel. Daniel had come into the side as Les Compton's replacement during the previous season and would miss only one game in the current season before moving to Sunderland in the summer of 1953.

Further up the field were several survivors from the 1950 Cup-winning side. Six years after Everton decided that he was past it Joe Mercer was still the captain and still, at the age of 39, inspiring the rest of the team with his performances on the pitch. Also still in the team were Alex Forbes, Freddie Cox, Peter Goring, Doug Lishman and Jimmy Logie.

Like Lionel Smith, Don Roper had arrived at Highbury just after the war – in his case from Southampton – but despite regularly playing 30 league games a season he had failed to establish himself as a permanent fixture in the team. Roper had been left out of the 1950 FA Cup final, in favour of fellow forward Peter Goring, but continued to turn out for the Gunners until the 1952–53 season when he found himself playing in all but one league game. Having scored a respectable 14 goals in the campaign, Roper saw his name appearing much more regularly from then on as he played in nearly every game for the next two seasons. Alongside him for much of the season was Cliff Holton or 'hot-shot Holton' as he was also known. Signed as a full-back from non-league Oxford City in 1947, Holton broke into the team some years later as a dashing forward with strength on the ball, a towering presence in the air and a powerful shot with both feet. With 19 goals in his 21 league appearances he made a major contribution to Arsenal's title challenge. Also making a vital contribution was Ben Marden. Signed in 1950, Marden never held down a regular first-team spot, but the speedy winger's appearances during the 1952–53 season invariably coincided with some of the Gunners' best and most important results.

THE BACKGROUND

Arsenal had a mixed start to the 1952–53 season. Wins over Aston Villa and Manchester United in their opening games and victory at White Hart Lane in September were offset by home defeats against Sunderland and Charlton. It was not really until mid-November when the Gunners travelled to Anfield that the Arsenal championship challenge really took off. Roper, who was injured, was replaced by Ben Marden who scored twice in a 5–1 win, but Marden's joy was short lived as he found himself out of the team for the next game. That victory over Liverpool, however, showed what the team was capable of and they proceeded to remain unbeaten for the rest of the year, including a remarkable 6–4 win at Bolton on Christmas Day.

The Gunners' run of success was interrupted on 3 January by Sunderland who went to the top of the table with a 3–1 win at Highbury, but Arsenal soon regained their form. In their next league game they beat fellow title chasers Wolves 5–3 and led the *Daily Mirror* to proclaim that: 'The "impossible" Cup and league double is not beyond Arsenal if they continue to play even half as well as they did in the first 50 minutes against Wolves. No defence in the world could have stopped the precision movements which produced three great goals by Lishman, Logie and Milton in a five-minute spell of perfect teamwork.'

February began with a 4–0 win over north London neighbours Tottenham, but the following Saturday was to be a much sterner test for Arsenal. Following two home games in the FA Cup against Doncaster and Bury – both of whom were despatched by a four-goal margin – Arsenal were drawn away to Burnley, one of the best teams in the country, in the fifth round. When Arsenal came away from Turf Moor with a 2–0 win, courtesy of goals from Holton and Lishman, talk of the double, which had not been achieved by any team since 1897, was rife. With a home draw against Blackpool in the sixth round and a place near the top of the First Division, the Gunners were well placed in both competitions. Within the space of a week, however, one team seemed to have wrecked Arsenal's chances in both the league and the Cup.

On 21 February Arsenal went to Blackpool in confident mood having put six goals past Derby in a midweek match; but they were in for a rude awakening. A 3–2 defeat had critics proclaiming that their dreams of the title and the double were over. The *Daily Mirror* reported that: 'It was an Arsenal dream, the annual mirage of the double . . . but the dream is dead . . . It was slaughter on the South Shore for a ragged Arsenal army. The Arsenal defence in the face of furiously brilliant Blackpool attacks creaked and groaned and trembled and there was a clear suggestion of loss of control in the side. That seldom happens with Arsenal but now, clearly, the pressure is on.' One week later the double was well and truly over when the same Blackpool team went to Highbury and won 2–1 to knock Arsenal out of the Cup. Now there was only the league left to play for.

An impressive 4–1 win at Sheffield Wednesday in their next game, with all four goals scored by Cliff Holton, left Arsenal just one point behind league leaders Burnley and Preston, but with a game in hand and a superior goal average. Only one win in the next six games, however, meant that, with just eight games to go, Arsenal had some catching up to do.

Their league position started to become more secure on the Easter weekend. While their championship rivals had poor results Arsenal followed a 1–1 draw at Chelsea on Good Friday with a 5–3 win over Liverpool the following day and a 2–0 win in the return match against Chelsea on Easter Monday – with the help of a goal from the recalled Marden. When the Gunners won at Manchester City on the following Saturday they were right back in the race. The *Daily Mirror* predicted that 'if Arsenal are to win yet another league title they may well look back on their 4–2 win . . . as the game that turned the trick. They went there to face a City unbeaten in ten straight home league games, a City just close enough to the relegation pot to put an edge on their play, yet Arsenal contrived to make it another example of efficiency football.' Just after the interval the score was 2–2 but, as the *Daily Mirror* went on to report, 'in the second half, Arsenal, this remorseless, fluid, killing machine, wrapped the match safely away with great goals from Logie and Roper. Still very much the team to beat your Arsenal.'

When Arsenal beat Bolton 4–1 four days later they went to the top of the league. Despite the scoreline the *Daily Mail* was unimpressed: 'Here was no championship form . . . there was much bad football on both sides and only in the second half did Arsenal really get on top of opponents disorganised by injuries.' But, as the top of the table showed, Arsenal were in the right position at just the right time:

	Played	Goals For	Goals Against	Points
1. Arsenal	38	91	59	49
2. Wolves	40	79	59	49
3. Preston	38	79	58	48

All was not entirely well in the Arsenal camp, however, as was illustrated in the programme for their next game against Stoke:

Under the heading 'I'm ashamed' the following appeared in a national newspaper just before Easter: 'What do footballers think of the fans who cheer (and jeer) them? One Arsenal player takes this straight from the shoulder crack at the Highbury crowd. "They have been bred on success and are fine when everything is going our or their way, but they have no appreciation of real football. Though I am proud to wear the Arsenal colours, I am ashamed of the crowd and consider them to be the most biased and unsporting collection in the country." Whether or not this remark was made by an Arsenal player we do not know, but we would like

41

to assure our loyal supporters, however, of the fact that this opinion is not held by the Arsenal club. We are zealously proud of the loyal and sporting nature of our supporters and we take this opportunity of publicly disassociating ourselves with the remarks made. Arsenal has always had reason to be grateful for the full and generous support of its fans and the above remarks by whoever they were made are certainly not in accordance with fact.'

The controversy did not seem to affect the team, as they gained a crucial 3–1 win with the help of the maligned Arsenal support. According to one report: 'With the scoreboard showing that Charlton were beating Preston 1–0 at the interval, the supporters decided to give the Highbury Roar.' With Preston going down 2–1 at The Valley, Arsenal now had the championship within their grasp.

On Wednesday, 22 April, Arsenal travelled to Cardiff while Preston visited Manchester City. A win for the Gunners and defeat for their rivals would virtually seal the title race. Ninian Park, however, was no easy place to get a result in those days. The large, passionate crowd regularly produced an atmosphere akin to a Wales v England encounter, while the Cardiff team were no pushover either as the Gunners had found out when they had been beaten 1–0 at Highbury earlier in the season. The game turned out to be a passionate and full-blooded affair with both defences coming under sustained pressure. At the final whistle, however, neither team had been able to make the breakthrough and the Arsenal players were, in the end, pretty happy to escape with a goalless draw, or at least they were until they heard that Preston had left Maine Road with a 2–0 win. The table now read:

	Played	Goals For	Goals Against	Points
1. Arsenal	40	94	60	52
2. Wolves	41	84	60	51
3. Preston	40	82	60	50

Despite not beating Cardiff, Arsenal were still in the best position and it would have appeared that they had a comfortable run into the championship if it had not been for the fact that their penultimate game was away to their strongest challengers: Preston.

When Preston and Arsenal met at Deepdale on 25 April the equation was simple: either Preston would win and open up the title race once more or Arsenal would win or draw to win the league. Wolves would have to win at Tottenham and hope that Arsenal lost to have any chance. But, just when they had the chance to wrap up the championship, Arsenal appeared to lose their nerve.

Arsenal had started the game well enough, but when Preston's Tom Finney went down in the penalty area after half an hour, the referee pointed to the penalty-spot despite the mutterings from the Arsenal players who felt that he had taken a dive. Finney himself stepped up to give the home team the lead and Preston dominated the game from then on. A further goal from Wayman 20 minutes from time gave Preston a well-earned 2–0 win and opened up the title race once more. According to *The Times*, 'only one side wore the look of champions and it was certainly not Arsenal. They were reduced to a very minor role by a Preston side that bore the authentic stamp of class and had them beaten at all points in pure skill and artistry. Indeed it is a long time since one has seen an Arsenal side look so thoroughly uncomfortable; unsure of themselves in defence and without method in attack.' With Wolves going down 3–2 at Tottenham it was now a two-horse race with both Preston and Arsenal level on points, but with the Gunners having a much better goal average. The two games that would decide the championship were Derby v Preston on the following Wednesday and Arsenal v Burnley two days later.

Preston took to the field at the Baseball Ground knowing that while defeat would give Arsenal the championship, a victory would mean Arsenal had to beat Burnley in their last game to win the title. It would be no easy victory as Derby were also desperate to win because any other result would see them relegated to the Second Division.

Preston made the all-important breakthrough two minutes from half-time when they won a penalty and Tom Finney scored from the spot. The second half was dominated by Derby as they swarmed around the Preston goal and on several occasions the ball was found bouncing around in the Preston penalty box, but there always seemed to be a defender on hand to clear the ball away. As hard as they tried, Derby were unable to score and as the final whistle blew, *The Times* reported that 'the white shirts of Derby were just a little more slumped as the players made that dreadful trek to the tunnel, and the blue shirts of Preston skipped and danced in what might well be a championship triumph'.

Preston then went on an end-of-season tour, not knowing whether they were about to be crowned champions or not. The Arsenal players were seemingly also in the dark as it was not until they arrived for training the next day that they were made aware of the result. Once they were told of Preston's win, however, they knew exactly what was needed. They would have to beat Burnley two days later or just miss out on the championship for the second year running.

THE MATCH

The build-up to the match was no different to that of any other for the Arsenal players. Tom Whittaker decided that they should stick to their normal routine in the hope that there would be no additional nerves on the night. There were no nights at a hotel or days out for the players, just eggs on toast at King's Cross station as usual.

The match was to take place on the evening before the FA Cup final in the hope that the gate would be boosted by fans of Blackpool and Bolton who had come down to London for the following day's game at Wembley. The fans did not materialise, most of them were probably put off, however, by the heavy rain which fell over London throughout the day and turned the Highbury pitch into a quagmire.

Despite the foul weather, 51,586 spectators packed into the ground to see the championship finally decided. From start to finish they roared the Gunners on and according to the *Daily Mirror* 'the whole stadium was alive and alight. 51,000 made as much noise as I've ever heard on a football ground.'

The match programme had been produced before Preston's last game and so no one was unaware of what would be required to take the championship. The *Voice of Arsenal*, however, was prepared to be generous in defeat if the Gunners were unsuccessful: 'If it is not to be we have no complaint, Preston beat us well and truly last Saturday and we may have to pay the penalty. Let us then conclude by expressing congratulations of a general nature to the boys of both Preston and Arsenal teams for the magnificent fight they have put up this season. Whichever side wins the honours, at least both teams have earned fame.'

The weather had taken its toll on the playing surface and apart from the wings there was little grass to be seen on the pitch but, as Ben Marden recalls, the Arsenal players were quite happy to play in the mud: 'We were that type of team, we were good in heavy conditions so that was in our favour. We had a lot of strong players as well as the likes of Jimmy Logie who could hold the ball up.' From the start there was no doubt that Burnley were doing their best to win the game; not only would a win see them climb from sixth to fourth in the table but they also had in goal Desmond Thompson, a player who had more reason than most to want a victory – his brother played in goal for Preston.

After eight minutes the opening goal was scored, and it was the determined Burnley who scored it. Holden found Billy Elliott who switched the ball to Stephenson, the outside-right, in the penalty area and he scrambled the ball home. Perhaps it was not to be Arsenal's night after all.

Those were the days of high-scoring matches, with Arsenal having already played in five games that season in which eight goals or more had been scored, so it was not quite the blow that conceding an early goal would be today. In many ways it dispelled any nerves in the Arsenal side and forced them to roll their sleeves up and get back in the game. Joe Mercer in particular seemed to react positively to the goal and he was at the heart of Arsenal's attacking play from then on.

The next few moments were to be vital. The Arsenal team could have let their heads go down and allowed the game to get away from them, but instead they responded with what Bob Wall described as 'some of the most spirited attacking play I have ever seen from an Arsenal side'; and within a minute they were level. It was man-of-the-match Alex Forbes who transformed the game with his first goal of the season – picking up the ball from right-half, Forbes went on a storming run before striking a 25-yard shot which deflected off the shoulder of Brown, the Burnley defender, and flew into the net. According to the *Islington Gazette*: 'The Highbury crowd's cheering could have been heard for miles around' as the Scotsman danced with joy.

Three minutes later it was 2–1 to Arsenal. Roper sent his corner into the penalty area where Logie, looking as if he was going to head the ball, suddenly ducked and, to the astonishment of the Burnley defenders, Lishman standing behind him, hit a low volley into the net. The Highbury crowd went wild, but still Arsenal came forward, determined to finish off their opponents.

With Forbes in startling form, running and probing, in tandem with Logie, Lishman, Marden and Roper, the Arsenal forwards were irresistible and, after another seven minutes Arsenal completed their incredible turnaround. Marden sent a deep cross to Roper who immediately sent the ball back to Marden. He then hooked the ball over his head into the penalty area where Logie was on hand to flick the ball goalwards from five yards out to score Arsenal's third. In the space of just 15 minutes Arsenal's amazing forward blitz had transformed the game and had once more put them back in the driving seat for the championship.

When the teams left the field at half-time the score remained at 3–1 and optimistic Gunners fans talked of scoring three more goals which would take Arsenal's goals tally to 100 for the season. More objective observers, however, were aware that the game was far from over. Apart from that incredible quarter of an hour in which the Arsenal forwards were simply unstoppable, Burnley had had a good share of the game and were by no means out of it at this stage. The mood in the dressing-room reflected the fact that they rarely lost a game in which they were two goals ahead, so if they just kept it tight in the second half they should emerge victorious.

As the second half got under way it was clear that the Arsenal players were much more concerned with winning the game than they were with achieving a century of goals; no longer were they throwing caution to the wind as they had done to score their trio of goals: now the emphasis was on defence. As a result it was Burnley who now dictated the tempo of the game as they came forward in search of the goal that would get them back into the match. The home team was now concentrating on defence so much that Goring was the only man left up front and, on the few occasions that he received the ball, he was forced to go it alone as there was no support from the rest of the team.

The Arsenal goal came under increasing pressure as Burnley went on the attack with their forwards, Shannon and Elliott, looking particularly dangerous. So desperate were the Arsenal players for the game to end that even in the early stages of the second half there was evidence of time-wasting. Yet with 15 minutes to go it seemed as though their tactics would pay off as the two-goal lead remained intact. It was at that moment, however, that the course of the game changed once more. Burnley won a corner kick and, having taken it short, the ball was swung into the area by Stephenson. Then, with an almost carbon copy of Arsenal's second goal, a Burnley forward ducked just as he was about to head the ball and the unmarked Elliott side-footed it into the net.

The Lancastrians now threw men forward in an attempt to find the equaliser. The Arsenal defence was compelled to work overtime to protect their goal and goalkeeper George Swindin was forced into several outstanding saves. The tension around the ground was unbearable – nowhere more so than on the Arsenal bench. Bob Wall recalled the reaction of manager Tom Whittaker in the game's dying moments: 'With ten minutes left Tom Whittaker couldn't bear the tension any longer. He jumped up and disappeared under the stand. I followed him in case he was feeling ill. When I went into his office he was sitting just behind the door mopping his forehead. I said, "You all right Tom?" "No, I'm not! I need a large brandy. I don't think I can take any more of that out there," he explained, gesturing in the general direction of the pitch. The cognac seemed to calm him and he insisted that I should return to watch the finish. "I'll stay down here Bob," said Tom. "It will be agony, but there's nothing I can do – only the lads can win us the championship."'

Arsenal began mounting a few forward raids again to relieve the tension with both Marden and Forbes almost getting through on goal. But as soon as the attacks broke down, the Burnley forwards would go back to bombarding the Arsenal goal. On one occasion Holden went down in the Gunners penalty area and the whole ground held its breath before the referee waved play on. Almost immediately a drive from Adamson forced Swindin to dive full length to save it. Time after time the ball fell to Burnley forwards in the penalty area, but they were unable to dig the ball out of the Highbury mud and the home fans could breathe again.

The clock seemed to have slowed to a snail's pace as every minute seemed like an hour and the home supporters whistled desperately at the referee but, eventually, just after eight o'clock in the evening, the final whistle went. Arsenal had held on and the championship was theirs. Bob Wall wrote that, 'under an appropriately red sky [the players] were lost to view, engulfed by thousands of jubilant Arsenal fans'. Ben Marden remembers the scenes vividly: 'I can see it now. At the end of the match there were hats and scarves and coats and everything going in the air.' A cordon of police took to the pitch and the players were able to stagger jubilantly from the pitch. As the captain entered the dressing-room he embraced Tom Whittaker who thanked the players for all their efforts. Mercer then shook hands with Bob Wall and said : 'It was absolute hell going through those last few minutes, Bob, but it's heaven now!'

In the end Arsenal had finished level on points with Preston, but their goal average was just 0.099 of a goal better than that of their challengers – the smallest winning margin of any league championship in history. Arsenal had now won seven league titles, more than any other team.

After the game Arsenal fans gathered outside the ground to celebrate and they refused to leave the street until they had seen Joe Mercer. There were cheers when, just 45 minutes after the final whistle had blown, the veteran captain emerged on the steps of Highbury's main entrance and waved at the crowd. Mercer then held his arm aloft to quieten the cheers and announced: 'This has been the most wonderful day of my life, but now I am sorry to tell you that you have seen me playing for the last time. I am retiring from football.'

Inevitably, Mercer's announcement meant that a memorable evening was tinged with sadness, but the sadness was short lived as Whittaker persuaded Mercer to play one more season. Mercer, however, did not quite make a whole season. When playing against Liverpool at Highbury the following April, Mercer broke his leg. As he was carried from the pitch on a stretcher he lifted himself up and waved to the fans. Everyone knew that his career was now over.

What happened on the evening of 1 May 1953 epitomises Arsenal's ability to reclaim great triumphs when it seemed as though they had thrown it all away. Arsenal should have made sure of a championship win before it got that far – but that would have been too easy. They were awarded just one point from their previous two games and then went a goal down in the decider. Even when they stormed into a two-goal lead they let a goal in near the end and then had to hang on for the final whistle. But in the end it was one of the greatest nights in Highbury's long history.

Unfortunately it also heralded a long period of Arsenal failure. It would be another 17 years before Arsenal would win another trophy. Many players would arrive and depart before glory would return to Highbury and many Arsenal supporters would grow up knowing only defeat and despondency. But through all the years, those that were there would remember 1 May 1953 as one of *the* great nights. A night of remarkable excitement, tension and drama. A night that was almost good enough to compensate for the next 17 years.

FINAL SCORE

Arsenal	3	Burnley	2
Forbes	9 mins	Stephenson	8 mins
Lishman	12 mins	Elliott	75 mins
Logie	19 mins		
Attendance:	51,586		

Arsenal:	Swindin, Wade, Smith, Forbes, Daniel, Mercer, Roper, Logie, Goring, Lishman, Marden
Burnley:	Thompson, Aird, Winton, Adamson, Cummings, Brown, Stephenson, McIlroy, Holden, Shannon, Elliott

Chapter 4

END OF THE FAMINE

Inter-Cities Fairs Cup final (second leg)
Arsenal v Anderlecht
Tuesday, 28 April 1970

Tuesday, 28 April 1970, was the night that Arsenal came in from the cold. It was 17 years since the league championship triumph of 1953 and since then the club had only managed a top three placing on one occasion, and had even been unable to reach an FA Cup semi-final. The only glimmer of success had been the League Cup finals that they had reached in the two preceding years, but a controversial defeat against Leeds and humiliation by third division Swindon Town had only made the Highbury faithful more desperate for success. The glory days of the 1930s and early 1950s were becoming a millstone around the necks of the players as they were constantly reminded of their predecessors' achievements and many of them used to curse the bust of Herbert Chapman which gazed down at them as they entered Highbury's famous marble halls.

Midway through the 1969–70 season it looked very much like the barren run was about to be extended to 18 years; Arsenal were stuck at mid-table in the First Division and had been knocked out of both domestic cup competitions in the third round. The only chance of success that remained was the Fairs Cup – or the UEFA Cup as it was later to become. If the ghosts of the past were to be finally banished the present-day team would have to win in Europe – something that no Arsenal team had achieved before.

THE PLAYERS

The Arsenal goalkeeper was Bob Wilson, a player noted for his bravery and reliability. Wilson, a former schoolteacher, had arrived at Highbury in 1963 but had only established himself as a regular in the team after the 1968 League Cup final defeat. Although born in Chesterfield, he went on to play for Scotland by virtue of his Scottish parentage

In front of Wilson was a solid defence containing many quality players. Bob McNab was signed from Huddersfield in 1966 for £50,000 – a record fee for a full-back. His success at left-back for Arsenal was reflected when in 1968 he made his England debut as a substitute against Romania and he went on to win another three caps. On the right side of defence was the hard-tackling Peter Storey. Along with the likes of Tommy Smith and Ron Harris, Storey was one of the classic 1970s hard men and his combative style earned him several caps for his country.

The captain and backbone of the team was Frank McLintock. Still regarded by many as the best captain Arsenal ever had, McLintock was bought from Leicester City in 1964. He had already played for Scotland and had undoubted ability and leadership qualities, but he did appear to be something of a Cup-final jinx. He had played in Leicester's losing FA Cup final teams of 1961 and 1963 and had left the club just before they won the League Cup in 1964. Then he had played for Arsenal in the 1968 and 1969 League Cup finals – both of which they had lost. It had begun to look as though he would never be a cup winner.

Alongside McLintock in the centre of defence was Peter Simpson. Simpson, from Gorleston in Norfolk, had come through the youth system and made his debut in 1964. Although he made sporadic appearances after that it was not until the 1966–67 season that he established himself in the team where he soon struck up a formidable partnership with the Arsenal captain.

In midfield was the promising Eddie Kelly. At 19 the young Glaswegian had only made his league debut earlier in the season, and he had already shown that as well as having great skill and a powerful shot, he also possessed the sort of determination that would make him a valuable asset.

George Graham had been signed from Chelsea in 1966. He was

the man who provided the style in the middle of the pitch, and such was the relaxed way that he cruised his way through games that he earned the nickname 'Stroller' from the Highbury fans.

Jon Sammels was a player who lacked only the confidence to go with his ability but, despite his unpopularity with Gunners fans, he consistently scored goals from midfield, some of which had been of crucial importance.

George Armstrong had already been at Highbury for several years and although he came from the north-east, he was Mr Arsenal. He was a vital member of the team who would run all day and his accurate crosses were the main source of ammunition to the forwards.

Also in midfield was a young player called Peter Marinello. Marinello had been a mid-season signing from Hibernian for £100,000 which, at the age of 19, made him the most expensive teenager in history. He was already known as 'the second George Best' and was expected to instantly transform the Arsenal team with his exciting wing play. Unfortunately, the media hype and the great weight of expectation combined to make Marinello's time in north London a difficult one for such a young man and, inevitably, he struggled to live up to his reputation.

In attack was the greatly underrated John Radford. Never a prolific goalscorer – he had never scored more than 15 league goals in a season for Arsenal – he was still a great leader of the line, a constant threat in the air, and a provider of many goals for his team-mates. Also up front were two youngsters from opposite ends of England who would go on to great things at Highbury – local boy Charlie George and Ray Kennedy from the north-east.

The man in charge was Bertie Mee. Until the summer of 1966, Mee had been physiotherapist at Highbury, but when manager Billy Wright left the club, Mee was the surprise appointment ahead of the big names that were expected to get the job. Mee had no experience of football management, but he had had a successful career in the military and also in medicine. He immediately instilled the team with discipline, professionalism and dedication – virtues which he himself exemplified. While his main role was in the art of management, the tactics and coaching of the team were the responsibility initially of Dave Sexton, but on his departure in 1967 the job went to former Gunners full-back Don Howe.

THE BACKGROUND

The Gunners' Fairs Cup campaign had started back in September 1969, yet to understand the motivation of the team one needs to go back to the previous season and the 3–1 defeat at the hands of Third-Division Swindon in the League Cup final.

It was a nightmare day for Arsenal and the press were quick to rub salt into the wound. One report was headlined 'The Shame of London' and proceeded to slaughter both the team and the individual players. Afterwards, Don Howe told the team that such an experience could either destroy them or be the making of them and Bob Wilson has no doubt that in the long run it had an incredibly positive effect: 'The whole thing was hideous at the time, but I would say that it brought us closer together . . . I would always quote that game as the reason that we had such a side the following year and went on to even better things.'

Arsenal's European season began with a comfortable 3–1 first-round victory over Glentoran of Northern Ireland. The fixture was significant on two counts, firstly for the sending-off of Charlie George for dissent in the second leg and, secondly, for the first appearance of Ray Kennedy in an Arsenal shirt when he came on as substitute in the same game.

A 3–0 win over Sporting Lisbon in the second round was also achieved with relative ease, but the following round was a much firmer test with Rouen beaten only by a Jon Sammels goal late in the second leg. Arsenal's Romanian quarter-final opponents Dinamo Bacau did not cause many problems – a fine 2–0 win in the away tie was followed by a 7–1 thrashing at Highbury to complete a resounding 9–1 aggregate win.

At the semi-final stage Arsenal were joined by Anderlecht of Belgium, who had knocked out the cup holders Newcastle in the previous round, and Internazionale of Milan, European Cup finalists three years previously. The one team that they wanted to avoid, however, were Ajax. The Dutch team contained the likes of Cruyff and Krol and had reached the European Cup final the previous year and would go on to be European champions for the next three seasons. Arsenal drew Ajax.

The first leg of the semi-final on a cold and damp evening at

Highbury saw what was probably Arsenal's best performance in the competition to date.

Charlie George scored an all-important early goal, shooting low from outside the penalty area after a quarter of an hour, as the home side took the game to the Dutchmen. Ajax had a team of skilful, elegant and creative players, but they seemed content to sit back in defence, confident that a one-goal deficit could be surmounted in the second game. As the clock ticked on it looked as though they would be successful in frustrating Arsenal but, with ten minutes to go, it was Sammels who struck home an Armstrong cross to make it 2–0, and just three minutes later Graham was tripped in the penalty area and scored from the spot to make it a 3–0 victory to Arsenal.

Arsenal were now clear favourites to reach the final, as were Inter who went back to Italy with a 1–0 advantage after their first-leg match against Anderlecht in Brussels.

In Amsterdam, Arsenal were utterly unshakable in the face of Ajax's surging attacks and even the threat by an Arab terrorist group to plant a bomb in the Olympic Stadium did not seem to upset them. A goal from Muhren after 17 minutes gave the Dutch side hope and increased the pressure on the Arsenal defence. But Arsenal remained resolute to the end and they reached a European final for the first time in the club's history. Their opponents would be Anderlecht, who had surprisingly won through with a 2–0 victory in Milan.

Manager Bertie Mee was understandably delighted after the match: 'I am tremendously proud of our efforts tonight. Ajax are a magnificent attacking side, but they were allowed to make little impression. This Arsenal team is improving with every performance and we feel very confident that we shall have the Fairs Cup to show for our season's hard work.'

Mee was even happier the following day when the draw gave Arsenal the advantage of playing the second leg at home: 'We're delighted to be away in the first leg. We want to collect that trophy in front of our own supporters.'

As the penalty shoot-out had yet to be introduced into European football, drawn games were usually settled by the toss of a coin. In order to avoid this the two teams decided to arrange a venue for a replay in the event of a draw. On winning the toss, Arsenal chose to play the game at Highbury.

And so, on 22 April, just a week after the semi-final, Arsenal went to Brussels to take on Anderlecht in the first leg of the final. Before the match Bertie Mee compared Anderlecht's Parc Astrid to Queens Park Rangers ground at Loftus Road – both allowing the crowd to be close to the pitch – and he hoped that his team would be more comfortable in such an English-style stadium. Helping them to feel at home were about 1,500 Londoners who had made the trip over to Belgium, but they struggled to make themselves heard above the roars of a 37,000 capacity crowd clamouring for English blood.

Mee and Howe decided that, with Anderlecht's defence having a reputation for being somewhat suspect, they would attack the Belgians in the hope of getting one or more valuable away goals, but they had not reckoned with their opponents ability to exploit the space that an attacking policy would provide them with.

Anderlecht tore into the Arsenal defence right from the off, combining breathtaking skill with rugged aggression. The atmosphere in the crowd was electric and the pressure on the Gunners defence was relentless. Two early penalty appeals rattled the visitors, and they were unable to show the sort of composure that had brought such success in Amsterdam.

After 25 minutes Anderlecht made the breakthrough. A pass from Nordahl found Devrindt on the edge of the penalty area. Devrindt slipped the ball through the legs of Peter Simpson and then drove it past Bob Wilson at the near post to give the Belgians the lead. Now was the time for the Arsenal defence to stay firm; but within five minutes they had gone further behind. Devrindt centred and Mulder swept the ball first time into the net from 15 yards.

For the rest of the first half and on into the second the trio of Devrindt, Mulder and Van Himst tortured the Arsenal defence with power, guile and speed that left the London team looking helpless and inadequate. As the attacks continued Arsenal had the bravery of Wilson in goal to thank for keeping the deficit to two, but there was nothing that the goalkeeper could do in the 77th minute – Devrindt and Mulder ran 25 yards through the middle of the Arsenal defence, interchanging passes, before Mulder slammed a shot into the net from 12 yards to give Anderlecht a seemingly unassailable lead.

Arsenal now had a mountain to climb and, to make things worse, Charlie George picked up an injury and had to be substituted after 80 minutes. The man who replaced him was 19-year-old Ray Kennedy. Arsenal desperately needed a goal to have any chance in the second leg and, with just five minutes to go, it was Kennedy who gave them a lifeline. With virtually his first touch of the game, Kennedy rose at the far post to meet a long cross from the right by Armstrong and send the ball firmly past the goalkeeper, Trappeniers, into the net. Arsenal had a precious away goal and were right-back in the tie as they managed to hold on until the final whistle.

The players had gone to Brussels, however, hoping to win the match and ensure victory, so there was an air of despondency as they returned to the dressing-room. None felt the disappointment more than McLintock who was faced with being a Cup-final loser yet again. But, as Bob Wilson later recalled, his mood soon turned to determination: 'Suddenly Frank started hurling things around, like a boot or something, and it was "we'll paralyse them at Highbury". It was crazy talk really, but suddenly he'd gone from depression to saying "in two weeks' time we'll slaughter them". If we could have gone back on the pitch we would have pulverised them there and then.'

Bertie Mee knew that Kennedy's strike meant that they were still in with a chance: 'It was a vital goal. It came just as we were all feeling terribly disappointed about taking a three-goal deficit back to London. It will be a tremendous second leg. I only hope our fans give us the sort of support Anderlecht had tonight.' Anderlecht coach Pierre Sinabaldi reflected that victory was no longer certain: 'I would have settled for a 3–1 win before the match. Now I must say it is no guarantee that we will win the Fairs Cup.'

After the game there was some surprise at the tactics that Mee and Howe had decided to adopt in such an important game. Jan Mulder who had certainly made the most of the space that Arsenal had provided commented: 'Arsenal played into our hands. We had heard so much about the strength of their defence, but found it surprisingly easy to get through it. We had expected a more disciplined defensive game, but they gave us so much room we could hardly believe it.'

Mee, however, was unrepentant: 'Don Howe and I had thoroughly checked out Anderlecht's strength and weaknesses. We had a choice of trying to exploit their suspect defence or to concentrate solely on containing their very fine attack. Our decision was to go for goals. We saw no reason to break the successful pattern we have followed during our last 18 matches.'

There was, however, no doubt who had been the outstanding player in the first leg. Dutch international Jan Mulder had demonstrated that he was a world-class player and had certainly made quite an impression on the Arsenal defence. Frank McLintock recalled the warning that he had received from Newcastle captain Bobby Moncur: 'He said that if you give this guy the scope he can destroy you. Well, he was certainly tremendous against us.' Bob McNab agreed: 'Cruyff was supposed to be the best thing in Dutch football, but Mulder's in a different class.' Even 25 years later Bob Wilson remembers how brilliant Mulder was: 'He had pace, his running off the ball was incredible and he just kept popping up all over the place. Peter Simpson and Frank McLintock were just pulled ragged by this guy's runs. We were just totally shellshocked. We didn't play badly, we were just outplayed.'

As the second leg approached, both teams were in confident mood. For the Belgian team, Mulder promised: 'We'll hammer Arsenal over there, I'm sure about that.' The Arsenal management, however, still felt that they could make up the deficit. Don Howe thought that the second leg would be very different from the first: 'We can pull back these two goals at Highbury and win this cup; make no mistake, because there are Anderlecht men who will not give as much away from home.' Bertie Mee also sensed victory: 'We have been averaging two goals a game in our past 15 matches and I would not be surprised if we put four or five past Anderlecht's suspect defence.'

As the big day approached, however, the tie was thrown into confusion as doubt was raised over whether away goals would count double in the event of a draw. The Fairs Cup Committee met on the morning of the game to make their decision but, on the eve of the final, FIFA president and chairman of the committee Sir Stanley Rous said that the clubs' decision to arrange for a possible third match had ruled out the normal methods of settling ties that ended level on aggregate: 'The principle of away goals counting double only applies, surely, when clubs, for one reason or another, cannot play a third match.'

Arsenal were understandably outraged that the rules that had applied throughout the competition might be changed at such a late stage. Anderlecht, after all, might not have been in the final if the rule had not applied beforehand, having knocked out both Dunfermline and Newcastle on away goals. Bertie Mee protested: 'They must not change the rules in the middle of a tie. Our tactics in Belgium were shaped by that rule and without it we would never have gone there to attack.' In the end it was decided, just a few hours before the game kicked off, that the away-goals rule would apply, and so Arsenal knew that a 2-0 win would give them their first trophy for 17 years.

THE MATCH

After the away ties against Ajax and Anderlecht, Bertie Mee had first-hand experience of how passionate support from the crowd could unnerve the visiting team and give the home side an advantage. In his programme notes for the match, Mee stressed the part the fans could play: 'One last plea on this, our Cup final night. Both the players and myself would like to hear the roar of encouragement which our players have faced abroad in this competition. The fantastic vocal support which Ajax gave their players in Amsterdam was almost unnerving. Believe us all, it really does make a tremendous difference. Give us all the help you can tonight, and I hope we will do the rest for you.'

As it was, over 50,000 packed Highbury and the atmosphere that they created is still talked about today by those that were there. For the first quarter of the game Arsenal appeared nervous and anxious while the Anderlecht defence stood firm. It was not until

McNab and Graham tested Trappeniers in the Belgian goal that the home team started to find their feet. Arsenal began to look more confident, a shot from Charlie George looked goalbound until it was deflected behind off a defender, and a George Graham header forced the goalkeeper to save just under the bar.

Then in the 25th minute the breakthrough was made. A corner from Armstrong was only half cleared and Eddie Kelly jinked inside Nordahl before crashing home a half-volley – over a wall of Anderlecht defenders – from 20 yards out. Kelly said afterwards: 'I didn't have time to take aim – I just let go and hoped for the best. I could have jumped out of the stadium when I saw it go into the top of the net.'

Both the crowd and the team now sensed that victory was within their grasp. In defence Arsenal regained their composure and showed the sort of determination that had proved so successful in Amsterdam, while up front the Anderlecht rearguard was subjected to continuous aerial bombardment. With the Highbury crowd urging their team on and the relentless pressure being exerted by the Gunners attack, the Belgians' confidence began to erode but, as time went by, they were still very much in the tie. Anderlecht knew that if they could snatch a goal, the Cup was almost certainly theirs.

Trappeniers did well to save from Graham and George but, despite the continuing pressure on the visitors' defence, half-time came and went with no further score. Ten minutes into the second half, however, Anderlecht almost sealed the tie; a skilful exchange of passes between Mulder and Puis ended with Nordahl hitting a close-range shot against the post. Just moments later, Wilson had to dive full-stretch to beat out Mulder's shot.

Arsenal may have been short on ideas, but they lacked nothing in determination and effort. As the team chased and challenged everything that moved, man of the match George Armstrong darted down the right-wing, and Graham and Radford won everything in the air. Anderlecht continued to look dangerous on the rare occasions that they got forward but, eventually, their defence had to give. It was in the 70th minute when Graham found McNab with a superb through pass and the cross found Radford unmarked in the penalty box to head powerfully into the net.

The ground erupted. After so many years of disappointment, Arsenal were just 20 minutes away from a trophy. All they had to do was hang on and the Cup would be theirs. Two minutes later, however, the controversy about the away-goals rule was made irrelevant when George's cross from the left found Sammels on the right-hand side of the box. Sammels chested the ball down, skipped a tackle and drove the ball into the far corner of the net from 12 yards.

In the space of two minutes the state of the tie had changed completely. Now Anderlecht had to score to take the game into extra-time. During those last, long 20 minutes the dangerous trio of Mulder, Devrindt and Van Himst converged on the Arsenal penalty area, desperately seeking the goal that would get them back into the match. The tension was such that someone in the crowd collapsed and died during the game's final few seconds. The Belgian forwards, however, could find no way through a defence that was less accommodating than it had been in Brussels just a week earlier. McLintock was determined that he would not be denied, and he marshalled his men superbly until the sound of the final whistle.

As the whistle was blown to end the match there were scenes of euphoric celebration as thousands of fans surged through the powerless police cordons onto the pitch to embrace the victorious players. Grown men wept with joy as Highbury witnessed the sort of jubilation that had not been seen there for many years. For the fans it was the end of a long wait for success, while for the players it meant an end to the endless comparisons with the great Arsenal teams of the 1930s as now they had a trophy that previous Arsenal teams had never won. As goalscorer Jon Sammels said later: 'This will make a huge difference to every player and every fan. No longer are we striving. After years of disappointment something has been won and we are in a position of strength.' For one player, however, this win was a particular relief. As Frank McLintock said after the game: 'At last I'm able to get rid of the feeling that I'm a jinx player. This is my fifth major Cup final and the first time I've finished on the winning side. I'm overwhelmed.'

After McLintock received the Cup from Sir Stanley Rous, the team was carried shoulder-high around the pitch by jubilant fans.

Charlie George had the shirt ripped from his back by souvenir-hunting fans, while Bob Wilson was paraded on the shoulders of fans as if he were a prized trophy. As Wilson said: 'We started to try and do a lap of honour and I was gaily careering round when suddenly the pitch was invaded and I was oblivious to the fact that the other players had made a run for it and gone and so I kept going and by the time I got back to the dressing-room my back was red raw from being slapped so many times.'

Once the players had escaped back into the dressing-room, the supporters gathered in front of the directors box chanting the manager's name until Bertie Mee, his assistant Don Howe and Frank McLintock appeared with the Cup to acknowledge their salute. Outside the ground hundreds of people gathered in Avenell Road and sang the names of the players who hung out of the dressing-room windows to greet them.

The celebrations both inside and outside the ground continued long into the night for Arsenal fans had waited a long time for this moment. Thousands danced through the North London streets as residents hung up flags and streamers in the team colours. One policeman commented: 'I've never seen scenes like it – not even when we won the war.' Arsenal secretary Bob Wall who had been with the club for 42 years said: 'I've witnessed many wonderful occasions here in the past, particularly in the pre-war days, but I must say I've never seen anything quite like these scenes at Highbury before.'

The Arsenal players, officials and guests celebrated with a champagne party which went on until the early hours of the morning, but even as the fans and players milked their triumph with almost hysterical delight, Bertie Mee and Don Howe were already planning for the future. It had been a memorable night and a great triumph. This was, after all, the first time that any team had ever won a European final after trailing by two goals from the first leg, but the Arsenal management had their sights set on even greater things, as Mee said shortly after the game had finished: 'Now we would like to win the league.'

The next day the *Daily Mirror* reported: 'Last night's result was pulsating proof that Arsenal are perhaps about to enter a new era of greatness.' As far as those Arsenal fans were concerned they were already there.

FINAL SCORE

| Arsenal | 3 | Anderlecht | 0 (4-3 on aggregate) |

Kelly	25 mins
Radford	70 mins
Sammels	72 mins
Attendance:	51,612

Arsenal:	Wilson, Storey, McNab, Kelly, McLintock, Simpson, Armstrong, Sammels, Radford, George, Graham
Anderlecht:	Trappeniers, Heylens, Martens, Nordahl, Velkeneers, Kialunda, Desanghere, Devrindt, Mulder, Van Himst, Puis

Chapter 5

AT THE DOUBLE

FA Cup final
Arsenal v Liverpool
Saturday, 8 May 1971

When Bertie Mee had said that the club's next aim was the league championship most people saw that as a long-term target. After all, despite their European success, Arsenal had only finished 12th in the First Division that season and would have to contend with strong teams such as Leeds, Manchester United, Manchester City, Chelsea and Everton amongst others. Yet, remarkably, by the end of the season Mee's team was not only on the verge of the championship, but also stood to gain the Cup and league 'double' which had only been achieved once before this century.

The Fairs Cup win may have banished many of the ghosts of the great teams of the 1930s, but if they could win the double this side would not only be remembered as one of the greatest teams in Arsenal's history, but also as one of the best English teams of all time.

THE PLAYERS
The main change that was made to the Arsenal team that had beaten Anderlecht was that Peter Storey was moved from defence into midfield. This had originally been a ploy to negate the influence of Alan Ball in the opening game of the season against champions Everton at Goodison Park, but the change was so successful that Bertie Mee continued with it from then on. The resulting vacancy at right-back provided the chance for the young Irishman, Pat Rice, to establish himself in the team.

A pre-season injury to Peter Simpson saw John Roberts, a Welshman signed from Northampton Town the previous season, form an effective partnership with Frank McLintock in the centre of defence. Roberts kept his place alongside the captain until Simpson's return in November and played an important part in Arsenal's strong start to the season.

In attack Ray Kennedy, who had already made his mark at Highbury, became John Radford's regular partner and soon struck up a formidable relationship that produced 47 goals over the season. Towards the end of the season, Charlie George also established himself in the team and he soon became Arsenal's superstar. George was a local Islington boy and the fact that he had stood on the Highbury terraces as a youngster, coupled with his fashionable long hair, made him a cult hero with Arsenal's young fans, while his genius on the ball made him popular with all Gunners supporters. He was a regular in the team during the latter half of the season and was to make many crucial contributions to the team's success.

THE BACKGROUND

By the new year of 1971 the optimism that had been prevalent at the start of the season had turned to expectancy. Over half the league season had been completed and only two games had been lost – one of which was a crushing 5–0 defeat at Stoke – the defence of the Fairs Cup was continuing after wins against Lazio, Sturm Graz and Beveren, and the FA Cup campaign was about to begin with an away game against non-league Yeovil.

With the defence marshalled so superbly by Frank McLintock and with Peter Storey closing down space in midfield, Arsenal had already kept 13 clean sheets in the league. With regular scoring from Radford and Kennedy, including a hat trick each, as well as Graham and Armstrong popping up with goals from midfield, the chase for the title was well and truly on.

The main threat to Arsenal's championship aspirations came from Yorkshire. Leeds United were considered by many to be the best team in Europe at the time. They had won the championship in 1969 and had been runners-up in both the league and Cup in 1970. Their team had a very similar look to that of Arsenal. Charlton and

Hunter were strong in defence, Billy Bremner snapped away in midfield and Clarke and Lorimer were lethal in attack.

At the beginning of 1971 there was little to choose between the two teams at the top of the First Division, but Arsenal's defeats at Huddersfield and Liverpool meant that by the end of January Leeds had opened up a five-point lead. Against a team that gave away as little as Leeds, this was a large gap to claw back. In the FA Cup Arsenal had already reached the fifth round – Yeovil had been comfortably dispatched 3–0, courtesy of goals from Radford and Kennedy, while Portsmouth had forced a replay after a last-minute equaliser cancelled out Peter Storey's penalty at Fratton Park. In the return match at Highbury another Storey spot-kick decided the match as the Gunners finished 3–2 winners.

By February Charlie George was back in the team and his goals from midfield were to prove vital. In the fifth round of the Cup Arsenal went to Maine Road where they took on Manchester City, holders of the Cup-Winners' Cup, and it was George's two goals – including a fierce shot direct from a free-kick – that won the game. Ten days later, however, a 2–0 defeat at Derby seemed to have killed off any hope of championship glory as Arsenal now found themselves seven points behind the mighty Leeds.

But from 2 March to 20 April, Arsenal played nine league games and won them all. In 810 minutes of league football only one goal was scored against the Gunners' defence. Not even Leeds could cope with such a powerful run of form as they found themselves slowly caught and passed by the ruthless Highbury machine.

There was no doubt that the key to Arsenal's run of success was a defence which, as Pat Rice recalls, had enormous confidence in each other: 'We had such a good understanding between the back five that once we went a goal up, you may as well have gone home. I don't think there were many times when we took the lead that the opposition came back to get a draw, let alone a victory. We practised a lot so everyone knew what the others were doing.' As the final championship run-in approached, Arsenal were in a strong position. After 18 years without a domestic trophy they were, amazingly, on course to win both the league and the Cup.

As the season began to enter its crucial final stage, Bertie Mee sat his team down in the dressing-room and mapped out the remainder of their campaign. Mee told his players that they had a chance to put their names in the history books and that if they were prepared to dedicate themselves to the cause they had a chance of achieving greatness. There were just two months left and the double was still within their grasp.

In the sixth round of the FA Cup Arsenal again found themselves drawn away from home, just as they had in every other round. This time they travelled to Leicester City (who would go on to win the Second Division championship that season). A goalless draw at Filbert Street was followed by a 1–0 win, courtesy of yet another Charlie George goal, and so Arsenal were in an FA Cup semi-final for the first time since 1952. At this point there was still the possibility of a remarkable treble but, on 23 March, the Gunners lost their grip on the Fairs Cup as they were beaten 1–0 in Cologne after a controversial penalty decision, and they went out on the away-goals rule. Just four days later they travelled to Hillsborough to play the team that had beaten them earlier in the season, Stoke City, in what was to be one of the most dramatic and important games in Arsenal's history.

It may have taken Arsenal nearly 20 years to reach an FA Cup semi-final, but it seemed that it would take them only 30 minutes to lose it. Firstly, Peter Storey tried to clear the ball from a Stoke corner, but succeeded only in hitting it straight onto the boot of Stoke's Denis Smith. The ball ricocheted into the top of the net. Then in the 29th minute a terrible back pass from Charlie George found John Ritchie who made it 2–0. The Arsenal players trooped disconsolately into the dressing-room at half-time having gifted the opposition two goals.

Pat Rice remembers what Don Howe said to the team during the break: 'He came in, and he wasn't really ranting and raving and singling people out, which made a change, he just said "you've got 45 minutes, give us 100 per cent and that's all people can ask of you".'

Early in the second half John Mahoney had a great chance to make it 3–0 and kill the game, but Wilson made a crucial save and almost immediately the ball went up the field where Kennedy lobbed the ball over his own head into the penalty area. The ball rebounded to Storey on the edge of the box, and he scored to give Arsenal some hope. For the remainder of the game chances came and went at both ends of the pitch – as the Gunners pressed forward in search of an equaliser, Stoke broke away in search of the deciding goal. As full-time approached, it was still 2–1 and it seemed that the dream of the double was over, but as the game entered injury time the Stoke goalkeeper Gordon Banks bundled a high ball out of play. He claimed that he had been fouled, but referee Pat Partridge gave a corner. As Armstrong crossed the ball in from the right, McLintock rose to head the ball towards the far corner of the net. John Mahoney, the Stoke defender, seeing that the ball was goalbound could only stick out his arm and palm the ball away. A penalty was awarded. Ten of the Arsenal players were ecstatic – they were sure that they were right back in the running. One player, however, was feeling the weight of enormous pressure on his shoulders; the destiny of the double was now in the hands of Peter Storey. All he had to do was put the ball past the best goalkeeper in the world. Bob Wilson could not bear to watch, but he had no need to worry. Storey hit it straight and low, Banks moved to his right.

In their dressing-room after the game the Stoke players were disconsolate, they knew that their big chance had gone. As a result the replay at Villa Park was a much less dramatic affair. A first-half header from George Graham was followed after the interval by a goal from Ray Kennedy to give Arsenal a comfortable 2–0 win. At last Arsenal were at Wembley where they would meet Liverpool, who had beaten Merseyside rivals Everton to reach the final. But now, for the first time in the season, they could concentrate completely on the league.

On 24 April Arsenal travelled to the Hawthorns to play West Bromwich Albion. They now had a two-point lead over Leeds with four games remaining – while their rivals had only three to play – but two days later Arsenal had to travel to Leeds for the game that could decide the destiny of the League title. Arsenal had won their previous nine games and if they could just win the next two the title was theirs. With five minutes remaining at the Hawthorns it looked as though Arsenal would win as they led 2–1, but a late Tony Brown equaliser ended their run of victories. Leeds's win that day meant that there was only a point between the two at the top of the table as they lined up for the big match at Elland Road on the following Monday. Arsenal knew that a win would seal the championship, but as the game reached its conclusion without a goal, they were happy to settle for the draw that would keep them on top of the table. In the dying moments of the game, however, Jack Charlton found himself behind the visitors' defence and while Arsenal's players appealed – incorrectly – for offside, he slid the ball into the net for the winning goal. It was a blow to the Gunners' title chances, but they knew that the destiny of the championship was still in their hands.

On the final Saturday of the league season both Arsenal and Leeds had home games, against Stoke and Nottingham Forest respectively. Both teams knew that if they won and the other lost, then the title was theirs.

At Highbury the home team seemed to be letting the pressure get to them, while their opponents were in no mood to do Arsenal any favours after the heartbreak of Hillsborough. Half-time came and went and still the Gunners could find no way through a tight rearguard. As news came through that Leeds were winning, the tension became ever greater as it seemed that Arsenal would never score. Then, with 25 minutes remaining, the goal came. As usual it stemmed from an Armstrong cross, Radford was there, as always, to win the ball and Kelly ran in to crash the ball home. In the last minute Mahoney's shot beat Wilson, but there was Radford on the line to clear. Arsenal held on to win 1–0, but Leeds's 2–0 win against Forest meant that the title win would depend upon the result from the last game. All Arsenal needed to do was to go to White Hart Lane and get either a win or a goalless draw, a score draw would mean that Leeds had a superior goal advantage. If there was one team that was not going to give Arsenal an easy game, however, it was Tottenham.

The championship was so tantalisingly close and for a team that had kept nine clean sheets in their last 12 league games, a goalless draw should not have proved too difficult. Yet they were not only playing away to their fiercest rivals, they were also up against a club that was proud of the fact that they were the only team during the twentieth century to have won the double. As Spurs captain Alan Mullery said beforehand: 'They are the last people we want winning the championship.'

With just a goalless draw required the pressure was on Arsenal to bring the championship trophy back to Highbury for the first time in 18 years, and yet this pressure did not seem to upset the Arsenal players. They were on such a good run that they almost expected to win every game and did not worry about the possibility of defeat. The manager, however, was not so calm. As he prepared his team for the match Bertie Mee's hands shook with nerves. This normally unflappable man had finally succumbed to the overwhelming tension that his team's success had brought.

He may have been affected by the problem of how to approach the match. Playing for a goalless draw was a dangerous tactic, and nothing could be left to chance now that the stakes were so high. On the eve of the match, Frank McLintock had no doubt as to how Arsenal should play: 'We know that a goalless draw would see us through. But that's not what we have in mind. We are going there to win.' Bob Wilson agreed: 'We shan't settle for anything but a win and it will be up to our supporters to roar us on. We need them like we have never needed them before.'

If it was support that Wilson wanted that was certainly what he got. Three and a half hours before kick-off White Hart Lane was completely ringed by the six-deep crowd, and an hour before the game was due to start the gates were closed on a crowd of 51,992. It is estimated that another 100,000 were locked outside. The streets around the ground were jam-packed and the chances of getting any vehicle to the stadium was virtually nil – Kevin Howley, the referee, had to abandon his car and walk the last mile, while the Arsenal bus took an hour from the team's meeting place at South Herts Golf Club which was normally only 20 minutes away. This may have been beneficial in the end as the players had to get changed and warmed up so quickly that they had little chance to dwell on the importance of the match and to lose their nerve.

There was an incredible confidence amongst the players that they could, at least, get the clean sheet that they required. They had got into the habit of winning and were sure that the title would be theirs by the end of the night.

The noise inside the ground was so loud that the referee struggled to make his whistle heard, and instructions that were shouted by players and managers were largely pointless. As the game began it became obvious that Arsenal were indeed going for the win that would make goal advantage irrelevant. The home defence was put under increasing pressure as Arsenal won seven first-half corners to their opponents one.

The best chances though fell to Tottenham, two efforts from Martin Peters, a 25-yard volley just over the bar and a shot that produced a diving save from Wilson, had Gunners supporters in a state of high anxiety.

In the second half, Tottenham continued to nearly score while, at the other end, George Graham headed an Armstrong corner onto the top of the crossbar. As the final minutes ticked away it seemed that the game was going to finish goalless and that the championship, with the top two teams level on points, would be won by a difference that worked out as one-hundredth of a goal. With just three minutes to go, however, Jennings punched away an effort on goal from Radford, the ball reached Armstrong on the left-hand edge of the penalty area and as he crossed the ball Ray Kennedy was there to head it just under the crossbar.

The Arsenal supporters and players went wild with delight, but within seconds the mood changed to one of concern. The game had been winding down as the teams settled for a draw. Now Tottenham would be determined to get back on level terms and a 1–1 draw would hand the title to Leeds. As Bertie Mee said afterwards: 'Ironically, when we scored, the realisation hit me that we could still lose if Tottenham equalised. It was strange to think that 0–0 could feel better than a 1–0 lead.'

During the last few minutes, Spurs threw men forward in an attempt to get the equaliser. A late Tottenham corner had Arsenal panicking, but Wilson dealt safely with the cross and moments later it was all over. Thousands of red-and-white clad supporters surged onto the pitch to celebrate. For the first time in 18 years Arsenal were the champions. Bob Wilson was so carried away that he hugged the nearest person to him – referee Kevin Howley, however, was not overjoyed at being manhandled in this way.

The pandemonium on the pitch meant that 20 minutes after the final whistle several of the players had still not made it back to the dressing-room, but they were too overjoyed to care. The manager summed up everybody's feelings when he said: 'It's the greatest moment of my life.'

Remarkably, Arsenal were only one game away from the double. Just five days after the emotional championship triumph, they were to take on Liverpool in the Cup final at Wembley. Whether or not they went on to win the Cup the season had been a great success, and yet the praise that came from the press and elsewhere was still grudging at best. Despite finishing four places and 14 points ahead of Liverpool in the league, Ladbrokes rated their opponents as 4/5 favourites to take the Cup. Critics accused the team of a lack of flair and adventure.

In the build-up to the final Bertie Mee spoke of how he had used such criticism to urge the team on: 'We have heard and read that we were not good enough but we have come out on top and no one can say we were not worthy of our success. There have been times when I have had to lift players up simply because they had been discouraged by criticism of their style and form, but in a way it was good for us. It made the players even more determined to do well.'

While Liverpool had been able to wind down their league campaign over the last few weeks and set their sights on Wembley, Arsenal had only a few days. After their White Hart Lane triumph, the players were told to enjoy themselves while remembering that they had an FA Cup final to play just five days later. The next day was used to recover both from the match and the celebrations that had gone on long into the night, and so it was not until the Wednesday of Cup final week that preparations could really get under way.

Jubilation soon turned to determination. The two League Cup final defeats were still fresh in everybody's minds and it was not just Frank McLintock who was desperate to ensure that they would be Wembley winners this time. The pitch at London Colney, Arsenal's training ground, was prepared as an exact replica of the Wembley surface and the players trained on it for the next two days.

The Liverpool players were also in confident mood. On the day before the game, Liverpool centre-forward John Toshack had no doubts: 'We've just never thought of losing. After coming all this way we just couldn't go back without the Cup.' His colleague Emlyn Hughes agreed: 'I just can't see us losing.'

It certainly wasn't going to be an easy game for Arsenal. Liverpool were building the first of their teams that would go on to dominate English football for the next 20 years. In goal was a young Ray Clemence who would go on to play regularly for England. In defence was the rugged pairing of Tommy Smith and Larry Lloyd, in midfield was Emlyn Hughes along with international wingers Ian Callaghan and Steve Heighway, while up front was the promising Welsh forward John Toshack, whose aerial power was a threat to any team. To add to this Liverpool also had the immense managerial skills of Bill Shankly. As well as his ability to prepare his team, Shankly was also a master of psychology as he showed on the eve of the Cup final. As the two teams walked around the rain-sodden pitch on the day before the game, Shankly went up to Bob Wilson and told him 'it'll be a nightmare for goalkeepers tomorrow'. Shankly, however, was not the only one with a few tricks up his sleeve.

THE MATCH
Cup final day, as it often is, was stiflingly hot and on the enclosed Wembley pitch it felt like a cauldron with temperatures up in the 90s. Many observers remarked that after Arsenal's busy build-up to the game the energy-sapping conditions would be to their opponents' advantage. The Gunners bus left from the South Herts Golf Club, as usual, but on this occasion virtually the whole of the club turned out to give the team a great send-off as they made their way to Wembley.

As kick-off time approached the two teams were called into the tunnel in readiness for their entrance into the stadium. Liverpool immediately left their dressing-room, but Bertie Mee kept them waiting as his team emerged only after the third request, having given their opponents plenty of time to get nervous. Standing at the end of the tunnel Shankly was fuming, he knew that for once he had been outwitted. Eventually the teams emerged into the stadium with bright sunlight shining onto Arsenal's change colours of yellow and blue.

As the game got under way, the Arsenal defenders seemed intent on letting the Liverpool forwards know that they were in for a hard game. In the first minute Storey brought Heighway down with a scything tackle on the edge of the penalty area. In the second minute, Toshack was brought down on the goal-line. In the third minute it was McLintock's turn to concede a free-kick and a minute later Simpson fouled Evans. Whether this was a deliberate policy to unnerve the opposition, or whether the Arsenal defenders themselves were showing signs of nerves, it was a scrappy start to the game and Liverpool were looking much the better and more composed team.

Four minutes into the match it was Arsenal who created the first real chance of scoring as Kennedy found himself with a clear run on goal. After the high-scoring season that he had enjoyed the Arsenal fans massed at the end opposite the players tunnel and roared with expectation as he bore down on goalkeeper Clemence, but Kennedy snatched at his shot and dragged the ball wide of the target.

All of a sudden the Arsenal team seemed to be reinvigorated; the defence tightened up, the midfield started to take control and the forwards kept the Liverpool defenders on the alert. George Graham in particular was enjoying the wide open Wembley spaces as he skipped past challenges and threaded accurate passes to his team-mates. Slowly and surely Arsenal imposed their game on the match but, apart from long-range shots from George and Storey that fizzed just over the bar, they were unable to convert their superiority into goal chances until just two minutes from half-time. Then, in a strange case of role-reversal, it was John Radford who found space on the right-wing and his cross was met by a diving header from Armstrong in the centre. Clemence could only parry the ball, but was quick enough to catch the rebound. This was the best chance of the game so far and yet a minute later Liverpool almost took the lead themselves. Simpson fouled Evans on the edge of the penalty area and as Callaghan knocked the free-kick to his left, Alec Lindsay hit a low and powerful shot from 25 yards that forced Wilson to make a diving save.

At the start of the second half the game continued in the same way. Radford cut in from the left and crossed to Kennedy in the middle, but he swiped and missed the ball. Some minutes later Charlie George hit two more rasping shots from the edge of the area that went just wide. It was not all one-way traffic, however. In the first half, the Gunners defence had won all the high balls that were delivered into their penalty area but, as the game wore on, John Toshack, the tall and powerful Liverpool forward, began to win balls in the air forcing the defenders to scramble the ball away. All it needed was for one of Toshack's colleagues to connect with one of his knock-downs in the penalty area and Arsenal would be in trouble.

After 18 minutes of the second period the limping Peter Storey, suffering with a recurrence of an ankle injury that he had picked up in the league game against Stoke, was replaced by Eddie Kelly. Four minutes later Liverpool replaced the ineffective Evans with Peter Thompson. Both of these substitutions were to have a significant effect on the match.

As the game wore on both sides continued to struggle to create clear chances in front of goal, but with just 15 minutes to go there was a flurry of activity in front of the Liverpool goal that almost won the game for Arsenal. Firstly, a low Radford cross from the right was met on the edge of the six-yard box by Ray Kennedy who side-footed the ball just inches past the near post. Three minutes later a long throw from Radford found Graham inside the penalty box and his header struck the crossbar. From the resulting corner it was George Graham again who shot towards goal, only to see the ball cleared off the line. This was the most concerted spell of pressure that either team had been able to manage, but the ball still refused to go into the net and so the stalemate continued right up until the final whistle.

There were 30 minutes of extra-time still to be played, but with so few goal chances having been created in the first 90 minutes, it looked like the first goalless Cup final was on the cards. If either team did manage to score it seemed that one goal would be enough to win the Cup. And so when, after less than two minutes of extra-time, Liverpool took the lead it looked as if Arsenal's double chances had gone.

It was the substitute, Peter Thompson who, finding himself in space in the middle of the pitch, played the ball out to Steve Heighway on the left-wing. Heighway accelerated past Rice and Kelly and approached the left-hand side of the penalty area. As he did so, Bob Wilson – anticipating the cross into the middle – moved a couple of yards away from his near post. Wilson had done this throughout the game in order to prevent Toshack getting on the end of Liverpool's crosses and had effectively dealt with everything that had gone his way, but now with his confidence high he had gone too early and was left off balance and well out of position. Heighway struck a low, firm shot into the gap that Wilson had created, leaving the goalkeeper watching helplessly on as the ball slipped between him and the post. Wilson remembers his feeling of horror as the ball hit the net: 'When he hit the ball, I then dived backwards towards the post and to my dying day I remember it hitting the bottom of the post on its way in. And as I turned around I saw Peter Simpson and Frank McLintock look at me as if to say "you stupid idiot, what have you done?". Suddenly I was on the verge of having done so much to win the championship with playing so well in the season, and yet costing us a chance of the double.'

Liverpool were in front and suddenly they seemed to be in control of the game. With their spirits raised by the goal they threatened to score yet again. A Liverpool corner fell to Hall on the edge of the penalty area and he turned and shot powerfully towards goal, forcing Wilson into a diving save. It was a great stop and, fortunately for Arsenal, it raised the goalkeeper's spirits after his costly error. Moments later, Liverpool had another chance to double their lead as Emlyn Hughes found himself through on goal, but his poor control and a saving tackle from Rice stopped him from threatening the Arsenal net.

The Wembley Kop found its voice as Liverpool seemed to be home and dry. 'We Shall Not Be Moved' rang out from the massed ranks at the tunnel end before the inevitable, 'You'll Never Walk Alone'. But Frank McLintock clenched his fist and urged his team on and, just as it seemed that the game was irretrievably running away from Arsenal, the equaliser came. Ten minutes into extra-time Radford received the ball with his back towards the goal and lobbed the ball over his head into the penalty area. As a crowd of players went up, the ball dropped to Eddie Kelly who stabbed the ball through a group of players towards the goal. George Graham ran in and appeared to deflect the ball past Clemence and into the goal. It was not a pretty goal by any means, but it was just what Arsenal desperately needed and now they were back on level terms.

As the ball rolled into the net, George Graham wheeled away in delight and everyone assumed that he had got the vital touch and scored the goal. All the Sunday newspapers credited him with the goal the next day, but when the goal was analysed on the television from behind the goal it seemed that Graham had not actually touched the ball and that this had deceived Clemence who had anticipated Graham getting the touch, only to see the ball roll agonisingly past him and into the net. As a result the goal has been awarded to Kelly, but George Graham and others who were in a close proximity to the pitch still maintain that he got a slight touch on the ball.

The first period of extra-time drew to a close with the teams level and with the match starting to take its toll on the players. George Graham, Chris Lawler and Larry Lloyd all suffered with cramp and, as the second period of extra-time began, Brian Hall fell to the ground with the same problem. As the game entered the last ten minutes it seemed that there was no way that the two teams could be separated on the day and that they would have to meet again at Hillsborough three days later, but all such thoughts were soon to be ended. With six minutes gone in the second period John Radford cut in from the left-hand side and passed to Charlie George; George looked up and drove in a shot from 20 yards out. The ball took a deflection off Larry Lloyd and flew past Clemence, high into the corner of the net.

With the two teams so closely matched on the day it was always going to take a great goal to win the match and, having been the man to score it, Charlie George was going to celebrate in style. Even to this day one of the most enduring memories in Arsenal's long history is of Charlie George turning away from goal and falling to the ground, lying on his back with his arms raised. As Armstrong and Kennedy hauled him to his feet the Arsenal supporters danced with delight – the darling of the North Bank had given them the lead and they were just minutes away from the double. Now 'We Shall Not Be Moved' rang out from the Arsenal supporters.

Those last few minutes may have seemed like an eternity but, in truth, the Liverpool players no longer had the strength to mount a concerted attack on the Arsenal goal. The greatest threat came with just 30 seconds remaining when Liverpool won a corner, but as the ball flew across the goal Wilson came out confidently to catch the ball and end the danger. Moments later referee Norman Burtenshaw blew the final whistle and the dream had become a reality. It was a truly remarkable achievement. At the start of the season no one would have given Arsenal much chance of winning either of the two major domestic honours and yet here they were having achieved something that only one other team had managed this century. In the next day's *Sunday People*, Mike Langley summed up how far Arsenal had come in such a short space of time:

> This is the side that finished last season in the wrong half of the First Division and were heaved out of the Cup in the third round by Blackpool. It's a side managed by a physiotherapist whose footballing career was ended by injury before he could play even one league game. A side with men who feared they were doomed never to be first up the steps at Wembley. Six of them had lost there twice, McLintock had been defeated there four times. And when Heighway scored in the second minute of extra-time that jinx fell on Arsenal like a sack of wet cement. Heads hung, bodies sagged. Yet from the memories of a nearly invincible league season they dredged up the spirit to hurl themselves forward once more.

The players were drained, Pat Rice was so shattered that he tried to persuade George Wright, the physiotherapist, to go up and get his medal for him, but they were able to summon up just enough energy for that climb up the steps to the royal box. The Duke of Kent presented the Cup and Frank McLintock, the man who had thought he would never see this moment, raised it aloft to the delight of the Arsenal supporters.

At the end of the game Charlie George had barely been able to contain his joy as he turned somersaults on the pitch. His excitement was still evident as he talked about his goal after the match: 'As soon as I hit that shot I knew it was a goal. What a way to end such a fabulous week. First the league championship and now the Cup. I feel fantastic . . . marvellous. What a week!' When asked about his goal celebration he said, 'I don't know, I really don't know. That's me, I suppose, it's just me.'

Before the match the experts had thought that with Arsenal's championship challenge going on until just five days before the final they would be more tired than Liverpool and that their opponents extra stamina would tell in the later stages of the game but, after the match, Pat Rice thought that the championship run-in had actually worked in their favour: 'We proved who was the fitter in extra-time. They were whacked on their knees. We kept going. It's possible that having nothing to fight for in their league games before the final told against them.'

Whatever the reasons, Arsenal had won the double. Along with their Fairs Cup win the previous year this team had managed something that the legendary team of the 1930s had never done, so ending forever the unfavourable comparisons that had been made. Individually the players may not have been as good as their illustrious predecessors but as a team they had won the ultimate domestic prize, and as such the team will go down as one of the all-time greats.

FINAL SCORE

Arsenal	2	Liverpool	1 (after extra-time)

Kelly	101 mins	Heighway	92 mins
George	111 mins		
Attendance:	100,000		

Arsenal: Wilson, Rice, McNab, Storey (Kelly),
               McLintock, Simpson, Armstrong, Kennedy,
               Radford, George, Graham

Liverpool: Clemence, Lawler, Lindsay, Smith, Lloyd,
               Hughes, Callaghan, Evans (Thompson),
               Heighway, Toshack, Hall

Chapter 6

THE BRADY FINAL

FA Cup final
Arsenal v Manchester United
Saturday, 12 May 1979

As the Arsenal team took to their open-topped bus and paraded the league championship trophy and the FA Cup around the streets of Islington in May 1971, the hundreds of thousands of supporters that greeted them had high hopes for the seasons to come. After 17 barren years it seemed that a period of concerted success had finally arrived with the European Cup and further domestic triumphs to look forward to. Yet, despite reaching the FA Cup final again in 1972 and the semi-final the following year, Arsenal failed to follow up on the remarkable success of the double season and over the next eight years there was not one single addition to the Highbury trophy cabinet.

In the opinion of many the double-winning team was broken up with undue haste. Players such as McLintock, Kennedy and George went on to play top-class football for several years after being transferred, and many of the players brought in to replace them were unable to make the same impact. By the mid 1970s the team consisted mainly of players that were past their best and promising but inexperienced youngsters. As a result the team found themselves battling at the bottom of the First Division.

Towards the end of the decade, however, things started to improve as the young players like David O'Leary, Liam Brady and Frank Stapleton started to fulfil their promise, and new manager Terry Neill managed to attract top players such as Pat Jennings,

Alan Hudson and Malcolm Macdonald to the club. So great was the improvement that the team began challenging at the top of the league table and, in 1978, Arsenal reached the FA Cup final.

Ultimately the 1978 Cup final was a huge disappointment as injury hit Arsenal, the pre-match favourites, froze on the day and produced one of their worst performances of the season to lose 1–0 to the underdogs, Ipswich Town. The fact remained, however, that Arsenal were on their way back, and even as the supporters trooped disconsolately home from Wembley, the players and management vowed that they would be back next year and this time they would take the Cup back to Highbury.

THE PLAYERS
When Bertie Mee resigned as manager in 1976 the Arsenal board looked to their north London rivals to find a replacement. Former Gunner Terry Neill leapt at the chance to leave Tottenham and take over at Highbury. Over the next two years, Neill hit the headlines as he signed big-name players such as Malcolm Macdonald and Alan Hudson, but probably his greatest coup was the signing of Pat Jennings.

Jennings had been goalkeeper for Tottenham for the past 13 years during which time he had built a reputation as one of the best goalkeepers in the world. His brilliance between the goalposts had kept Arsenal at bay during many north London derbies over the years and Highbury fans had had good reason to curse him. In the summer of 1977 Tottenham decided that, at the age of 32, Jennings' best days were behind him and that they needed a younger goalkeeper. Neill jumped at the chance to sign Jennings and brought him across north London at a cost of just £40,000. Jennings went on to produce some of his best form over the next few years and was instrumental in the revival of Arsenal's form.

In defence Pat Rice, the one remaining player from the double-winning side, was now captain. The other full-back was Sammy Nelson, an Irishman who had broken into the team just after the double win, with over 200 league appearances to his credit he was a model of consistency and had now been a fixture in the side for several seasons.

In central defence was the partnership of David O'Leary and

Willie Young. O'Leary was a quiet Irishman who had come up through the youth team and made his first-team debut in 1975. Since then he had established himself in the Irish national team and was regarded as one of the most promising defenders in the league. Young, on the other hand, was a tough uncompromising Scot. He was another player that Neill had signed from White Hart Lane and, at just £80,000, was another bargain. Despite previously playing for Spurs, Arsenal fans soon took Young to their hearts with his no-nonsense approach to defending and his entertaining forays into the opponents' half of the field.

In midfield Terry Neill and his assistant Don Howe, who had returned to the club after brief managerial posts elsewhere, had managed to blend craft with graft. The latter was provided by Brian Talbot and David Price.

Talbot had played against Arsenal in the 1978 Cup final but became the club's record signing early in 1979 when he moved from Ipswich for £450,000. His industry in the middle of the field had already earned him five England caps and he could be relied upon to get forward in support of the strikers, scoring many crucial goals in the process. Price was the unsung member of the midfield. Although he was a powerful and hard-working player, he was also very underrated but, as would be shown in the 1979 Cup final, his absence could have a very detrimental effect on the team.

The two players that brought skill and subtlety to the team were Graham Rix and Liam Brady. Rix, a recent product of the youth team, was in his second full season in the side and had replaced the departed Alan Hudson. With his left foot he was able to deliver stunning passes, accurate crosses and spectacular free-kicks, and was definitely one of the most promising young players in the country. The star of the team, however, was undoubtedly Liam Brady. Another Irishman, Brady had made his debut as a teenager in 1973 and soon made an impression on the Arsenal fans. With his touch, control, dribbling skills, passing ability and regular goalscoring, Brady was possibly the greatest midfield player in Highbury history and would certainly be in most supporters all-time greatest Arsenal team.

Early in the season, Arsenal's superstar centre-forward Malcolm Macdonald was sidelined with a knee injury and did not play again until the last game of the season. This brought together two players who would form one of the Gunners' most effective forward partnerships. Frank Stapleton was the sixth of Arsenal's Irish players. He had come through the youth ranks with O'Leary and Brady and made it to the first team in 1975. He was never a really prolific scorer, but his ability in the air and on the ground provided a constant menace to the opposition and he would invariably create as many goals as he scored. The same could be said about Alan Sunderland. A signing from Wolves the previous season, his pace and skill was enough to keep any defence on its toes.

THE BACKGROUND

The day of the third round of the FA Cup is one of the highlights of the year for most football supporters but, on 6 January 1979, due to the bad weather that swept the country, only three games were completed. One of these was Sheffield Wednesday v Arsenal at Hillsborough. Wednesday were struggling near the bottom of the Third Division and had won only two league games at home all season. Arsenal, on the other hand, were lying fourth in the First Division having lost only once in their last 12 games. Despite this Sheffield Wednesday were probably the toughest opponents that Arsenal faced during their Cup campaign as the two teams battled out the sort of marathon cup-tie that, with the advent of penalty shoot-outs, we no longer see.

The match was played on an ice-rink of a pitch in front of 33,635 spectators – almost 20,000 more than Wednesday's best league crowd that season – and is remembered by many as the game when Pat Jennings found himself bombarded by snowballs thrown by the home fans.

An Alan Sunderland goal gave the Gunners a first-half lead, but a goal from Jeff Johnson after the break earned Wednesday a replay. Three days later at Highbury Arsenal were expected to cruise comfortably into the next round but in the end they were lucky to get another draw. According to the *Daily Telegraph*: 'It was a case of "Lucky Old Arsenal" again at Highbury last night as a goal almost into injury time saved them from embarrassing defeat.' An early goal from Rodger Wylde looked as though it would give

Wednesday a shock win, but as the 90 minutes came to an end Rix crossed the ball from the left, Stapleton nodded the ball down at the far post and as Liam Brady and 18-year-old defender Mark Smith lunged together, the ball found the net. Smith hung his head in despair as Brady celebrated. Extra-time saw no further goals and so another game was needed.

The following Monday the two teams met at Filbert Street, home of Leicester City, and yet again they could not be separated. Goals from Brady and Sunderland cancelled out two goals from ex-Gunner Brian Hornsby and meant that everyone had to come back two days later. When the third replay was drawn as well the tie became the talk of the nation. Despite two goals from Frank Stapleton and another from Willie Young, a penalty miss by Brady meant that Arsenal could only draw 3–3 and this forced a fourth replay.

On Monday, 22 January, a crowd of 30,275 – over 9,500 more than Leicester's biggest home gate of the season – packed into Filbert Street for the next instalment of this Cup saga. With the fourth-round ties due to be played just five days later, Notts County still didn't know whether they would be travelling to Yorkshire or London for their next game. At half-time Arsenal led 2–0 through goals from midfielder Steve Gatting – brother of cricketer Mike Gatting – and Frank Stapleton. Everyone waited for the expected Sheffield Wednesday comeback but, finally, Arsenal held on to win and bring an end to one of the longest Cup ties ever. In the end five matches were played over 540 minutes in front of 143,996 spectators.

After the drama of the third round, the fourth round was much more comfortable as five days later the Gunners beat Second Division Notts County 2–0 at Highbury with second-half goals from Willie Young and Brian Talbot – who was making his debut for the club.

The fifth-round draw paired Arsenal with Notts County's neighbours Nottingham Forest at the City Ground. They could not have been given a more difficult task. Forest were the reigning league champions and would go on to win the European Cup a few months later. Furthermore, they had not lost a home game since April 1977. On 17 February the weather put paid to the whole FA Cup programme, and so it was not until nine days later that the game was played on a pitch that was more akin to a mudbath than a football ground. Arsenal's defence soaked up incessant Forest pressure and Pat Jennings had to be at his brilliant best. The Gunners rearguard held firm and, on one of their rare breakaways, Stapleton headed the winning goal to give Arsenal a famous victory – Forest's first home defeat in 52 games.

Pat Rice still regards that as one of Arsenal's great performances: 'That was a brilliant win. They absolutely bombarded us and we defended really well – not just the back four but the whole team.' The *Daily Telegraph* reported that Arsenal's win was 'the most blatant example of floodlit robbery even this competition has produced in recent seasons'.

Being drawn away to Southampton in the sixth round was no easy task either, especially as just five days after beating Forest Arsenal went to the Dell for a league game and were beaten 2–0. As the Cup game drew to a close it looked as though there would be a similar outcome as Southampton led through a Phil Bowyer goal, but a late equaliser from David Price earned the Gunners a replay at Highbury which, despite the appearance of a certain Charlie George for the Saints, Arsenal won 2–0 with both goals coming from Alan Sunderland.

The perception that Arsenal had been lucky throughout their Cup run – presumably this did not include being drawn away in three out of four rounds – increased when the semi-final draw saw them avoid the big guns of Liverpool and Manchester United. Instead they would meet Wolves at Villa Park.

Arsenal were not so lucky, however, when their star player, Liam Brady, was hit by injury before the semi-final. Remembering how he had performed in the previous season's final when injured, he missed the match and was replaced by Steve Gatting. Even without Brady, the players were confident that they were too good for Wolves and so it proved. Goals from Stapleton and Sunderland, against his old club, were enough to send the Gunners back to Wembley.

There was understandable delight in the Arsenal camp. Most defeated Cup final teams vow to return the following year, but Arsenal were one of the few that had actually done it. They may have had a little luck on the way but it would be difficult to recall a Cup final team that hadn't. A draw in the other semi-final meant that Terry Neill did not know yet who their Wembley opponents would be, but he was unconcerned: 'We don't care which of them we meet – we're just delighted to have got there.' Four days later a Jimmy Greenhoff goal gave Manchester United victory.

After reaching Wembley, both finalists struggled to keep their form in the league. Arsenal won two of the ten games that followed the semi-final, while United could win only two out of 12. None of the players wanted to risk injury, particularly at Arsenal where injury to key players had been one of the reasons for their defeat the previous year.

Terry Neill and Don Howe decided to give the team a varied schedule in the run-up to the game so they started the week at Bisham Abbey before training at London Colney on the Thursday and then at Highbury the following day. After training on the Friday the team went for lunch at the Grosvenor Hotel in Mayfair where they stayed the night and prepared for the big day.

In contrast to the previous year, the only doubt for Terry Neill was whether Willie Young would shake off a knee-ligament injury, but the Scotsman proved his fitness during Cup final week giving the manager a full squad to choose from. On the eve of the final he was understandably relieved: 'I spent the run-in to the game last season disguising all sorts of injury problems. It has been marvellous to concentrate on the game instead of worrying about a player's leg strain or whatever. The team is fully fit. We have had a superb week's training without any reaction to any player.'

The players seemed confident that with the lack of injuries, coupled with their Cup final experience they would do much better this time around. The big difference this year was that Liam Brady was 100 per cent fit and feeling far more confident: 'This time I feel fit and I feel good, and there isn't the tension in the camp that there was this time a year ago.'

Pat Rice also noticed the difference from the previous year: 'I firmly believe we will win the Cup. Last year we had about five players struggling with injuries. This time we are all fit. We know we are going out against United to compete and that's the big difference. We are feeling a lot more confident. We are not as tense as against Ipswich when we knew we let a lot of people down.'

The Arsenal team contained no surprises with ten of the 12 men who had played against Ipswich – Alan Hudson had left the club and Malcolm Macdonald was injured – starting the match. While those ten members of the team were out to make up for the previous year's defeat, the eleventh, Brian Talbot, was hoping to make history as the first player ever to win successive Cup-Winners' medals with two different teams. This year Talbot knew that there was much more pressure on him to win: 'It is altogether different being with Arsenal. Last year with Ipswich it was a one-off affair, the greatest day in the club's history. Here at Arsenal you are conscious of the tradition, the fact that you are expected to win any major competition.'

Without doubt the same was true at Old Trafford. This was United's third Cup final appearance in four years, so their players were unlikely to be overawed by the occasion. The possible exception was their young goalkeeper Gary Bailey. Aged only 21, this was Bailey's first full season at Old Trafford and, despite his impressive showing over the past months, it was bound to be a nerve-wracking experience for him. He did have the advantage, however, of having two experienced central defenders in front of him. The Scottish pairing of captain Martin Buchan and Gordon McQueen was one of the most formidable in the league and was guaranteed to give any forward a hard time.

In midfield was the creative threat of Steve Coppell on the wing along with fellow internationals Mickey Thomas and Sammy McIlroy, while Lou Macari would have the onerous task of marking Liam Brady. In attack was big Joe Jordan, who was at his most dangerous in the air, and Jimmy Greenhoff, thought by many to be one of the best English players never to win an international cap. It would, therefore, be no easy game for Arsenal, but their spies felt that they had spotted a weakness in the United team. Assistant manager Wilf Dixon and former Arsenal great George

Male reported to Neill and Howe that the full-backs Nicholl and Albiston tended to over cover for Gordon McQueen on crosses and left the far post vulnerable. Howe stressed to his team the importance of reaching the by-line and sending in good crosses, any player coming in behind the United defence might reap rewards.

As the big day approached many experts found the teams too closely matched to be able to make a prediction. William Hill gave odds of 8/5 for both teams with the draw at 11/5. Frank McGhee of the *Daily Mirror* who had tipped Manchester United, Liverpool and Arsenal in the last three finals (all lost) went for United, while in the *Evening Standard* Brian Talbot wrote that he had a strange feeling that there could be an unusual Cup final scoreline: 'I can't explain why . . . but, for some reason a 3–2 Arsenal win keeps coming into my mind. I haven't had any premonitions about the actual scorers, but I like to think I'm due for one myself.'

THE MATCH

Just as it had been in 1971 Cup final day saw the sun beating down on Wembley Stadium. Britain was basking in a heatwave with pitch-level temperatures reaching record levels, On the pitch there could not have been a greater contrast from Arsenal's game at Hillsborough back in January. Just as they had done in 1971 and 1978, Arsenal kicked off the game in their change colours of yellow and blue.

For the first ten minutes the teams seemed determined to show how evenly matched they were, with neither team being able to create anything to seriously worry their opponents. Then the one man capable of single-handedly changing the course of the game decided that enough was enough.

Liam Brady picked up the ball just inside the United half and ran at their defence. He shrugged off the challenges of three players before finding Stapleton on the right-hand side. Stapleton fed the ball through to David Price whose run inside the penalty area towards the goal-line drew Bailey away from the goal and, as he knocked the ball inside, Talbot and Sunderland arrived together to put the ball into the empty net. Just as in 1971 it was unclear who had scored the goal, television replays were unable to show who had got the final touch to the ball and while the goal was credited to Sunderland over the stadium tannoy, Talbot was adamant that he had been the scorer.

Having gone a goal down, Manchester United were forced to go on the offensive, creating most of the chances during the remainder of the first half. Thomas found space in the penalty area only to shoot weakly into Jennings' arms, Jordan twice sent headers narrowly over the bar, Greenhoff shot over from close range and a Thomas header from seven yards went straight to the goalkeeper. Then, after 37 minutes, it seemed as though Manchester United had levelled the score. A corner at the tunnel end was floated across the Arsenal area and McQueen rose to put the ball into the net. The big Scot turned away in triumph as the supporters at the far end of the ground cheered, but referee Ron Challis disallowed the goal. The television replay clearly showed that McQueen had knocked the ball into the net with his hand. Fortunately this 'hand of God' had not got away with it.

Apart from a couple of threatening shots from Graham Rix and an overhead kick from Frank Stapleton that cleared the bar Arsenal created few chances in the remainder of the half, seemingly content to soak up the pressure and sit on their lead. With less than two minutes remaining before the interval, however, it was Brady again who turned the game even further to Arsenal's advantage. Running at the United defence again he went past the hapless Albiston and Buchan to find space on the right-hand side of the penalty area. Brady saw Frank Stapleton free at the far post – just as Don Howe had predicted – and he sent over a perfectly weighted cross which his Irish team-mate headed into the corner of the net. Moments later the whistle blew for half-time and Arsenal returned to their dressing-room to the cheers of their delighted supporters. It was 13 years since a team had scored two goals in an FA Cup final and lost.

All Arsenal had to do in the second half was sit on their lead and the Cup would be theirs. For most of the time they had little difficulty in doing so. The back four stayed firm and Jennings was required to do very little behind them. Willie Young in particular was a rock in defence as he kept the menacing Jordan covered. The action went from one end to the other as United pressed forward in a desperate search for the goal that would get them back into the game, while Arsenal broke away and threatened to end the game as a contest. Time after time Brady would bring the ball out of defence and beat players with his pace and skill to set up another Arsenal chance. Up front, Stapleton worked tirelessly and, with 13 minutes gone in the second half, he nearly put the game out of United's reach; Brady fed the ball to Rix on the left and Stapleton met Rix's cross at the far post only to see the ball turned away off Bailey's legs.

Manchester United had their chances, but Jennings was never called upon to make the kind of world-class save which he was renowned for and as the game entered its last few minutes it seemed that both sides were just playing out time until the final whistle.

Then, with just five minutes remaining, Arsenal made a substitution – replacing David Price with utility player Steve Walford. Most people saw it merely as a chance to give Walford a winners' medal, but both Terry Neill and Don Howe later insisted that it was a positive move replacing the tiring Price with the fresh legs of Walford. David O'Leary, writing in *David O'Leary – My Story*, was sure that it had a detrimental effect: '[Walford] was a centre-back replacing a midfield man and it upset the balance of the side.' Whichever is true, Walford later revealed that he and Price had discussed the situation before the game: 'I always share a room with Pricey. We were talking on Friday night and he promised he would come off five minutes from time so that I could have a taste of Wembley. It was an amazing coincidence the way it happened, but he was knackered . . . he had done so much running.' Either way the substitution changed the course of the match.

Within 30 seconds of Walford taking to the field United were awarded a free-kick some 30 yards from goal after O'Leary fouled Greenhoff. Coppell's cross evaded everybody as it ran across the penalty area and, as Jordan turned and knocked the ball back into the box, the Arsenal defence seemed to stop as McQueen stuck out a leg and turned the ball past Jennings and into the net.

Suddenly there was a glimmer of hope for United. The team

which had seemed to have given up hope were suddenly reinvigorated, while their supporters who had previously been silent now roared their encouragement. Arsenal, meanwhile, seemed unnerved and their calm, controlled play disappeared. As the red shirts poured forward it took only two more minutes for United to draw level. Coppell's long ball found McIlroy running towards the Arsenal penalty area. His twisting and turning run left O'Leary and Walford sprawled across the Wembley turf and as Jennings dived at his feet he rolled the ball under the goalkeeper's body and into the net.

The Manchester United supporters danced with delight as McIlroy ran ecstatically towards them with most of his team-mates frantically giving chase. From nowhere they were back in the game and with extra-time just moments away it seemed that a distraught Arsenal would have little chance against their jubilant opponents. Just as those two goals had made the Gunners players more tired and weary, United were rejuvenated.

After the game Terry Neill described his feelings at that moment: 'When their two goals went in I was numbed from the neck up. We had only to suffer three minutes and here they were level. I knew that after all our running we would have the harder task in extra-time.' Substitute Steve Walford was in a state of shock: 'I went on and I just couldn't believe what was happening. Suddenly it was 2–2 and I couldn't even remember whether I'd had a kick yet.'

Arsenal restarted the game to the sound of ecstatic United fans still celebrating their team's comeback and with their substitute Brian Greenhoff warming up for extra-time. The ball found its way to Brady who surged into the United half. Again Macari was left trailing in his wake as Brady fed the ball through to Rix on the left. Rix looked up and sent a high cross to the far post. Bailey at the near post leapt despairingly as the ball sailed over his desperate grasp and, as the ball came down, there was Alan Sunderland to slide the ball into the gaping net.

Rarely can a football match have caused such a dramatic swing in the moods of the two sets of supporters. The United fans who, for just one minute had seen their team on the verge of Cup glory, held their heads in disbelief, while their Arsenal counterparts, who had watched their side throw away certain victory, leapt with delight as Sunderland wheeled away to celebrate his dramatic goal.

It looked like the Cup was back in Arsenal's hands but after the events of the previous three minutes nobody could be sure. There was still time for United to mount one last attack and Arsenal could only look on anxiously as Jordan's head met a cross at the far post, but Jennings leapt to clutch the ball above his head and Arsenal were safe. Moments later, referee Challis blew his whistle to bring an end to the most dramatic FA Cup final of all time.

There was a sense of shock all around the stadium. United players fell tearfully to their knees while their opponents struggled to take in the enormity of what had just happened. The players were almost too tired to celebrate after such an emotional and gruelling match.

Wille Young summed up the Arsenal players' feelings after the final whistle: 'I honestly don't know how I managed to make it up the stairs. I was dead on my feet. I can't think how the United lads felt. I couldn't believe it when United pulled one goal back. I was completely shattered when Sammy McIlroy hit the equaliser, and I would have been quite happy to be carried off on a stretcher when Alan Sunderland scored our winner with 50 seconds left. There wasn't an Arsenal player who believed we could still win it in ordinary time – and that includes Liam Brady. He told me that when he started the run which ended with Graham Rix getting the ball over for Sundy's winner, all he was doing was trying to do was to keep the ball in their half. Thank goodness he reacted that way. I'm convinced if we hadn't scored then, United would have gone on to win the Cup.'

There were two great debates after the match. The first concerned the scorer of the first goal. At the end of the game Talbot was too happy to care: 'I thought I got a touch for our first goal and so did Alan Sunderland, but who cares? There was no disputing Alan's winner. It was a beauty.' Having scored the crucial third goal, however, Sunderland was happy to give Talbot the first: 'I didn't even see Brian Talbot but it seems we both kicked the ball at the same time. I'm happy, though, for Brian to have it. I got the winner . . . and there's no dispute about that.'

The second big talking point concerned Gary Bailey's positioning for the winning goal. There were some commentators who criticised him for attempting to catch the ball at the near post, only to see it sail over his head into Sunderland's path, but his manager Dave Sexton defended his performance: 'Gary had a good sound game and acquitted himself well in a difficult situation for a young goalkeeper.' Goalkeeping coach Harry Gregg also insisted that Bailey was not to blame: 'If I thought Gary had been wrong I would have been the first to have a go, but I couldn't fault him over any of the goals.'

And so it was that Pat Rice climbed the Wembley steps to receive the FA Cup from Prince Charles and for the Arsenal captain it was a truly special moment: 'It was fantastic, I couldn't get my hands on it quick enough. You see other people go up and collect it and you always hope that one day it may happen to you, so it was a dream come true.'

There was little doubt amongst the millions watching on television or the 100,000 in the stadium that the man who had won the Cup was Liam Brady. He may not have scored, but all three goals owed something to his surging runs and accurate passes, and throughout the game his constant threat had blunted United's attacks. Not since the Matthews final of 1953 had one man dominated English football's showpiece game to such an extent. Just as Matthews had hauled Blackpool back from the brink of defeat in the closing stages of the game, so Brady's final burst into the United half and his pinpoint ball to Rix set up the goal that turned the game back in Arsenal's favour. Without him the Cup would surely have gone to Old Trafford. It was with good reason that Arsenal fans called him 'The King of Highbury'.

The game will always be remembered for that final dramatic five minutes where both teams experienced emotions of jubilation and despair. At the end of it all it was Arsenal who had a famous victory, but the final word goes to the man who seemed to have turned the game decisively in United's favour, Sammy McIlroy: 'It was like picking eight draws and then finding the pools coupon still in your pocket. I'm still numb. I still can't believe it.'

FINAL SCORE

Arsenal	3	Manchester United	2

Talbot	12 mins	McQueen	85 mins
Stapleton	43 mins	McIlroy	87 mins
Sunderland	88 mins		
Attendance:	100,000		

Arsenal: Jennings, Rice, Nelson, Young, O'Leary, Talbot, Price (Walford), Rix, Brady, Stapleton, Sunderland

Manchester United: Bailey, Nicholl, Albiston, Buchan, McQueen, Coppell, Macari, McIlroy, Thomas, Greenhoff, Jordan

Chapter 7

TRIUMPH IN TURIN

European Cup-Winners' Cup semi-final (second leg)
Juventus v Arsenal
Wednesday, 23 April 1980

The 1979–80 season saw Arsenal become the cup specialists of England. Long runs in the League Cup, FA Cup and European Cup-Winners' Cup led to the Gunners playing more games in one season than at any other time in their history. In all Arsenal played 27 cup games in that hectic season, games which would provide plenty of drama, delight and, ultimately, despair.

In the end the record books show that Arsenal won nothing that year, but for much of the season they had looked capable of achieving a memorable double. Ultimately it all ended in disappointment, yet along the way Gunners supporters were treated to some memorable performances. Few people will forget the epic battles with Liverpool in the FA Cup semi-final, but above all else they will always remember one night in Turin.

THE PLAYERS
Immediately after their Cup final triumph against Manchester United, the newspapers had been full of speculation regarding the futures of Arsenal's best young players: Liam Brady, Frank Stapleton and David O'Leary. All were seen as being transfer targets for other clubs from both home and abroad. At the start of the new season, however, the team was almost exactly the same as it had been during the previous campaign, although Brady had announced that this would be his last season at Highbury before he

moved abroad. Not only had there been no major departures, but the only arrival of any note was that of veteran midfielder John Hollins who joined from Queens Park Rangers with over 580 league appearances already under his belt.

During the course of the long season, a number of young players would have the chance to play in the first team. One who established himself in the first-team squad was yet another Irishman, John Devine. Injuries to Pat Rice and Sammy Nelson meant that he was able to play over 20 games in the season and prove himself to be more than adequate cover for both full-back positions.

It was obvious that manager Terry Neill was happy with the team that had won the Cup. As the new season got under way, the team that won 4–0 at newly promoted Brighton on the opening day was exactly the same as that which had triumphed against Manchester United at Wembley just three months earlier.

THE BACKGROUND

The opening games of the season found Arsenal at their most inconsistent. Home defeats by Ipswich and Wolves contrasted sharply with the 7–0 demolition of Leeds in the League Cup which left opposing manager Jimmy Adamson saying: 'Arsenal were magic, we were rubbish.'

The Gunners' European campaign began against Fenerbahce of Turkey. The first leg at Highbury saw Alan Sunderland give his side the lead, but Willie Young's crucial second goal did not arrive until the dying moments of the game. A two-goal lead was sufficient, however, as a goalless draw in Turkey saw them through. In the second round against the East Germans of Magdeburg it was never going to be an easy victory and so it proved. Arsenal struggled to a 2–1 home win courtesy, again, of goals from Young and Sunderland. In the second leg Arsenal battled bravely to gain a 2–2 draw, with Price and Brady scoring the all-important goals that enabled Arsenal to qualify for the quarter-finals in March.

After a poor start, Arsenal's league campaign soon clicked into gear. From the beginning of October to the end of March they lost only three league games and climbed as high as third position in the table, but Liverpool always had points in hand at the top and Arsenal never really threatened to catch them.

In the cup competitions, the Londoners were very much in the hunt for honours. Despite a shock defeat at the hands of Third Division Swindon Town in the quarter-finals of the League Cup, by March Arsenal were in the quarter-finals of both the Cup-Winners' Cup and the FA Cup. Victories over Cardiff City, Brighton and Bolton Wanderers had seen the Gunners through to the sixth round of the FA Cup where they avoided the likes of Liverpool, Tottenham and Everton when they were drawn against Watford.

The European draw was also kind to Arsenal as a tie against Gothenburg spared them the task of meeting either Barcelona or Juventus.

On 5 March Arsenal played the first leg of their tie against Gothenburg and virtually booked their place in the semi-final. Two goals from Alan Sunderland added to others from Young, Price and Brady which gave the Gunners a comfortable 5–1 lead.

A goalless draw a fortnight later saw the Gunners safely through, but the trip to Sweden was not without drama. In *David O'Leary – My Story* the Arsenal centre-back recalled that: 'Flying into Gothenburg . . . the pilot of our special charter announced over the intercom that he had a problem with the landing gear. There was a sudden silence. I think quite a few aboard – players, officials and press – made a few promises to themselves about the misdeeds they wouldn't commit again if we got down okay. We did – after circling round and round the airport jettisoning fuel. It was a false alarm. A light on the flight-deck panel had failed to function properly.'

In between those two games, Arsenal visited Vicarage Road in the FA Cup. It was a close match throughout, but two Frank Stapleton goals were enough for a 2–1 win over Watford.

They may have had favourable draws in the quarter-finals, but in the semi-finals of both competitions Arsenal drew the strongest remaining team. In the FA Cup they would take on a Liverpool team that was about to win its fourth championship in five years, and in Europe they would face the mighty Juventus.

Beating two of the best teams in Europe would be difficult at the best of times, but Arsenal were going to have to do it by playing five games in 12 days. What was more, with a UEFA Cup place still up for grabs in the league, all their remaining matches were vitally important. Arsenal's fixture congestion was now so bad that they were due to play a home game against Southampton on Easter Saturday, followed by the derby match at Tottenham on Easter Monday, the first leg against Juventus at Highbury on the following Wednesday and the semi-final against Liverpool three days later. Arsenal asked Tottenham if their fixture could be moved to a later date, but their North London rivals refused to help – although they might later have wished that they had.

On Saturday, 5 April, Arsenal began with a 1–1 draw at home to Southampton in the week that would make or break their season. Despite the importance of league points, it was obvious that the minds of the Arsenal players were on the crucial games to come. The following day – while Juventus cruised to a 2–0 win over Avellino to keep them in third place in Serie A – the wounded trooped into Highbury. David Price had five stitches in a shin wound that he had picked up the previous day and Sammy Nelson had pulled a hamstring. Liam Brady, Graham Rix, Brian Talbot and John Hollins were also under treatment, while Steve Gatting had the flu.

Don Howe expressed the feeling at Highbury that they were being asked to do too much in the space of too few days: 'It's not only hard on the club and players, but also for our supporters and the image of English football throughout Europe. We have three things to do this week. We must go for European points at Tottenham because there is no guarantee we will survive in either of the cups. Allied to that point is the fact that we want to do well at White Hart Lane for the sake of our supporters. Secondly, when we play Juventus we are fighting for the prestige of the club and for the good of English football abroad. Finally, the players want to get back to Wembley and to do that they must beat Liverpool.'

With the ever-growing injury list and the need to rest players for the crucial semi-finals to come, Terry Neill decided to put out what was almost a reserve side for Monday's game at White Hart Lane. Jennings, Nelson, Price, Rix, Sunderland and Stapleton were rested and in came reserve goalkeeper Paul Barron, Steve

Walford, John Devine, John Hollins, Paul Vaessen and Paul Davis, a young 17-year-old making his first-team debut.

Davis's potential was obvious to all at the match and he went on to become one of the club's most long-serving players. The other of the youngsters who the club had very high hopes for was centre-forward Paul Vaessen. Vaessen was born in Bermondsey to Scandinavian parents and had worked his way through Arsenal's youth teams to the verge of regular first-team football after less than a year as a professional. He had made his debut in the final game of the previous season at Chelsea and although he had yet to score in any of his eight league appearances, he had put two goals past Brighton in the League Cup. Tragically, his career was to be finished by injury at an early stage, but not before he had made his mark for Arsenal.

Despite the weakness of their team, it was Arsenal who created the best chances in a fairly mundane encounter at White Hart Lane. Tottenham were easily contained and according to the report in *The Times*, Paul Davis 'strolled into the game with almost veteran assurance'. The game was goalless until the 84th minute when Talbot's corner was volleyed back across the penalty area by O'Leary and Vaessen headed his first league goal. Moments later Sunderland broke away and lobbed Daines in the Spurs goal from 30 yards to make it 2–0. Tottenham managed to get one goal back in the game's dying seconds, but it was too late to avoid defeat. How they must have wished they had agreed to move the game to a later date. Losing at home to their greatest rivals was bad enough, but losing to their reserves would take some living down. As far as Arsenal were concerned it had all worked out rather well; they had picked up two points with less than half their first-choice team and so had given the watching Juventus team few clues as to how they would play two days later.

Juventus arrived in London with some of the best-known players in Europe in their team. Famous internationals such as Dino Zoff, Franco Causio, Roberto Bettega and Marco Tardelli were able to strike fear into the hearts of many teams, but they were aware that their opponents had one or two players that they would have to be wary of.

Tardelli would be given the job of marking Liam Brady and he knew he was going to be in for a tough time: 'I have seen Brady play twice and I have been very impressed. He will be the danger man . . . there are, however, others at Arsenal who could give us problems. We hear and we know, for instance, that Graham Rix is also an outstanding player.' Italian teams had a reputation for caution and defensiveness. When Tardelli was asked how Juventus would approach the first leg he replied: 'We have come to Arsenal not to lose.'

The team which Terry Neill named for the first leg had only two changes from the FA Cup-winning team with Devine and Walford replacing Rice and Nelson at full-back, while Willie Young was to play with a broken nose that he had received in the Tottenham game and David Price still had stitches in his leg. Arsenal needed to establish a lead if they were going to have any chance of reaching the final and Terry Neill was confident that if they took the game to the Italians they could force them into making mistakes: 'In Italian football they are not normally hustled in their own penalty area and that is what we shall be trying to do.'

As the game got under way in front of nearly 52,000 fans, it became clear that Juventus had no intention of playing for a goalless draw. They played the ball around the pitch in brilliant fashion as they attacked the Arsenal goal. While the Italians played positively the home team looked tentative. Brady was effectively shackled by Tardelli and Juventus overran the midfield as they looked for an all-important away goal.

In the course of just eight minutes the game would change completely. After ten minutes of the match, Claudio Gentile became the first player to receive a yellow card when he scythed Graham Rix down with a tackle from behind.

A minute later Walford dangerously lobbed the ball back to Devine and, as he came under pressure, the young Irishman attempted to head the ball back to Jennings in goal, but all he could do was plant the ball in the path of the onrushing Bettega. With just the goalkeeper to beat, Bettega was hauled down by Talbot and referee George Corver pointed to the spot. Cabrini's penalty kick was saved by the diving Jennings, but before the Highbury crowd could cheer with relief, the Italian seized on the rebound and drove the ball high into the net. Juventus were in the lead.

Having scored a precious away goal, Juventus now reverted to type as they attempted to kill the game off. Suddenly the tackles became nasty and malicious. First, Cabrini was booked for a foul on Price. Then, after 18 minutes, came the flashpoint of the game; David O'Leary was felled by a brutal tackle from Bettega which Terry Neill described as 'probably the most vicious foul I have seen in 20 years in the game'. O'Leary was later told by the club doctor: 'If you hadn't been wearing shin pads your leg would have been snapped in two.' The Irish defender was carried off with a gashed leg. Amazingly Bettega received only a yellow card – most onlookers felt the card should have been a red one. Tardelli was then booked for failing to retreat ten yards for a free-kick before, after 32 minutes, he received his second yellow card for a foul on Brady. Juventus were down to ten men, although most people thought that it was Bettega rather than Tardelli who should have left the field.

The Italians were now forced to adopt a more defensive stance, something they were well practised in. Brio and Scirea, the sweeper, snuffed out the joint menace of Sunderland and Stapleton, while Dino Zoff in goal was in imperious form. He held on to every Arsenal cross, dived to save at Stapleton's feet and flung himself to his left to keep out a shot from Brady.

After the break the Italians committed themselves totally to defence. Fanna was left isolated in attack as Juventus created a defensive wall around their goal. Arsenal had almost constant possession, but even Brady and Rix could find no way through. With five minutes to go it seemed that Juventus were going to achieve the clean sheet that they had played for, but Arsenal were about to get the stroke of luck that they so desperately needed. Arsenal won a free-kick on the edge of the penalty area, Brady floated the ball across to Young who headed it back across the area where Bettega, under pressure from Stapleton, headed the ball into his own net. After his assault on O'Leary it seemed that justice had been done.

Bettega's own goal gave Arsenal a lifeline, albeit a slender one. They would now have to go to Turin and win to reach the final. In the last ten years, Juventus had lost only one of their 33 European home ties, and in their 11 previous meetings with British clubs they had won eight of the encounters and drawn three. Terry Neill was putting on a brave face as he insisted that they could still win: 'It is not over yet. We tend to play better away from home and I'm sure we can still win it out in Italy.'

The main talking point after the game was not the scoreline but the foul on O'Leary by Bettega. Neill was incensed and in the post-match press conference he pointed to an Italian journalist and said: 'You must be ashamed. It must be difficult admitting you are an Italian tonight.' He went on to describe O'Leary's injury: 'David has two vivid stud marks just below the knee. It was a disgraceful foul and in that moment Bettega destroyed a reputation that has taken him years to build.' He added: 'We have taken the studs out of O'Leary's shin and handed them back to Bettega.'

Giovanni Trappatoni, the Juventus coach, tried to play down the incident: 'I know Arsenal are angry about Bettega's tackle but I am unable to say whether it was deliberate or not.' The normally placid O'Leary, however, was in no doubt: 'Bettega knows what he did. He even thought about it before he did it. He knows it was a criminal tackle. His studs smashed through my pad and into my leg. The pad saved me from a break. I always thought more of Bettega, that he was an exception.' The next day O'Leary was on painkillers and antibiotics and was still upset at what Bettega had done: 'I can put my weight on my right foot now, but it's desperately sore. Bettega didn't come to see me afterwards. Cuccuredu, the right-back, was the only Juventus player to come into the dressing-room to see how I was. I do know that what happened taught me the value of shin pads.' The day after the match, Neill was still angry: 'Nothing will ever change my mind about the brutality of Bettega's tackle. He will have to live with that on his conscience. My lads didn't retaliate and I was proud of them.' In Italy, meanwhile, widespread anger was building up over the strong comments that were emanating from Highbury, leading to Juventus chairman Giampiero Boniperti saying: 'Neill's behaviour was unacceptable and he should be fired.' This, in turn, upset Arsenal chairman Denis Hill-Wood: 'I resent the fact that

Juventus officials should try to tell me how to treat my own manager. Their suggestion . . . is scandalous. I totally agree with what Terry said . . . I would have said something even stronger.'

All the controversy concerning the European semi-final tended to obscure the fact that Arsenal had an FA Cup semi-final to play on the following Saturday. The team travelled up to Hillsborough as underdogs yet again, but buoyed up by the news that O'Leary had recovered sufficiently to take his place in defence. The game, however, was a great disappointment as tired players struggled unsuccessfully to create goal-scoring chances. A dour game ended with a 0–0 draw which meant that the two teams would have to meet again at Villa Park three days later. In the replay Liverpool took the lead, but an equaliser from Alan Sunderland squared the scores and extra-time failed to produce a winner. The teams would have to try again. By a strange quirk of the fixture list, the two teams met for the third time in eight days when they played a league fixture at Anfield. Again they could not be separated as they played out a 1–1 draw.

Arsenal now had the rare luxury of three free days to prepare for their next game, the second leg with Juventus. In Turin, however, feelings were running very high. Juventus general manager Pietro Giuliano warned Arsenal players and supporters that they were likely to receive a less-than-friendly welcome: 'The atmosphere will be very tense. Feelings have been inflamed by newspaper reports of what was said at Highbury. We fear our fans may be planning something for Arsenal. They are very angry that Juventus players have been called animals. Now we will need extra police to guard Arsenal in their hotel and on the way to the stadium, but we can't protect their supporters. They will be easily picked out by their red-and-white colours and they won't get a friendly reception. The reception for Arsenal's officials won't be too friendly either. They will be greeted politely but coolly.'

The man who had caused relations between the two clubs to be so strained now attempted to defuse the situation. Roberto Bettega had his own show on Italian television and he invited Neill and O'Leary to appear on it with him: 'I realise the publicity the last game aroused has created the wrong atmosphere for the return [match] and it's not a situation I'm happy with. If a chat with Neill and O'Leary would help to smooth things over I would love to have them on my show.' O'Leary declined the invitation but Neill agreed to appear. During his television interview Bettega asked Neill why his reaction had been so violent. The Arsenal manager replied: 'I am not a violent man, but I reacted to the situation as I saw it. I don't regret a word I said. My loyalty is entirely to my players. The players didn't retaliate after what happened at Highbury and I am sure that attitude will continue on Wednesday. David, I am sure, will not take the law into his own hands.'

In their retreat at Asti, some 20 miles from Turin, Arsenal made their preparations for the match ahead. Their chances were boosted by the injury that Brio had picked up in a friendly match the previous week. Gentile was to be moved from full-back into a more central position, a move which Terry Neill felt would make the Italians vulnerable to aerial attack: 'Both our front men are accomplished in the air. It will be important for us to use them well as Juventus will miss a key player like Brio.' Also missing would be Tardelli following his dismissal in the first game. Neill's only injury worry was Sammy Nelson whose knee problems failed to pass an injury test. John Devine took over his place at left-back.

There was little doubt about how Juventus would play the game. The masters of the 0–0 draw knew that this would be sufficient to send them through. Gentile freely admitted that they had no intention of pushing forward but would concentrate on killing off the game: 'I think it will be 0–0 which, with our away goal in London, will put us into the final. We shall concentrate on trying to stop Arsenal scoring.'

THE MATCH

The 66,386 supporters in the Stadio Communale created an atmosphere of almost hysterical proportions. The two teams were greeted by a wall of sound and a colourful array of fireworks. In the opening minutes of the match Arsenal – yet again in yellow and blue – and Juventus, in their famous black-and-white stripes, played tensely and tentatively, showing great respect for each other. Devine looked particularly nervous as he lost possession several times in those first few moments. The game soon found its pattern, Arsenal would push forward only to come up against a solid defensive wall, while Juventus broke away quickly, only to find insufficient players in support up front to take advantage.

Without the close attentions of the suspended Tardelli, Brady dominated the midfield. He organised, pushed forward into the space Juventus allowed him and produced some faultless passing. It was proving impossible, however, to break through the defence. With Juventus showing no ambition, there were precious few goal chances and precious little excitement. Not that this bothered the fanatical crowd who were quite happy with the way the game was going, although at times it seemed that Juventus were hampered by their support as they seemed to hurry the few attacks that they had.

Half-time came and went without either goal being seriously threatened. Both teams were reasonably happy with the situation at the interval – Arsenal had not conceded a goal which would make their task so much harder, while Juventus were on course to achieve their desired scoreline.

The second half began in much the same way as the first half had ended with chances at a premium. Juventus's only real chance came after 70 minutes when a free-kick by Cabrini was met with a header by Bettega which was cleanly plucked out of the air by Jennings. Arsenal's best chance came when Stapleton had a header saved by Zoff. Fortunately the match was not filled with vendettas from the first game. Willie Young was the only man to be booked after a foul on Causio in the 61st minute.

With 15 minutes remaining the tiring Talbot and Price were replaced by Hollins and Vaessen. Arsenal now knew that they had nothing to lose – they had to score a goal. Big Willie Young left his position at the centre of defence and went forward to give the Italian defenders something else to worry about. Yellow shirts poured forward in an attempt to get the crucial goal that they required, but still the Italian defence remained firm. As the game entered its 88th minute it looked as though Juventus were going to succeed in getting the goalless draw that they had played for – Arsenal were on their way out. The home crowd celebrated their impending triumph as the stadium became a sea of black-and-white flags and the fans sang victory songs. Just then, however, Graham Rix won the ball on the left-wing, he took it down the flank before kicking over a high cross which had Zoff grasping at air, much as Gary Bailey had done almost a year earlier, and there at the far post was Paul Vaessen who had the simplest of tasks to nod the ball over the line and into the goal. Suddenly, for the first time in the match, the crowd was silenced; the Juventus players and supporters were stunned. They had thought that they were home and dry. The players tried to regain their composure and make one last attack, but it was too late. Before they had a chance to launch themselves at Pat Jennings' goal, referee Eric Linemayr had blown the final whistle. Arsenal had done it.

The celebrating Arsenal players went to applaud their small, brave band of supporters in one corner of the ground, but unfortunately this only drew attention to their presence and bottles and stones were soon raining down on top of them. One Arsenal fan was later taken to hospital with a broken leg following the trouble on the terraces. Although the aftermath was a frightening experience those fans had seen one of Arsenal's greatest ever performances.

Terry Neill was ecstatic: 'It has got to be one of the best European results ever. The performance of my players showed just what a remarkable bunch they are. Nothing they do amazes me any more. I am so proud of them.' Chairman Denis Hill-Wood paid the team the ultimate compliment: 'I believe they are better than the team that won the double because their level of consistency has been so remarkable. They just never know when they are beaten and they work so hard for each other.'

The players celebrated jubilantly in the dressing-room before crossing to the Juventus changing area to exchange shirts. Sportingly, Marco Tardelli who had been somewhat harshly dismissed in the first game, wished them well for the final. On their return to the hotel there were further celebrations which involved, amongst other things, John Hollins driving down the hotel corridor on a moped.

If the night belonged to any one person it was young Paul Vaessen who was understandably elated to have scored such an important goal at such an early stage of his career: 'Incredibly I had a dream last night that I would come on as substitute and score the winning goal. It is all so exciting.' At such a young age, Vaessen appeared to have the world at his feet and a great footballing future ahead of him. Sadly his goal in Turin proved to be the highlight of a short career as within two years he was forced out of the game with a serious knee injury. As Terry Neill later reflected: 'One of the grimmest truths about football is that every player can be one tackle away from the end of his career.'

Such thoughts were far from people's minds on the night of 23 April 1980 as they savoured Arsenal's incredible achievement. Few people had given Arsenal any chance after the first leg, but they had persevered and eventually triumphed against all the odds. Together with Nottingham Forest who had beaten Ajax to reach the European Cup final, they had given the English game an enormous boost. When the team ran out at Highbury three days later for their game against West Bromwich Albion, they were greeted with a standing ovation.

Arsenal still had many important games to play. On 28 April they drew yet again with Liverpool in the FA Cup, but three days later in the fourth meeting they took the lead through Brian Talbot and held on to reach their second Cup final of the season and their third FA Cup final in a row. From there the season went sharply downhill.

At Wembley they were unable to even approach their top form and were beaten by Second Division West Ham. Three days later they faced Valencia of Spain in the Cup-Winners' Cup final at the now infamous Heysel Stadium in Brussels. Arsenal had the better of the game but, after extra-time, there was still no score and so the game went to a penalty shoot-out. Brady for Arsenal and Kempes for Valencia both missed before Rix's penalty was saved and the Cup went to the Spaniards.

Even now Arsenal still had two league games left to win if they were to qualify for the following seasons UEFA Cup. Somehow they managed to find enough energy to beat Wolves at Molineux, but their 70th game of the season at Middlesbrough was one game too many as they crashed to a 5–0 defeat. As Pat Rice later recalled: 'Never mind beating us 5–0, Middlesbrough could have been five up at half-time because no one had a gallop left in them. It was really, really hard.' A season that had promised so much had ended with nothing.

On the plane journey back from Middlesbrough Terry Neill insisted on opening the champagne that they had brought. They may have finished the season empty-handed but in the end it was only fatigue that had stopped them from adding to the contents of the trophy cabinet. In the 48 days from 2 April to their final match on 19 May, Arsenal had played 17 games, including six semi-finals and two finals. Throughout the season the team had achieved many great victories, but in the end the one that stood out above all else was that historic night in Turin.

FINAL SCORE

| Arsenal | 1 | Juventus | 0 (1–2 on aggregate) |

| Vaessen | 88 mins |
| Attendance: | 66,386 |

| Arsenal: | Jennings, Rice, Devine, Talbot (Hollins), O'Leary, Young, Brady, Sunderland, Stapleton, Price (Vaessen), Rix |

| Juventus: | Zoff, Cuccureddu, Cabrini, Furino, Gentile, Scirea, Causio, Prandelli (Maracchino), Bettega, Tavola, Fanna |

Chapter 8

ONE–NIL DOWN
TWO–ONE UP

Littlewoods Cup semi-final replay
Tottenham Hotspur v Arsenal
Wednesday, 4 March 1987

The 1985–86 season had not been a happy one for Arsenal supporters; not only was the trophy cabinet empty – again – but there had not been a realistic challenge in any of the major competitions. Despite having a team full of top internationals including Kenny Sansom, Viv Anderson, David O'Leary, Graham Rix, Steve Williams, Charlie Nicholas, Tony Woodcock and Paul Mariner, Arsenal had managed to score just 49 goals in 42 league games, finishing the season in seventh position. In the big games they had been outfought and outplayed, beaten at home by struggling Aston Villa in the League Cup, and humiliated 3–0 by Luton in the FA Cup.

Changes were needed and so, on 14 May 1986, George Graham returned to Highbury to take over as manager. Things soon began to change. Arsenal rediscovered their battling qualities and team spirit and they began to get the better of teams that appeared, on paper, to be superior. Suddenly, Arsenal were challenging in all three competitions and Highbury was, once more, a place that opponents visited with some trepidation. A new golden age was beginning.

THE PLAYERS

On arriving back at his old club, George Graham immediately decided that some of the well-paid star players had to go and that several of the club's young players would be given a chance to play in the first team. Out went Woodcock and Mariner and in came youngsters like Adams, Rocastle and Quinn. As has been the case with most successful Arsenal teams, the majority of the players were now products of the club's youth system.

Several of the big name players may have been sold, but there was still plenty of experience in defence.

John Lukic had joined Arsenal from Leeds as understudy to first-choice goalkeeper, Pat Jennings, but his form had earned him a regular place in the team in December 1984 and he had been a permanent fixture in the team ever since. Although occasionally suspect on crosses, he was a great shot-stopper and had a particularly good record at saving penalties.

Arsenal had arguably the two best full-backs in England in Viv Anderson and captain Kenny Sansom. Anderson at right-back had become the first black player to play for England when he was with Nottingham Forest and had collected more than 20 caps since then. In defence he was a difficult man to beat with his long legs sliding in for the tackle, while in attack he was quick to get forward and provide crosses for the front men. Sansom had arrived at Highbury in 1981 in bizarre circumstances when he was exchanged for Clive Allen, who had arrived in a blaze of publicity but had left without playing a game. Sansom had been a regular in the England side and, with 77 caps in his time at Highbury, is still Arsenal's most capped player. Despite his regular Wembley appearances for the national team he had yet to visit the twin towers in his club colours.

One of the two survivors from the Cup-winning team of 1979 was David O'Leary. Although the two other Irish stars from that team – Brady and Stapleton – had left to join Juventus and Manchester United respectively, O'Leary had stayed loyal to Arsenal despite their lack of success in the intervening years. He had seen several central defensive partners come and go, but his new partner was possibly the best of them all. Tony Adams had made his debut as a 17-year-old in 1983, but had yet to establish himself as a regular in the team. The arrival of George Graham soon changed that. Graham immediately saw Adams's potential and before a ball had been kicked in the new season he described him as a future England captain. With the departure of fellow central defender Martin Keown to Aston Villa the way was open for Adams, alongside O'Leary, to make the position his own and he went on to play in every game of the 1986–87 season.

The other member of the 1979 team still at Highbury was Graham Rix. He had started the season in the first team, but the injury problems that were to blight his Arsenal career from then on meant that he did not play after the first couple of months. In his place came 20-year-old Martin Hayes. Hayes had previously made only a handful of appearances but his arrival in the team had a dramatic effect. In their first nine league games Arsenal won only three times and scored only six goals, but in the 15 games after Hayes had joined the team they won 12 games and drew three – with Hayes scoring 11 times. The 1986–87 season was definitely the best of Hayes's Arsenal career. In all, despite not being an out-and-out forward, he scored 24 times to be the club's top scorer.

On the right-hand side of midfield was David Rocastle. Another fresh product of the youth system, 19-year-old Rocastle also had only had a few first-team appearances. It was not long, however, before he too became a regular first-team player, and with his ability to take on and beat defenders when going forward and his tough tackling in defence, 'Rocky' soon became a firm favourite with the Highbury crowd.

The two playmakers in midfield were Paul Davis and Steve Williams. After his promising debut at White Hart Lane in 1980 Davis had initially struggled to live up to expectations, but by now he was, in his own calm and unassuming way, playing some of the best football of his career and his simple passing and calming influence was at the heart of much of the team's play. Alongside him was Steve Williams who had been signed from Southampton for £600,000 in December 1984. Due to injury the England international had yet to make a significant impact on the team, but now he was able to form an effective partnership with Davis at the heart of the side.

Although some of the star names had left Highbury in the summer, the biggest star remained – Charlie Nicholas had signed from Celtic in 1988 and was seen as the man who would transform Arsenal into a championship-winning side. Having scored 48 goals for his club during the previous season, Nicholas was the hottest property in British football. He had been expected to sign for either Liverpool or Manchester United, but had surprisingly opted for Arsenal instead. Despite his obvious ability and a number of outstanding performances, Charlie had struggled from the start to play consistently well and, after three seasons, had scored only 30 goals in 120 league appearances. Despite this he was still hugely popular with Highbury supporters as his occasional brilliance had provided most of the few highlights in recent seasons.

Alongside Nicholas in attack was six-foot four-inch-tall Niall Quinn. At 19 he was yet another of the youngsters to be part of the first-team action. Quinn had hit the headlines during the previous season when, on his debut, he had scored in a 2–0 win over mighty Liverpool. With the departure of Mariner and Woodcock he was now a first-choice player and, with his obvious aerial skills allied to Nicholas's ability on the ground, it was hoped that they would make an effective forward partnership. The only other player at the club who had previously appeared up front for the first team was Ian Allinson who, in his 83 appearances since his free transfer from Colchester United, had scored 16 goals.

All of these players were at Arsenal when George Graham arrived, and during the summer only one player was added to the squad. Graham's first signing was Perry Groves who came from Colchester for just £50,000. It was not exactly a signing to set the world alight, but Groves would go on to make many valuable contributions to this and many more seasons. Unfortunately he found that he was not popular with some sections of the Highbury crowd, but his pace and willingness were valuable assets to the team.

THE BACKGROUND

The first day of the season had brought a very encouraging 1–0 win over Manchester United courtesy of a goal from Charlie Nicholas, but it seemed to be a false dawn as after that match the

Arsenal forwards struggled to find the net. During September the Gunners went for four consecutive league games without a goal and slipped into 15th place in the table. On 4 October, however, a Steve Williams corner went directly into the goal to give Arsenal a 1–0 win at Everton, and from then until 7 March they lost only one league game. In their next seven league games Arsenal won six and drew one, and a 4–0 win at Southampton in November took them to first place in the championship.

By then Arsenal's Littlewoods Cup campaign had begun. In the second round they were drawn against Second Division Huddersfield Town. The first leg was won 2–0 with goals from Paul Davis and Niall Quinn. This seemed as though it would be sufficient to see Arsenal comfortably through to the next round but, when Huddersfield took the lead in the second leg, things did not look so easy. Fortunately, Martin Hayes, who had come on as a second-half substitute, scored a vital goal which allowed Arsenal to ease through to the third round. Ironically, Hayes had been poised to move to Huddersfield earlier in the season, but the deal had fallen through.

In the following round a deflected shot from Rocastle, a penalty from Hayes and a last-minute 25-yard shot from Davis gave Arsenal a 3–1 home win over struggling Manchester City. Three weeks later at Highbury, Charlton Athletic were beaten 2–0 thanks to an Alan Curbishley own goal and a header from Niall Quinn, to send the Gunners through to the quarter-finals.

Arsenal's unbeaten run continued through November and December and as 1987 began they had a four-point lead over Everton at the top of the First Division. On New Year's Day Wimbledon came to Highbury for the first time in their history and were beaten 3–1. Three days later Arsenal travelled to White Hart Lane for the 100th north London league derby.

The trip to Tottenham was seen as a great test of Arsenal's championship credentials. As well as having many big name international stars such as Ray Clemence, Richard Gough, Glenn Hoddle, Ossie Ardiles and Chris Waddle, the Spurs team included England's most in-form striker – Clive Allen – who had so far scored 32 goals in 29 games. Tottenham were also on a run of form which had seen them rise from eleventh place in the middle of November to their current position of fifth. The Gunners were in no mood to surrender their unbeaten run, and certainly not at White Hart Lane.

With the rain pouring down over north London they immediately took the game to Tottenham and soon found themselves in the lead. An Arsenal corner saw a Viv Anderson shot cleared off the goal-line, but the ball found its way to Kenny Sansom whose cross was knocked down by Quinn. Tony Adams, who had stayed forward after the corner, beat Clemence to the ball and sent it spinning into the empty net. Five minutes before half-time, a Williams back-heel found Rocastle who fed Nicholas who sent a defence-splitting pass through to Hayes, who was then fouled on the edge of the penalty area. From the free-kick Davis threaded the ball through the defensive wall and past Clemence to give Arsenal a two-goal lead. Tottenham pulled one goal back, but that was to be the end of the scoring and Arsenal held on to gain a tremendous 2–1 victory. In fairness, some of the credit should also go to the Arsenal mascot for that game, 13-year-old Stuart Nethercott, who went on to play Premiership football – for Spurs!

Just over two weeks later, following a 3–1 FA Cup win at Reading and a goalless draw with Coventry, Arsenal's Littlewoods Cup campaign continued with another home game; this time against Nottingham Forest. Forest were in a determined mood following their FA Cup defeat against Crystal Palace as the Littlewoods Cup now represented their only real chance of success for that season. After only two minutes and 11 seconds Arsenal were ahead as Charlie Nicholas shot past the Forest goalkeeper at the second attempt. Later in the first half Martin Hayes's impressive turn on the edge of the penalty area and shot that found the top corner of the net increased Arsenal's lead. Forest looked as though they would come back into the game when they were awarded a second-half penalty, but John Lukic dived to his left to save Stuart Pearce's spot-kick and Arsenal were 2–0 winners.

The semi-final draw paired Arsenal with either West Ham or Tottenham, depending on the result from their quarter-final tie. In their first game the two teams drew 1–1 at Upton Park, but in the replay Tottenham were 5–0 winners – with Clive Allen scoring a hat trick in just eight minutes. While Tottenham were on a roll and in the mood to get revenge for their league defeat, Arsenal had received a blow to their confidence, just three days after their win over Forest, when they lost their unbeaten record to Manchester United in a bad-tempered 2–0 defeat at Old Trafford and which saw David Rocastle sent off. Although Arsenal recovered to beat Plymouth 6–1 in the FA Cup the following Saturday, they were to be hampered by the loss of both Viv Anderson and Rocastle for the first leg of the semi-final. This was a serious blow to the Gunners as so many of their goals came from Anderson and Rocastle linking up so effectively down the right-hand side of the field.

The first leg of the semi-final took place at Highbury on Sunday, 8 February in front of 41,306 people. George Graham's biggest decision beforehand was who to play at right-back in place of the suspended Viv Anderson. His choice rested between two youngsters: Gus Caesar who had made only a handful of appearances, most of which were as substitute, or Michael Thomas who had been playing at Portsmouth on loan and had yet to play for Arsenal. In the end Graham opted to play Caesar and picked Perry Groves in place of Rocastle.

Arsenal started the game well and, had Quinn and Hayes been able to take advantage of chances presented to them, could have taken an early lead, but Tottenham soon got into their stride and Hoddle, Ardiles, Claesen and Waddle began to assert their authority on the match. Waddle, in particular, was able to show off his skills on the left-wing as he ran poor Caesar ragged. As the report in *The Guardian* said the next day: 'You had to have some sympathy for Caesar as Waddle led the queue along the Tottenham left to bury him.'

The decisive moment in the game came after 38 minutes when a shot by Clive Allen was adjudged by the referee to have been tipped over the bar by Lukic, although it was not clear to many spectators that the Arsenal goalkeeper had managed to get a touch. From the resulting corner the Arsenal defence tried to clear the ball but it fell to Mabbutt. Lukic did well to save the Spurs defender's shot, but the rebound fell to Clive Allen – who many felt was in an offside position – and he volleyed the ball into the net.

Allen turned away in triumph and leapt into the air before falling to the ground where he was mobbed by his team-mates. A minute later Allen should have doubled his tally when Caesar attempted to clear the ball from defence, but only managed to slice the ball into Allen's path who then had only Lukic to beat. As the North Bank waited for the inevitable goal, Allen, uncharacteristically, hit his shot wide of the post.

The closest that Arsenal came to scoring in the second half came when Groves's dipping shot caught Clemence off his line but the ball hit the post. From the rebound, Hayes fed the ball into the six-yard area where Davis incredibly missed an open goal from two yards out when he sent the ball over the bar. The linesman subsequently raised his flag, but to many it seemed he was merely trying to save Davis from embarrassment rather than signalling any infringement. Soon afterwards, not to be outdone, Hoddle hit a curling free-kick against Lukic's left-hand post.

At the final whistle the Tottenham players turned triumphantly to applaud their jubilant supporters. With a one-goal advantage to take into their home leg they appeared to be well on the way to Wembley. Tottenham manager David Pleat was very happy with his team's all-round performance: 'We have a lot of attack-minded players in the team, but as a group they did extremely well. The team is defending more solidly and we restricted Arsenal to just a few chances.' He also revealed that the league game at White Hart Lane had helped him in his planning for the match: 'We learnt a few things from our defeat in the league . . . earlier this month. Then we made a lot of uncharacteristic errors during the first 20 minutes which we did not today.'

George Graham was not too downbeat after the match: 'I am not unhappy with our display. We took the game to Spurs to try to get something back. Spurs scored their goal when we should have been ahead.'

The three weeks that preceded the return leg saw Arsenal beat Barnsley 2–0 to reach the sixth round of the FA Cup. But draws at Sheffield Wednesday and Oxford meant that they had now failed to win any of their four league games since the victory at White Hart Lane and they had dropped behind Liverpool and Everton in the championship. Tottenham, meanwhile, played three games and scored eight goals without reply to record three victories. With Tottenham running into form at just the right time and Arsenal seeming to be experiencing problems, the pundits were predicting a comfortable win for Spurs in the return leg.

Even though Steve Williams was out with an injured arm and had to be replaced in midfield by young Michael Thomas, with Rocastle and Anderson returning to the team, the Arsenal players and supporters still felt that they were in with a chance. If Tottenham got an early goal, however, they knew that their task would be a very difficult one.

After 16 minutes of the game it appeared that Tottenham had booked their Wembley place. Richard Gough sent his free-kick high into the Arsenal penalty area, John Lukic attempted to punch clear, but succeeded only in knocking the ball to the feet of Clive Allen who evaded Quinn's challenge and found the net with ease. Just as at Highbury in the first game, Allen should have scored again shortly after his goal. As the ball was crossed in low from the left, Allen slid in right in front of the goal, but he failed to connect properly with the ball and sent it wide of the post.

Despite being two goals down the Arsenal team refused to give up, and slowly they began to work themselves back into the game. Rocastle found space on the right side of the penalty area and forced Clemence to make a diving save, while Charlie Nicholas beat the goalkeeper from the edge of the area, only to see the ball come back off the crossbar.

As the half-time whistle blew the aggregate score remained 2–0 and few in the Tottenham camp doubted that their Wembley appearance was assured. Their supreme confidence rebounded on them, however, as Kenny Sansom recounted in his book *Going Great Guns*: 'We were low in the dressing-room at half-time. We won here in the league and yet how many teams win twice in succession at White Hart Lane! Then something happened that transformed the match and turned our sullen mood into one of determination. Spurs announced on their public address system how their fans should apply for tickets for the final and the message boomed into our dressing-room. Then they switched on their old FA Cup final song, "Spurs are on their way to Wembley", and that took the lads' determination over the top. This is difficult to describe because it is a feeling that rarely happens to you. You get a goosepimply feeling and you know that you are not going to lose the game. The young faces in the team suddenly wanted to get out for the second half and it was obvious to me as we trotted out that Arsenal were not going out of the competition.'

David O'Leary recalls in *David O'Leary – My Story* how George Graham also urged his team on: 'What the boss had to say was inspirational. Part of what he said was, "We'll keep our heads. We won't panic. We will continue to create chances . . . only we will put them away this half." What he did was settle us down. He was under pressure himself – but it didn't show.'

It took only five minutes after the interval for Arsenal to get themselves back into the match and their goal came courtesy of the two players who had missed the first leg. Rocastle won a throw-in near to the Tottenham corner flag and took the throw himself, hurling the ball into the area where Niall Quinn flicked it on. The ball bobbled around the near post and in the confusion Viv Anderson managed to stab the ball home.

During the next ten minutes, with Arsenal pressing forward in search of the goal that would level the aggregate scores, Clive Allen twice found himself through on goal with only Lukic to beat, but his first effort was blazed over the crossbar and his second was saved by Lukic's outstretched leg. With Allen passing up the sort of chances that he had been putting away all season, Arsenal must have thought that it might just be their day, and in the 64th minute they got their crucial second goal. Davis picked up the ball in midfield and slipped the ball out to Rocastle on the right. Rocastle ran towards the by-line and sent the ball low across the six-yard area, eluding Clemence and the Tottenham defenders, and Quinn slid in at the far post to send the ball high into the roof of the net.

The Arsenal fans massed at the other end of the ground danced with delight. They were right back in the game and, from then on, Arsenal took command of the match. The Tottenham midfield which had looked so composed became overrun as Thomas and Rocastle denied them any space and Davis started to find his forwards with his probing passes. Neither team, however, could score the winning goal and, despite the end-to-end nature of the game, there was no further score in normal time. Extra-time proved similarly goalless as two tired teams struggled to carve out chances.

With the aggregate score standing at 2–2 a replay was needed, and it took place three days later. The two managers took to the field at the final whistle for the toss of the coin that would decide the replay venue. Even then it looked as though the two teams could not be separated as the coin stuck horizontally in the mud – George Graham wondered if it was pointing towards Stamford Bridge – but eventually it came down as heads, David Pleat's choice.

With both teams having won at their opponents' ground the decision was not necessarily as straightforward as normal. As Pleat admitted: 'Arsenal have come here twice and won this season and we've won at Highbury so it was a tough decision to go for home advantage again.'

George Graham also admitted that had he won the toss he would have been tempted to choose to play away, but Pleat knew that it was in Spurs' best interest for the replay to take place at White Hart Lane for as he said later: 'If Arsenal come back on Wednesday and get a hat trick of wins good luck to them.'

The Arsenal manager was certainly proud of his players and felt that the way that most people had written off Arsenal's chances had helped him to motivate his team: 'We don't get the credit we deserve. A few guys said we would lose by two or three to nothing. That fired the players up. We had two players out there just 19 and three aged 20. That's half our team 20 or under. Allen's goal came from a mistake by John Lukic, but I thought we were still excellent throughout. Young players like Tony Adams, David Rocastle and Martin Hayes were outstanding – and what about Niall Quinn? These players are still learning the game and yet produce displays like that.'

David Pleat was forced to be more philosophical as he rued the chances that Clive Allen had missed: 'Clive will feel he might have scored from a couple of chances, but that's Clive. He's scored a lot and has missed a few this season, but he took his goal well today. There were four occasions I thought "This is it" when we were through one against one, but we didn't put it away.'

THE MATCH

Arsenal's chances of reaching Wembley were boosted before the replay began by the news that Glenn Hoddle had a stomach strain and would be missing from the Spurs team. In Gary Stevens Spurs had another England international to take his place, but the absence of Hoddle was a huge blow to Tottenham. They still had home advantage, however, as well as the determination not to lose their third north London derby at White Hart Lane in just two months.

The significance for both teams of the match could not be overstated. Semi-finals against your deadliest rivals are big occasions, but both teams were desperate to reach Wembley after a lengthy absence. Arsenal had not visited the twin towers for seven years and it was five years since Tottenham's last appearance. For the winners it would be a great evening to remember, for the losers it would be an evening of desperate disappointment. With the stakes being so high, it was no surprise that the 41,005 spectators that crammed into the ground created an atmosphere of incredible passion and intensity.

Despite the importance of the match it had been decided that no further replays would be allowed and that a winner had to be found on the night with, if necessary, a penalty shoot-out following extra-time. Neither team wanted to resort to penalties and this may explain why, instead of the sort of cagey start that one might expect in such a crucial game, both teams made it clear from the kick-off that they were going for goal.

Barely two minutes had been played when the first clear opening of the game arrived. A long ball was played up to Quinn in the Arsenal attack. The big Irishman brushed off the challenge of Mabbutt and bore down on goal. His shot across the diving Clemence looked goalbound, but just sneaked past the far post. Soon afterwards Claesen's acrobatic overhead kick looped just past Lukic's post and, moments later, Waddle found himself in a dangerous position at the far post, only to volley the ball into the side netting.

With both teams so evenly matched the players and supporters knew that the first goal was likely to be crucial, and on two occasions in the opening 45 minutes, Arsenal's top goalscorer

Martin Hayes looked as though he might make the breakthrough. On the first occasion he found himself through on the goalkeeper, but Clemence denied him with a diving save. Moments later a fine pass from Rocastle found Hayes in acres of space, but he was easily hustled out of the danger area by the Tottenham defence.

As half-time came the game was still goalless. After the interval the game continued as it had in the first half with the play going from one end to the other at breakneck speed, but with an hour of the game gone there was still no score.

With 62 minutes on the clock, however, the deadlock was broken, and once again it was Clive Allen who was responsible. Michael Thomas was penalised for a foul on Ardiles near the touchline just inside the Arsenal half. As Spurs pushed their big men forward, the Argentinian took the free-kick himself and lofted the ball towards the penalty area. Gough, on the edge of the box, rose above the Arsenal defence and nodded the ball down into the area where Allen pounced to beat Lukic and score his 12th goal of Spurs' Littlewoods Cup campaign – a new record for the competition.

It seemed as though that would be the killer blow for Arsenal. Surely Tottenham would not let their lead slip at White Hart Lane again? Even George Graham admitted after the game: 'When Spurs scored I thought "that's it".' Worse was to follow just moments later when, following a fierce tackle from Gough, Charlie Nicholas was carried from the field with an ankle injury. With Nicholas's replacement being Ian Allinson – who had yet to score a goal that season – Arsenal fans had little cause for optimism.

With the home crowd roaring them on and a 1–0 lead in their favour, now was the time for the experienced Tottenham players to take a grip on the game and make sure of their trip to Wembley, but the Arsenal team did not appear to have read the script.

The young players in their red-and-white shirts refused to admit defeat as they continued to perform with sheer guts and determination. As time began to run out, George Graham decided that it was time to gamble and he threw Anderson, Rocastle and Allinson forward to support Quinn in attack.

As the game entered the last ten minutes Arsenal desperately needed a breakthrough and, with just eight minutes remaining, it was Ian Allinson who made himself an unlikely hero. Paul Davis, again finding space in midfield, played the ball over the Tottenham defence and found Allinson running towards goal. With Gough alongside him blocking his route to the net, Allinson stopped and turned his back to goal by the left corner of the six-yard box, but just as it looked as though the danger had passed for Spurs, the Arsenal substitute turned and shot through Gough's legs and beat the surprised Clemence at the near post.

In the delirium that followed Allinson's equaliser, Kenny Sansom felt that the game was now Arsenal's. As he wrote in *Going Great Guns*: 'I knew then that we were going to do it. The Tottenham players "went" in that split second. They were asking themselves the question: "Not a third time", and I noticed Chris Waddle with his head on his chest. I began to shout anything at the top of my voice to keep the lads going. This was the time to go for the kill although I fully expected the match to go into extra-time. I would have been happy with that, we were strong now while Spurs looked tired and ready for the worst.'

From then on it was Arsenal who were on all-out attack with the Tottenham goal under almost constant siege. As they had in the second leg, the Arsenal players had got stronger as the game went on while their opponents had wilted under the pressure. In the few minutes that remained both Michael Thomas and Martin Hayes found themselves in positions to win the game, but they put their shots narrowly past the post and into the side netting respectively, and with the game entering the first minute of injury time it looked as though this marathon tie would go on for another 30 minutes.

When Arsenal were awarded a free-kick just inside their half it seemed that this would be the last chance for either team to win the game in normal time. O'Leary's ball towards the penalty area was deflected out to Allinson on the left-wing. Allinson went for his second goal of the night, but his shot was blocked and fell invitingly to Rocastle in the penalty box. Rocastle's first touch took him through the Tottenham defence and his left-footed shot crept under Clemence and into the net.

The 10,000 Arsenal supporters behind the goal could barely

contain their joy, while the Arsenal players mobbed Rocastle in celebration. Most people thought that the final whistle was imminent but, in fact, referee Joe Worrall played another three minutes of injury time, although this did not surprise Rocastle too much for as he admitted after the match: 'I was so involved in the game that I thought there was still 15 minutes left on the clock.' In all that time, however, the nearest that Tottenham came to the Arsenal goal was when Sansom headed the ball away from the edge of his penalty area following a Spurs free-kick. Moments later the referee blew the final whistle and Arsenal were back at Wembley for the first time in seven years.

As the distraught Tottenham supporters left the ground and their tearful players left the pitch, the jubilant Arsenal players stayed to celebrate in front of their ecstatic supporters. As their young heroes embraced each other, the fans sang 'Arsenal are back'. By the time that the players left the field, the three sides of the ground that had housed the home supporters were completely empty.

The moods of the two managers could not have been more different after the game. David Pleat was understandably dejected: 'I think I'll die tomorrow. To lose to a last-minute goal like that is almost as bad as going out on a penalty shoot-out. We gave away two unbelievably bad goals, but perhaps you have to start believing in fate. Maybe it was meant for Arsenal to win. We are demoralised but we wish Arsenal well in the final and hope they win it for London.'

George Graham, on the other hand, was overjoyed: 'This equates to anything I achieved as a player and I hope it's just the start of a new era for this club . . . I'm so proud of my team. I told you on Sunday not to underestimate them and they've proved it again. I didn't expect to come back this time, but I wasn't surprised. We are very resilient and have that wonderful never-say-die attitude.'

In his many post-match interviews, David Rocastle was keen to talk about his winning goal: 'That is the most important goal I've ever scored. For a moment I could not believe it. I had to check with the linesman to make sure the flag was down before I started celebrating.' Rocastle also spoke about the spirit in the Arsenal team: 'Everybody fights for each other. We are friends as well as team-mates. That kind of togetherness breeds a tremendous team spirit.'

That team spirit was evident again when Arsenal played the great Liverpool team in the final at Wembley on 5 April. Again they were underdogs – since beating Tottenham they had been knocked out of the FA Cup and failed to win a single league game – but again they came from a goal behind to win 2-1 and take a trophy back to Highbury for the first time in eight years. It was another performance of character and determination in the face of adversity and it captured the imagination of the Arsenal supporters.

In a short space of time, George Graham had instilled these qualities into the team, and their success would be the launching pad for the golden era that Highbury would witness over the next seven years. As *The Sun* said on the day after their White Hart Lane victory: 'George Graham's bunch of Arsenal kids will go down in history as the team that refused to die.'

FINAL SCORE

Arsenal	2	Tottenham Hotspur	1
Allinson	82 mins	C. Allen	63 mins
Rocastle	90 mins		
Attendance:	41,005		

Tottenham Hotspur: Clemence, D. Thomas, M. Thomas, Ardiles, Gough, Mabbutt, C. Allen, P. Allen, Waddle, Stevens, Claesen (Galvin)

Arsenal: Lukic, Anderson, Sansom, M. Thomas, O'Leary, Adams, Rocastle, Davis, Quinn, Nicholas (Allinson), Hayes

Chapter 9

ONE MINUTE

On 26 May 1989 millions of people throughout Britain settled down in front of their television sets ready to watch Liverpool win the championship – again. Once more they would see the all too familiar sight of the Liverpool captain holding the championship trophy aloft before the cheering Kop to the strains of 'You'll Never Walk Alone'.

For the first time since 1952 – when Arsenal had lost 6–1 against Manchester United – the championship would be decided by the final game when the top two teams of the season played each other. The outcome, however, was in little doubt; Liverpool had won the championship six times in the previous eight years and had won 17 and drawn one of their last 18 games. All they had to do to retain the championship was to avoid losing by more than one goal at home to a young Arsenal team that had led the championship for so much of the season but had let a commanding lead slip since February and who had appeared to have lost their nerve at a crucial stage. Not only had Arsenal not won at Anfield for 14 years, but it was three seasons since any team had beaten Liverpool on their own ground by two goals or more.

Despite this George Graham and his Arsenal team felt that they had a chance. All logic pointed to a comfortable Liverpool victory, but at Highbury they still thought they were capable of pulling off one of the most remarkable results of all time and they were determined to do so.

THE PLAYERS

The Arsenal team that won the Littlewoods Cup in 1987 was not really George Graham's team. It was only Graham's first season in charge at Highbury and he was effectively just doing his best with the players that had been left by the previous manager Don Howe. Two years later, however, many changes had been made and the team that the manager wanted was beginning to take shape. Out were Kenny Sansom, Viv Anderson, Steve Williams, Graham Rix and Charlie Nicholas to be replaced by a mixture of transferred and home-grown talent.

John Lukic remained first-choice goalkeeper but the rest of the defence had seen several changes over the past two years. The two new full-backs were Lee Dixon and Nigel Winterburn. Dixon had arrived midway through the previous season to take over from Viv Anderson who had left for Manchester United. Signed from Stoke City after several years in the lower divisions, Dixon made an instant impression on his debut against Luton and, although he only played a handful of games that season, looked set to establish himself in the team with his sound defending and his speed when going forward. Winterburn had arrived from Wimbledon at the start of the 1987–88 season but had initially been unable to get into the team while Kenny Sansom was filling the left-back berth. After Christmas, Winterburn had filled in at right-back and played remarkably well for someone who could barely kick with his right foot and, at the start of the 1988–89 season, he took over as the regular left-back, allowing Dixon to take over on the right. Once he was in his proper position Winterburn soon showed his true ability and his tough tackling became an important feature in the club's success.

In the centre of defence Tony Adams and David O'Leary remained. Adams's rise had been meteoric and he had been picked for England in 1987 at the age of 20. He had played well enough to keep his place over the next year and was chosen to play in the European Championships in Germany in 1988. In his second game there, however, he was given a torrid time by the player of the tournament Marco van Basten who scored a hat trick for Holland in their 3–1 win over England which knocked the English team out of the tournament. Being given the runaround by the best striker in the world was hardly a disgrace, but opposing fans in England were determined to punish Adams for it and he was unmercifully taunted with 'donkey' chants for years to come. Arsenal fans, however, never doubted his importance to the team. In his new role as captain, he held both the defence and the team together as a whole and he had saved them with many a last-ditch tackle. To the Highbury crowd he was still the best defender in England and, gradually, supporters of other teams began to realise this as well.

David O'Leary was still at the club, but his place was threatened by the arrival in the close season of Steve Bould from Stoke. It had been assumed that Bould had been signed as cover for Adams and O'Leary, but on the first Saturday of the season he was picked to play alongside the captain. Bould continued to be the first choice for the rest of the season, but, with injuries and suspensions affecting both him and Lee Dixon, O'Leary was still able to play 30 times that season.

In midfield Paul Davis, David Rocastle, Martin Hayes and Perry Groves remained. Michael Thomas, who had made such an impression in his debut against Spurs two years earlier, was also still at the club. In addition, George Graham had picked up two bargain buys; winger Brian Marwood had been signed from Sheffield Wednesday for £600,000 towards the end of the previous season. The Arsenal manager had been chasing Marwood for some time as he saw his skilful wing play and accurate crossing as being ideal for the side. Kevin Richardson, meanwhile, had been bought for just £250,000 from Watford. This proved to be a great bargain as Richardson's hard work in midfield, although often unnoticed, was crucial in allowing the rest of the team the freedom to go forward.

Alan Smith had been signed from Leicester City for £800,000 towards the end of the 1986–87 season. In his first full season at Highbury he had scored a respectable 16 goals, but the 1988–89 campaign was to be the season where Smith showed his true worth. The tall centre-forward not only scored a mass of goals, but with his ability to hold up the ball and his accurate distribution he created many scoring opportunities for the rest of the team. Alongside Smith in attack was another product of the Highbury youth system. Twenty-year-old Paul Merson had been in and out of the first team over the previous year and in his 22 appearances he had impressed both the management and supporters, with his eight goals showing that he had the ability to score. George Graham realised that now was the time for Merson to prove his ability and he was to be a regular in the team throughout the season.

THE BACKGROUND

Even before the season started it was clear that Arsenal were capable of making a championship challenge after they had beaten both Tottenham and Bayern Munich in the pre-season Makita Tournament at Wembley. This was reinforced on the first day of the season when an emphatic 5–1 win away to FA Cup-holders Wimbledon served as a warning to the rest of the country.

After just six league games, Arsenal had scored 17 goals, the bulk of which came from Smith (nine) and Marwood (four). By the end of October they had reached second place in the First Division standings, with their first real test about to arrive.

The draw for the third round of the Littlewoods Cup had given the Gunners an away tie with a Liverpool team that had won the previous year's championship by a huge margin and had only missed out on the double when they lost to Wimbledon in the FA Cup final. Arsenal, however, were undaunted and travelled to Anfield with confidence.

Right from the start of the match they tore into the Liverpool team. Rarely can a visiting team have dominated a game at Anfield as much as Arsenal did that night, and only a succession of fine saves by goalkeeper Mike Hooper kept them at bay. Arsenal's dominance continued into the second half, but still they could not find a way past Hooper. Despite their superiority Arsenal found themselves falling a goal behind, courtesy of a superb individual goal from John Barnes. The thousands of travelling supporters could not believe it. Salvation came shortly afterwards as Rocastle, from the corner of the penalty area, sent a crashing shot past Hooper and into the top corner of the net. Even then, Arsenal continued to push forward and they seemed to have won the game in its final moments, but Marwood's goal was disallowed for pushing. Television replays suggested that Arsenal were unfairly penalised and the overwhelming feeling amongst the players was one of annoyance that they had not won the game.

It was certainly a moral victory for the Gunners but, unfortunately, moral victories don't get you through to the next round and, following a 0–0 draw watched by over 54,000 people at Highbury, Liverpool were 2–1 winners at Villa Park. Defeat was a great disappointment but at least Arsenal had shown that they could compete with the reigning champions, this was emphasised just a few days later when the two teams met again in the league and played out a 1–1 draw.

The confidence that Arsenal gained from these close encounters with Liverpool showed in their following games. A draw away to surprise league leaders Norwich City was followed by wins over Manchester United, Charlton, Aston Villa and Tottenham. Arsenal were at the top of the table by the new year.

Arsenal's run of wins was interrupted in mid-January when, following a 2–2 draw at Upton Park, West Ham knocked the Gunners out of the FA Cup with a 1–0 win at Highbury. As disappointing as this was it meant that Arsenal were now, as the old saying goes, free to concentrate on the league. This they proceeded to do, winning three and drawing one of their next four games, including a fine 3–1 win at Everton which saw them applauded off the pitch by the home supporters.

When Arsenal took to the field at Loftus Road to play struggling Queen's Park Rangers on 18 February they were very much in form as far as the championship was concerned. They had a three-point lead over second-place Norwich – who had played a game more – while third-placed Manchester United were a further eight points behind. While Liverpool were in sixth place, 14 points behind the Gunners. With a comfortable run-in within their grasp, however, the young Arsenal team appeared to succumb to the pressure of bringing the title to Highbury for the first time in 18 years.

Alan Smith later recalled what can happen in such a situation: 'You get a bit on edge and you forget what got you there in the first place, how you were playing. You don't relax as much and a bit of edginess creeps in.' The goalless draw at Loftus Road was the first of six games that yielded only one win. During that time Liverpool won all four of their league games and the race for the championship was on once more.

A fine 3–1 win at Southampton saw Arsenal back to winning ways, but Liverpool's charge from behind was relentless as they proceeded to win all their games. When Arsenal played Manchester United at Old Trafford on 2 April both they and Liverpool had eight games left to play, with the Gunners having an advantage of just two points. Manager George Graham knew that they could no longer afford to lose and so he announced to the players at the start of the week that they would abandon the 4-4-2 formation that they had played all season and introduce a sweeper at the back. David O'Leary was the man chosen to play just behind Bould and Adams in defence, with Dixon and Winterburn pushing forward on the flanks and Rocastle and Marwood supporting lone striker Alan Smith in attack.

The plan appeared to be working perfectly when Tony Adams dived into a cluster of flying boots to head home a corner and give the Gunners a vital lead. Up until then Manchester United had struggled to get to grips with Arsenal's new formation and had rarely threatened to score but, with the match drawing to a close, disaster struck. A hopeful ball was lofted into the Arsenal penalty area and Tony Adams attempted to hook the ball clear, but the ball sliced off the top of his boot and looped over the helpless Lukic into the net. That one error had cost Arsenal a vital two points. The next day, the *Daily Mirror* printed a picture of Tony Adams with donkey ears on the side of his head under the headline 'EE AW'. Adams was understandably upset and considered taking legal action before deciding that it wasn't worth it. There was little doubt, however, that the persecution of their captain increased the sense of togetherness within the team.

The next weekend saw Liverpool kick off their home game with Sheffield Wednesday in the morning so as not to clash with the Grand National. Liverpool's 5–1 win knocked Arsenal off the top of the table for the first time since Boxing Day and put added pressure on to the Gunners' home game with Everton in the afternoon. A hard-fought 2–0 win sent Arsenal back to the top, but Liverpool's subsequent midweek win over Millwall meant that on Saturday, 15 April 1989, the two teams were level on points at the top of the table.

On 15 April Arsenal beat Newcastle 1–0, but by the end of the match few in the Highbury crowd really cared. Throughout the game news had filtered through from Hillsborough where Liverpool were playing Nottingham Forest in an FA Cup semi-final. There had been a crush at the end of the ground which housed the Liverpool supporters and it soon emerged that there had been many injuries. By the time the final whistle had gone at Highbury the full enormity of the situation had become clear with the news that 95 people had died. The league race was put on hold as the football world stopped to mourn.

Arsenal did not take to the field again until 1 May against Norwich. The two games that they had been due to play in the intervening period against Wimbledon and Liverpool had been put back to the end of an extended season. Continuing the good form that they had shown before Hillsborough Arsenal proceeded to thrash Norwich 5–0 and followed that with a crucial 1–0 win at Middlesbrough the following weekend. These two wins, coupled with Liverpool's draw at Everton, meant that when Derby came to Highbury and Liverpool visited Wimbledon on 13 May, the Gunners had a five-point lead over their championship rivals. Arsenal had only three games remaining while Liverpool had four, but if Arsenal could beat Derby and Liverpool lost to Wimbledon, the title would almost certainly be going to Highbury.

Early in the first half, with the game still goalless, a roar went up on the Highbury terraces and became louder and louder as it spread around the ground: Wimbledon had scored. The crowd was jubilant, but instead of being spurred on the team let their nerves get the better of them and the mood of the crowd was soon changed when Dean Saunders volleyed Derby into the lead. With both Arsenal and Liverpool a goal down at half-time there was everything to play for, but Arsenal simply could not find their way through the Derby defence. As the game entered its final few minutes Tony Adams brought down Dean Saunders for a penalty and Saunders put the visitors 2–0 ahead. Although Alan Smith scored for the Gunners in the final minute it was not enough to save the game. To make matters worse news came from Plough Lane that Liverpool had come back and won 2–1. The Anfield team were now firmly in control of the championship.

With the league title in their sights the Arsenal team had been affected by the great weight of expectation that existed at Highbury. Alan Smith recalls: 'We were diabolical, we played terrible, just didn't perform at all.' Dean Saunders remarked after the match, 'Arsenal were tense, the pressure was on them. You could see it.' Saunders also claimed that it was one of the most important goals of his career, which did not make him very popular in the Arsenal dressing-room.

Now Liverpool were the favourites and they were very confident. Liverpool midfielder Steve McMahon proclaimed, 'We're not worried about Arsenal now. The great thing is that it's in our hands. All we have to do is win our matches.' Three days later Liverpool's confidence was increased even more when they beat Queen's Park Rangers 2–0 to move a point clear at the top. QPR manager Trevor Francis had no doubt that the title was on its way back to Anfield saying, 'They are easily the best team in the First Division and the best Liverpool side in my time in the game.'

The following evening saw Arsenal play their penultimate game of the season at home to Wimbledon. George Graham knew what they had to do: 'We must win to keep our championship chances alive. We have to claim three points to take the title run-in to Anfield. Losing to Derby was a terrific disappointment but that is forgotten now. Our heads are not down. I see no signs of nerves, but then only tonight will tell . . . We all know what is expected of us – that is why all the talking has to be done on the pitch now.' With tension rife throughout the crowd and amongst the players Arsenal really needed an early goal. Fortunately they got one, and what an incredible goal it was. Receiving the ball 30 yards out from goal Nigel Winterburn hit a scorching shot with his right foot – previously thought to be used only for standing on – right into the top corner of the net to send the Highbury crowd wild. After that Arsenal always had the better of the game but were never able to dominate and when Alan Cork headed Wimbledon's equaliser the tension returned. Half-time came and went with the Arsenal players knowing they had to win the game in the next 45 minutes. When Paul Merson volleyed the ball home from close range it looked as though the home side would be victorious, but Wimbledon refused to be beaten and when the ball flew across the Arsenal penalty area, young Paul McGee on his debut fired the ball into the net from the edge of the penalty area. Try as they might Arsenal could not score a third goal and the game finished 2–2. Arsenal and Liverpool were now level on points with the decider at Anfield still to come, but Liverpool also had a home game against struggling West Ham to play beforehand. Arsenal's title dream was all but over.

Alan Smith remembers the mood amongst the players: 'We thought we'd blown it. We did a lap of honour afterwards to thank the crowd . . . the crowd clapped us as if to say "you've done well lads, hard luck", and even the chairman came in afterwards to say "you've had a great season, you've done us proud". He didn't say you've had it now, but you could read between the lines, so the feeling was then that we might have blown it.'

The press agreed. Under the headline BLOWN IT, the following day's *Daily Mirror* reported that: 'Arsenal's championship dream is all but over . . . They have blown it with two disastrous results in the last five crucial days, and the loss of five precious home points has almost certainly handed the crown on a plate to Liverpool.' Even London's *Evening Standard* conceded that 'barring a miracle Liverpool now look certain to end this harrowing season with a record 18th league title as a memorial to those who died at Hillsborough'. Wimbledon manager Bobby Gould agreed saying: 'I am going for Liverpool to be champions again.'

George Graham, however, remained defiant: 'We don't concede anything. Why should we? You've got to be a super optimist in this game and I am.'

On the following Saturday Liverpool beat Merseyside rivals Everton 3–2 at Wembley to win the FA Cup. All they had to do to win the double was to avoid defeat in their two remaining games – at home to West Ham on Tuesday and to Arsenal on Friday. Considering that they had not lost a game since New Year's Day and that in the 23 games since then they had won 20 and drawn three, this was not likely to prove too difficult.

How well Arsenal had to do at Anfield depended on Liverpool's result against West Ham. The two teams were level on points and goal difference, but Arsenal had scored more goals. This meant that if Liverpool beat West Ham by one or two goals Arsenal would *only* have to win at Anfield to take the title. If Liverpool won by more than two the Gunners would need a two-goal victory, and if West Ham were beaten by more than four goals, Arsenal would have to go to Anfield and win by three goals.

As West Ham needed to win to avoid relegation, they were certainly going to give 100 per cent and Arsenal prayed that they would be able to produce a shock result, but their hopes proved to be in vain. West Ham were steamrollered 5–1 which meant that Arsenal required a two-goal victory in the final match of the season to take the title. The *Daily Mirror* headline was YOU DON'T HAVE A PRAYER, ARSENAL.

West Ham midfielder Mark Ward gave Arsenal no chance: 'Arsenal won't have a hope in hell if Liverpool play like they did tonight, they're incredible. We felt we were doing okay but it was no good. We thought Liverpool would be tired after the FA Cup final and the celebrations afterwards, but Liverpool were stronger than ever. Arsenal haven't a prayer, they just drive through you.'

Liverpool striker Ian Rush was still preaching caution: 'It's still possible for Arsenal to do it. If it was us who had to go to Highbury and try to win by two clear goals then we would fancy our chances. But we will not be looking for a draw on Friday. We will be going flat-out to win it.'

During the previous four and a half years, Liverpool had been beaten by two goals at Anfield on only one occasion – against Everton over two years ago – and few people gave Arsenal any chance of emulating that feat. On the morning of the final match, *The Sun*'s John 'gives it to you straight' Sadler wrote: 'Arsenal, I'm afraid, appear to be there only to make up the numbers, to complete the season's fixture list. To win the title now they need to beat Liverpool by a minimum of two clear goals. In any season that would be unlikely. At this stage of this particular season it looks impossible.'

In the build-up to the final game there seemed to be a change in the mood at Arsenal. One day at training a group of players sat outside the dressing-rooms at London Colney when Bob Wilson walked past and said, 'Cheer up lads, this is the week that we're going to win the league.' This buoyed up the confidence of the players and their remarks to the press became more upbeat. David O'Leary still refused to abandon his dream of winning a championship medal saying: 'Miracles do happen. One thing's for sure, we'll give it a hell of a go.' George Graham also refused to admit defeat as he plotted a way for Arsenal to pull off a remarkable victory: 'It doesn't bother me that people think we have already lost the title – we've been fighting that all season. I firmly believe we can win at Anfield and my players do as well.' Alan Smith recalls: 'We were very relaxed that week because we thought we had got nothing to lose. I can't remember it ever being as relaxed as it was in the build-up to that game.'

Despite the new-found confidence George Graham did have a major worry in the run-up to the game. With Paul Davis and Brian Marwood already out through injury the manager could not afford to lose any more players, but as the game approached there was a serious doubt over the fitness of Michael Thomas. Thomas later explained: 'I had a slight knee-ligament injury that our physio thought would keep me out of the game. It was certainly touch and go. I didn't train all week and only managed to be involved in the set-piece play on Thursday's training session. I was far from fully fit but there was no one else, I had to play.'

THE MATCH

At eight o'clock on the morning of Friday, 26 May 1989, the Arsenal players and staff gathered at their London Colney training ground to take the coach to Anfield for the club's most important game in 18 years.

George Graham sat alongside his assistant Theo Foley. David O'Leary, Tony Adams, Niall Quinn and Brian Marwood sat together playing cards. A newspaper article by Graeme Souness saying that Arsenal had no chance was passed around for everyone to read. At noon the coach arrived at their Liverpool hotel and the players went to their rooms to get some rest before the big match build-up began.

At five o'clock the manager gave a team-talk while the players ate a light snack. Graham's words were almost prophetic as he told them, 'Be patient, we don't want the game won in the first five minutes. If it's 0–0 at half-time I won't mind. Score in the second half and Liverpool won't know whether to go forward or defend and then the next goal will come.' The team bus, along with police escort, left for the ground at 6.30 p.m. and arrived at Anfield 20 minutes later. Most of the players walked straight out to inspect the pitch. As the eight o'clock kick-off time approached the teams were informed that the game would start ten minutes late as 24 coaches carrying Arsenal supporters had been held up on the motorway. As the teams prepared to go out the Arsenal manager emphasised to the players the importance of denying the Liverpool defenders the chance to bring the ball out from the back and the need to deny their opponents time and space when they did have the ball. Graham's last words to his team were, 'You've got nothing to lose. Go out and play and don't be frightened.'

The Arsenal players took to the field with bouquets of flowers which they presented to the Liverpool supporters in memory of those who had died at Hillsborough. That, however, was where the goodwill ended. The Arsenal players had 90 minutes in which to win the championship; the odds were stacked against them but they were determined to give it their best shot.

George Graham had decided to stick with the sweeper system that had been so effective up until the last two games and so O'Leary played along with Adams and Bould in defence. The system could be used either to bolster the defence or the attack, but in the early stages of the game the emphasis was on making sure Liverpool did not score. Having to win by two goals was hard enough, but if Liverpool managed to score Arsenal's task would be virtually impossible.

The game started at a frantic pace and with both sides determined not to concede an early goal neither team really threatened the goal in the first few minutes. After eight minutes, however, the Gunners nearly took a shock lead: Thomas forced his way to the goal-line on the right-hand side of the area and crossed to the far post, there Steve Bould leapt up and headed the ball past

Grobbelaar and towards the goal. It looked as though the deadlock was about to be broken but Nicol, standing on the goal-line, managed to head the ball away from danger. Moments later the ball flashed across the Liverpool penalty area once more but Smith, in a good position, failed to make contact and the danger was cleared.

Liverpool now knew that they were in for a tough game and they responded almost immediately. Alan Hansen sent a long ball towards the Arsenal area where Bould lost Aldridge for a moment. As the Liverpool forward received the ball he found himself with a sight on goal but he could only put the ball well wide. Ten minutes later Rush played a sharp one-two with Aldridge and hit a powerful shot from the edge of the penalty area, but the shot was straight at Lukic and the Arsenal keeper made an easy save. Rush, however, had picked up a groin strain when making the shot and after 32 minutes he was substituted. Unfortunately for Arsenal this was not a cause for too much celebration as Liverpool were able to replace him with Peter Beardsley. In the remainder of the first half the greatest threat to either goal came when Whelan hit a 20-yard shot which Lukic palmed over the bar.

With the game still goalless at half-time, both managers were fairly happy. George Graham was very calm, he told his team that 'this is fine, we haven't conceded. Get a goal early in the second half and we only need a second to score the next one'. Now it was all down to the last 45 minutes of the season to decide the destiny of the championship.

The opening minutes of the second half continued in the same vein as the first 45 minutes, but after seven minutes the breakthrough was made. Arsenal were awarded an indirect free-kick some 25 yards from goal on the right-hand side of the field after Whelan fouled Rocastle. The ball was curled across the penalty area by Nigel Winterburn and Alan Smith stooped to send a glancing header past Grobbelaar and into the net for his twenty-third league goal of the season. While the Arsenal players and supporters celebrated, the Liverpool players surrounded the referee. They believed that Smith had not touched the ball and with the free-kick having been indirect the goal should not stand.

Referee David Hutchinson was persuaded to consult his linesman who, the Liverpool players and coaches believed, had raised his flag and then put it down again. The two officials were under great pressure as the members of the Liverpool bench were standing just yards away and the Liverpool players hovering menacingly around them. As the two officials conferred, the watching millions held their breath. Referee Hutchinson later explained: 'My immediate gut reaction was that an Arsenal player had touched it on into the net. The Liverpool protests were so strong that in the interests of man-management I consulted my linesman. He was happy about it. It was a goal.' As the referee pointed to the centre spot Arsenal were understandably relieved, although Smith had had no doubts: 'I made a good contact. It didn't change the flight path of it too much but I just clipped it with the side of my head and then the Liverpool lads started to complain to the linesman . . . When the referee pointed to the spot we were relieved.'

Television replays showed that Smith had definitely got a touch but several of the Liverpool players were incensed, particularly Ronnie Whelan who continued to argue with the linesman long after the decision had been made.

Now Arsenal knew that they were in with a real chance and they began to put consistent pressure on the Liverpool goal. Twice in the next few minutes Gary Ablett in the Liverpool defence came to his team's rescue. First he managed to clear the ball after his goalkeeper dropped a cross and then he made a vital tackle as Richardson found himself in space in the penalty area. Arsenal were determined to score that crucial second goal and with just 17 minutes remaining they almost got it.

Kevin Richardson knocked the ball forward to Michael Thomas who was unmarked in the penalty box. Thomas turned towards goal and had only the goalkeeper to beat, but he hurried his shot and merely stabbed the ball towards the onrushing Grobbelaar. It was unlikely that Arsenal would have as good a chance as that again.

Almost immediately after Thomas's miss George Graham decided that changes would have to be made. After 29 minutes of the second half had been played Martin Hayes replaced the tiring Merson and just three minutes later the sweeper system was dispensed with as Perry Groves came on for Steve Bould. As the minutes ticked by the Arsenal players became more desperate and both Richardson and Rocastle had their names taken by the referee. With the game entering its final ten minutes, Arsenal pushed more and more players forward which inevitably left gaps at the back for Liverpool to exploit. With eight minutes remaining Liverpool almost ended the suspense when an Aldridge flick found Houghton who was storming towards the Arsenal goal, but his volley from just ten yards out went over the crossbar.

In the last minutes, both teams tried desperately to get the goal that would put the championship issue beyond doubt. With three minutes remaining an Arsenal throw-in caused havoc in the Liverpool area but the ball was finally cleared. Moments later Hayes found space near the goal but was closed down before he could get a shot in. With two minutes left Aldridge was clean through on goal on the edge of the penalty area but his first touch let him down and sent the ball safely into Lukic's arms. Thirty seconds later Kevin Richardson went down with cramp and the game was halted while he received treatment.

As the clock ticked past the 90-minute mark there was no doubt amongst the Liverpool players and supporters that they had done enough on the night to clinch the championship and the double. The Kop sang 'We Shall Not Be Moved', Aldridge and Barnes shook hands in congratulation, while Steve McMahon assured his team-mates that there was just one minute remaining. The man who had earlier missed Arsenal's best chance, however, was still determined to make amends.

Michael Thomas said later: 'There were just a few minutes left when Kevin Richardson went down with cramp. I said to him, "See you later, I'm moving forward to try to get a goal." I just had to do something to make up for my miss.'

As the game restarted Liverpool attacked the Arsenal goal and Barnes dribbled his way to Lukic's six-yard box before he was tackled by Richardson. The ball went back to the Arsenal goalkeeper who immediately threw the ball out to Dixon on the right who fired the ball up to Smith near the halfway line. As usual Smith controlled the ball with his first touch and then hooked the ball into the centre towards Michael Thomas who was running into the Liverpool half. As the ball came to Thomas he tried to lob the ball over the defender Steve Nicol but the ball hit the Liverpool player and rebounded back to Thomas who suddenly found himself with a clear run on goal. As Thomas brought the ball under control, he had defenders bearing down on him from behind and Grobbelaar racing towards him in front. As the thousands in the stadium and the millions watching at home held their breath, TV commentator Brian Moore cried: 'It's up for grabs now!' The fate of the championship was completely in the hands of Michael Thomas.

Thomas describes what happened next: 'Everybody was going mad, they were shouting "put it in!", I was told that Paul Davis and Gus Caesar were behind the goal with the Arsenal fans yelling at me and so were George Graham and Theo Foley on the bench. I didn't hear anything. I know it seemed like a long time before I put it in and it was. That was because I was simply waiting for Bruce to commit himself. All that was in my mind was Bruce Grobbelaar. I didn't think about what rested on that one shot. I didn't think of the championship. I waited for Bruce to make the first move and he took such a long time making up his mind whether to come out or not. I was also told later that Ray Houghton was closing in for the tackle, but he was way off when Bruce finally came off his line and I placed my shot. I did my usual handstand – I was really elated. I knew Liverpool couldn't come back. There wasn't enough time.'

As Grobbelaar had come out to meet him, Thomas had flicked the ball over the goalkeeper's legs with the outside of his right boot and into the corner of the net. Pandemonium broke out among the Arsenal supporters and on the Arsenal bench. The frustration of having been so close had suddenly turned into elation as the championship was almost theirs. There was time, however, for one final attack from Liverpool and as the ball was crossed into the Arsenal penalty area the Gunners fans were in a state of anxiety but as the ball came down it was none other than Michael Thomas who brought the ball under control and guided it back to his goalkeeper. As Lukic sent his goal-kick down the field the whistle blew – Arsenal were the champions.

The impossible had been done. The championship would be back at Highbury for the first time in 18 years. No one connected with Arsenal could conceal their glee as they hugged each other and danced with delight. The Liverpool players could not hide their desperate disappointment as they sunk to their knees in despair. David O'Leary's attempts to sympathise with his Irish counterpart John Aldridge were shrugged off by the inconsolable centre-forward, while the Kop looked on in stunned disbelief. As the championship trophy was presented to Tony Adams the Kop sportingly applauded while the travelling fans saluted their heroes with cries of 'Champions, champions'.

Along with all the other players, Alan Smith was overjoyed: 'I didn't want to come in, I don't think any of the lads did, we were out there for a long time. The stewards were really good, they all patted us on the back and said, "well done, you deserve it", which we thought was nice, and then we did a lap of honour and the Kop clapped us which we really appreciated, so we didn't want to come off. The champagne was out in the dressing-room – a lot of it was a blur from then on. Every director – some that you'd never even seen – came in. The ITV cameras came in but I was drunk by the time I did the interview.'

George Graham was quick to round on those who had written his team off beforehand: 'Who the hell expected us to come up here and beat a great team like Liverpool by two goals? I'll tell you: nobody outside Highbury. So many critics have done my job for me. They have motivated my players simply by trying to knock them down all the time. One in particular kept on about George Graham freeing all his men from the chains and letting them play real football. I hope that particular critic is eating his words right now.'

Goalscoring hero Michael Thomas was almost overcome with emotion: 'I just can't put my feelings at this moment into words that make sense. We have come to Liverpool and done it in style. To clinch it in the last seconds makes it even better for all of us.'

Liverpool manager Kenny Dalglish was not gracious in defeat saying, 'Arsenal made it difficult for us the way they play. They came to do a job, but it's not the way we like to play.' Nothing, however, could spoil the Arsenal party.

At 10.19 p.m. George Graham left the pitch with the championship trophy in his arms. As he returned to the dressing-room he went round to congratulate his players one by one. Moments later Bruce Grobbelaar and Peter Beardsley sportingly came in to congratulate the team. At 10.45 p.m. the Arsenal party boarded the coach and more champagne was opened. As they drove back towards London a convoy of celebrating Arsenal supporters gathered along the motorway to salute their conquering heroes. When the players returned to London some three hours later they moved on to the appropriately titled Winners nightclub. George Graham's final piece of advice to his players was 'don't drive'.

Despite the great moments that Arsenal had produced in the past and whatever they go on to achieve in the future, it is hard to imagine a time when any other game will be regarded as the greatest in the club's history; 26 May 1989 is a date etched onto the minds of all Arsenal supporters who saw their team triumph in such incredible circumstances that night and the mere mention of it brings back all sorts of different memories. The drama of Smith's goal, the pain of Thomas's missed chance, the premature celebrations by the Liverpool players, the winning goal, the contrasting agony and ecstasy at the final whistle, Tony Adams triumphantly lifting the championship trophy aloft.

One memory that will stand out for many people, however, was that of a tearful David O'Leary. Throughout the lean years of the early 1980s O'Leary had stayed loyal to the club, despite the fact that he could have made millions if he had moved to any of the clubs that were keen to take him, and during all this time he had consistently said that his greatest footballing wish had been to win a championship medal with Arsenal. In the 14 years since he made his debut for the club this had rarely looked likely to happen and he must have doubted whether it ever would. But now, at last, in the most dramatic of circumstances, Arsenal had done it. David O'Leary finally had his championship medal and as the final whistle blew Arsenal's most loyal player, along with many of their supporters, cried tears of joy. It had been an unforgettable night.

FINAL SCORE

Arsenal	2	Liverpool	0

Smith	53 mins
Thomas	92 mins
Attendance:	41,783

Arsenal: Lukic, Dixon, Winterburn, Bould (Groves), Adams, O'Leary, Thomas, Richardson, Rocastle, Merson (Hayes), Smith

Liverpool: Grobbelaar, Nicol, Hansen, Ablett, Staunton, Houghton, Whelan, McMahon, Barnes, Aldridge, Rush (Beardsley)

Chapter 10

REVENGE

FA Cup semi-final
Arsenal v Tottenham Hotspur
Sunday, 4 April 1993

On Sunday, 14 April 1991 Arsenal and Tottenham made history by taking part in the first-ever FA Cup semi-final to be staged at Wembley. Tottenham had world-class players such as Gascoigne and Lineker in their team, but over the course of the season they had failed to mount any sort of championship challenge and were, at that time, lying eighth in the table – 27 points behind Arsenal. With a five-point lead at the top of the First Division and a record of only one league defeat in 33 matches, Arsenal were hot favourites to reach the final and take a step closer to the second League and Cup double in their history.

As with so many FA Cup games in the past the match did not go to form and a Gascoigne-inspired Spurs were 3–1 winners. The Tottenham fans were sent into raptures of delight, while the Gunners supporters sank into depression. From then on, that day was known at Highbury as 'Black Sunday'.

For the next two years, Arsenal fans were constantly reminded by their rivals of that fateful afternoon. At every opportunity, White Hart Lane would reverberate to the strains of 'We Beat the Scum 3–1'. It seemed that no matter how many times Arsenal beat their North London neighbours in the league they would never be allowed to forget the events of 14 April 1991.

Having gone more than a hundred years without meeting

Tottenham in an FA Cup semi-final it was unlikely that the Gunners would be able to exact revenge in the near future. And yet, incredibly, only two years later the two teams met again at the same stage of the competition. Once more the game was to be played at Wembley and again Arsenal were going for a double, having already reached the Coca-Cola Cup final.

After just two years Arsenal had the chance to avenge their most painful defeat in recent memory. A victory would surely erase the sad memories of their previous semi-final defeat. On the other hand, if Tottenham were to beat them again life would truly be unbearable for everyone at Highbury. With that in mind it is possible that as far as Arsenal fans are concerned this was the most important game in the club's history.

THE PLAYERS

The arrival of goalkeeper David Seaman at Highbury in the summer of 1990 was not met with universal approval amongst Arsenal fans. His predecessor in goal, John Lukic, had been popular with Gunners' supporters and Seaman's signing was seen as unnecessary. Any doubts were soon erased, however, as Seaman was in inspired form throughout Arsenal's 1991 championship-winning season, conceding only 18 goals in 38 league matches. It was a truly remarkable season for Seaman and he was able to celebrate it with a championship medal and an England call-up. There was, however, one blot on his copybook. In the FA Cup semi-final against Tottenham he had been at fault for at least one and possibly two of the goals that Arsenal had conceded. Since then he had continued to be the cornerstone of the miserly Arsenal defence, but he more than anyone else in the Arsenal team was determined to atone for the events of 'Black Sunday'.

The rest of the Arsenal defence was virtually unchanged since that famous night at Anfield. Dixon, Winterburn, Adams and Bould were still the first choice for the back four, while David O'Leary, in his last season at the club, remained in reserve. The only significant addition to the defence was Andy Linighan who was signed from Norwich in 1990. Linighan had not been an immediate success at Highbury but he had ably deputised for Tony Adams during the last championship-winning campaign, and in the 1993 Cup run he played in every game from the fourth round onwards due to Steve Bould's thigh injury.

The midfield had seen a major overhaul in the previous four years. The likes of Thomas, Rocastle, Richardson, Marwood and Hayes had all departed and only Paul Merson remained from the triumphant Anfield team. Most of the replacements were fresh products of the youth system. Over the past two years David Hillier, Ray Parlour, Stephen Morrow and Ian Selley had all emerged as first-team players but, unfortunately, they all seemed to be more adept at working hard and tackling back than they were at passing accurately and beating defenders. The same could be said for George Graham's one pre-season signing Danish international John Jensen. Bought following his performances in helping Denmark win the European Championships, it became obvious that Jensen was able to supply little skill or guile to the Gunners midfield and he soon became known mainly for his inability to score. There were, however, two players in the squad who possessed the sort of flair that the team required. Paul Davis was still with the club and was still Arsenal's most elegant and effective playmaker, while Anders Limpar had thrilled the Highbury crowd with his skilful wingplay ever since he joined the club before the triumphant 1990–91 season. Both players, however, had fallen out of favour with the manager and only made fleeting appearances during the Cup run.

In attack were two players who between them had won the Golden Boot award for highest league goalscorer three times in the last four years. Alan Smith had won the award in Arsenal's 1988–89 and 1990–91 championship-winning seasons while Ian Wright, signed from Crystal Palace for £2.5 million early in the 1991–92 season, had gone on to be that season's top scorer with 29 goals. Wright had been an instant hit with Arsenal fans as he injected pace and excitement into the Arsenal attack. Towards the end of his first season he had set Highbury alight with 13 goals in Arsenal's unbeaten last 14 games to enhance his position as the crowd's favourite. Unfortunately, Wright's arrival coincided with a drop in Smith's form. In the nine league games before Wright arrived Smith had scored seven goals, but during the rest of the season he only managed to find the net five times. This inevitably raised questions as to the compatibility of the two strikers.

The other notable forward at Highbury was Kevin Campbell. Following his prolific goalscoring in both youth and reserve teams, Campbell had been brought into the team at a late stage in their last championship-winning campaign and his nine goals had proved crucial in securing the league title. With a further 13 goals the following season most people expected Campbell to be leading the Arsenal attack for many years to come.

THE BACKGROUND

Having won the championship in such convincing style in 1991 great things were expected of Arsenal for the following season. By February of 1992, however, they were out of all the cup competitions and were only eighth in the league table. There was a great sense of anti-climax around Highbury as the team seemed destined just to play out the last three months of the season. All this changed on 15 February when Arsenal beat Sheffield Wednesday 7–1 and proceeded to win nine and draw five of their last 14 games. As a result, Arsenal were strong pre-season favourites with the bookmakers to win the inaugural Premier League championship in 1993.

The opening game of the season was a taste of things to come. Arsenal looked to be cruising to victory over Norwich when they took a 2–0 first-half lead, but they proceeded to lose 4–2 and leave the Highbury crowd stunned. A run of six straight wins did see the Gunners briefly top the table in November, but they were immediately beaten 3–0 at Leeds and went on to win only six of their remaining 27 league games.

There were various theories for Arsenal's lack of form. One was the lack of atmosphere at Highbury. The North Bank terrace had been knocked down during the previous summer and the new North Bank Stand was now being built. In the meantime the ground was only occupied on three sides and the vocal support from the North Bank was missing. With the reduced ground capacity and the strict ticketing arrangements the average attendance for the season was only 24,403. Yet the team's form was poor when playing away as well as at home.

In midfield, new signing John Jensen was struggling to come to terms with life in the Premier League and his partner David Hillier was doing little to set the world alight.

On the flanks Paul Merson was struggling to find any consistency while Anders Limpar was in and out of the team. Kevin Campbell was being switched between forward and wide positions in an attempt to find some form and Alan Smith was failing to find the net.

Arsenal were increasingly relying on Ian Wright to win games for them. In the 30 league games that Wright started that season, Arsenal only scored in three games where Wright failed to hit the net – in other words if Wright didn't score the team didn't score.

With Arsenal in such poor form, a draw away to non-league Yeovil in the third round of the FA Cup meant the media vultures were out in droves. Having been knocked out by Wrexham at the same stage in the previous season the Gunners were certainly taking nothing for granted, although optimistic supporters pointed out that the last time Arsenal had been to Yeovil, in 1971, they had gone on to win the Cup. In the event a hat trick from Ian Wright gave Arsenal a comfortable 3–1 win and saw them proceed to the fourth round.

Despite their poor early-season form in the league Arsenal were still going strong in the Coca-Cola Cup. Four days after their win at Yeovil Arsenal faced another tricky tie when they travelled to Scarborough for their fourth-round Coca-Cola tie. This was a much tougher test, particularly as much of the game was shrouded in thick fog, but a rare goal from Nigel Winterburn saw them through, and a 2–0 win over Nottingham Forest just six days later sent the Gunners into the semi-finals.

The Gunners' next test in the FA Cup was the home game against reigning champions Leeds United who had beaten them so comprehensively at Elland Road earlier in the season. Due to Leeds's poor away form – they had yet to win a league match away from Elland Road that season – Arsenal should have been hot favourites, but with Ian Wright suspended and Steve Bould and Anders Limpar missing with injuries, it was never going to be an easy game.

As the Arsenal players trooped into their dressing-room at half-time it looked as if their FA Cup dreams were about to be ended for another year. Goals from Gary Speed and ex-Gunner Lee Chapman had given Leeds a 2–0 lead which, on their first-half performance, looked to be more than enough to see them through to the next round. George Graham said later: 'The game never ignited in the first half. I just relied on my players' pride in themselves to have a go. I did not have to say much. I know the spirit and the character in the team.'

If they were going to find a way back into the tie Arsenal needed an early goal to get them back into it, and after 51 minutes it came. Ray Parlour picked the ball up near the Leeds penalty area and muscled his way through the Leeds defence before threading the ball between the goalkeeper's legs. With only one goal in it Arsenal's spirits were raised and as the *Daily Mirror* reported they were 'steamed up and raring to go, the Gunners pressure stretched Leeds to breaking point'.

Despite the pressure it was not until eight minutes from time that Arsenal drew level in spectacular style. Picking the ball up around the halfway line Paul Merson ran at the Leeds defence before cutting inside and unleashing a 25-yard drive that flew past the goalkeeper and into the top corner of the net. The Highbury crowd went wild and urged the home team on to get a late winner. In the final moments of the game it looked as though they would do it as Campbell found himself through on goal, but a diving save at his feet by former Highbury favourite John Lukic saved the day for Leeds and set up a replay nine days later.

The good news for Arsenal was the return of Ian Wright for the replay, but on the other hand with the absence of Jensen (suspended) and Hillier (injured), George Graham had to draft in the inexperienced Ian Selley and Stephen Morrow. Along with Ray Parlour, this midfield trio had less than 30 league appearances between them and would be up against experienced players such as McAllister, Strachan, Speed and Batty.

It was soon clear, however, that Arsenal's youngsters would not be letting the side down as they matched Leeds during a hard-fought first half. The Gunners midfield was further weakened at half-time when Parlour had to be replaced by Kevin Campbell, but still they refused to be beaten and, as in the first game, they managed to score early in the second half. For once it was Ian Wright who was the provider as he beat his man on the left-wing and reached the by-line where he crossed for Alan Smith to volley emphatically past Lukic from four yards to give Arsenal the lead.

For the next 20 minutes Arsenal looked to be in comfortable control of the game but, after 70 minutes, they lost concentration in defence as the ball bounced in the Arsenal penalty area and Carl Shutt pounced to slot it past Seaman for the equaliser. Ten minutes later it looked once more as though Arsenal were on their way out as McAllister struck a 30-yard free-kick of incredible power and accuracy into the top corner of the Arsenal goal.

Yet again Arsenal were on the verge of defeat and yet again they refused to be beaten. With just three minutes remaining the ball fell to Ian Wright some 20 yards from goal, quickly he sent a low drive towards the corner of the net. The ball was not hit cleanly and Lukic appeared to have time to save it, but it was the accuracy of the shot that beat the Leeds keeper and sent the game into extra-time.

As the extra period went on without any further goals a penalty shoot-out looked increasingly likely, but with eight minutes to go Ian Wright won the game for Arsenal. Merson's pass found Wright unmarked in the Leeds area and he hit a shot that was the exact opposite of his previous goal. This time he hit the shot right over Lukic's head but with such ferocious power that the goalkeeper had no time to react. Arsenal were through after an epic battle.

With a home game with Nottingham Forest to come in the next round Arsenal had high hopes of progressing further. Forest were struggling at the bottom of the Premier League and had been beaten at Highbury just a few weeks earlier in the Coca-Cola Cup quarter-final by two Ian Wright goals to nil.

Before their next FA Cup game, however, the Gunners travelled to Selhurst Park where they virtually booked one Wembley visit with their 3–1 win over Crystal Palace in the first leg of the Coca-Cola Cup semi-final.

Six days later Arsenal took another step nearer to a second trip to the twin towers and once again it was Ian Wright who proved to be the thorn in Nottingham Forest's side. In a tight game with few clear goalscoring chances it was going to take something special for either team to score. Fortunately for Arsenal their star striker managed to do just that on two occasions. Firstly, on 20 minutes he latched on to a header from Ian Selley just inside the Forest half before sending a powerful dipping volley past the hapless Forest goalkeeper and into the top corner of the net. Then on the stroke of half-time he again received the ball from Selley and proceeded to bamboozle two Forest defenders before slamming the ball into the roof of the net. If ever a man had won a game single-handedly, it was Ian Wright.

With Wembley now in sight on two fronts, Arsenal had to travel to Portman Road for a quarter-final clash with Ipswich who were in fourth place in the Premier League. With their opponents having their best season for many years this was going to be a tough match for Arsenal, and it was to be made tougher by injuries and suspensions which meant that Paul Davis came in for only his second game of the season and winger Jimmy Carter was called upon to make a rare appearance. In addition to this, just ten days before the match Tony Adams required 29 stitches for a head wound after falling down a flight of stairs, casting grave doubt over his appearance in the game.

As the teams took to the field the 2,000 travelling Arsenal fans and the 4,500 watching on a giant screen at Highbury, were relieved to see Adams leading out his side, although he did have a huge plaster just above his left eye.

Ipswich set about Arsenal from the start and gained a deserved lead after 15 minutes when Chris Kiwomya stabbed the ball home after a goalmouth scramble. This got the capacity crowd going and the home team were roared on by their enthusiastic supporters. Gradually, however, the Gunners clawed their way back into the game and on 28 minutes they got the crucial equaliser. A free-kick from Paul Merson was left by everybody as it curled across the goal before the irrepressible Tony Adams popped up at the far post to head the ball home.

From then on it was Arsenal's game and in the second half it was Ian Wright who made sure of a Gunners victory. First he scored from the penalty spot, after being brought down by John Wark, and then he pressurised Phil Whelan into scoring an own goal to make it 3–1.

There were a few jitters in the Arsenal camp when sloppy

defending allowed Guentchev to pull one back with ten minutes remaining, but a late goal from Kevin Campbell finally put the game out of Ipswich's reach and the final scoreline of 4–2 meant Arsenal were through to the semi-finals.

Having witnessed such an impressive performance, most Arsenal fans settled down the following day to watch the televised quarter-final between Manchester City and Tottenham in the hope that a City win would make their weekend complete. Tottenham were not to be outdone, however, as they also impressed in a 4–2 away win. In the draw that followed the match, the inevitable happened and Arsenal and Tottenham were paired together in an FA Cup semi-final for the second time in three seasons.

Four days later Arsenal beat Crystal Palace 2–0 to reach the final of the Coca-Cola Cup where they would meet Sheffield Wednesday who had also reached the FA Cup semi-finals.

THE MATCH
There was certainly no love lost between the two north London rivals on or off the pitch. In their previous meeting at White Hart Lane in December Ian Wright was seen to have struck Tottenham midfielder David Howells and was banned for three games. George Graham had also been heavily critical of the referee in the same game.

With the Arsenal players determined to make up for their last semi-final meeting and the Tottenham players wanting to crown the Chinese Year of the Cockerel with another Cup triumph there was no lack of motivation on either side.

The build-up to the game was definitely to Tottenham's advantage. Four days before the semi-final England took on Turkey in Izmir for a vital World Cup qualifying match. Tony Adams (who was England's man of the match), Lee Dixon (who was substituted after damaging his shin) and Ian Wright all played, while Paul Merson and Alan Smith, who were both in the squad, were ruled out with ankle injuries. Back at Highbury Paul Davis had hamstring problems and Steve Morrow had a thigh injury. John Jensen and Steve Bould were also ruled out with injury. Spurs, meanwhile, had a clean bill of health and were free of international call-ups.

With both Davis and Jensen unavailable, George Graham was once again forced to play Ian Selley, Ray Parlour and David Hillier in a midfield short of years and experience. But the manager was confident that they would be up to the task and that the presence of so many products of the Arsenal youth system – the semi-final team contained six such players – would make victory even sweeter.

The day before the game saw the people of Sheffield descend on Wembley to see United and Wednesday play the first semi-final. Wednesday won 2–1 after extra-time to increase the possibility of Wednesday and Arsenal meeting in the final of both domestic cup competitions. Most of the headlines, however, were concerned with the infamous Grand National that never was following farcical events at Aintree.

On 4 April over 76,000 Arsenal and Tottenham supporters descended on Wembley but, unlike the previous day, there was no sense of enjoying a day out at the famous stadium. The two sets of supporters were racked by tension and it showed. This was not a day to enjoy the game or for playing entertaining football; this was a day for getting a result. Both sets of players and supporters were desperate to win and both teams were petrified of losing.

Whereas the Sheffield derby match had been an open and entertaining contest, it was clear from the start that the north London encounter would be a much different one. Remembering their last Wembley encounter – when Tottenham had the game virtually won within ten minutes – both teams started cagily, determined not to make any crucial mistakes. The opening 20 minutes saw Arsenal in command as far as possession and pressure was concerned, but neither team was able to create much in the way of scoring opportunities. Seaman had to save a Sheringham shot from the edge of the penalty area, while Austin was twice forced to intercept dangerous Arsenal crosses, but neither goal was seriously threatened. But as the game approached the half-hour mark referee Philip Don made a crucial decision.

A rare Tottenham attack saw Anderton on a twisting and

dodging run towards the Arsenal penalty area but as he approached the box he was challenged by Andy Linighan. The Spurs forward fell to the ground and the ball ran away over the goal-line. The two questions were whether Linighan had fouled Anderton and, if so, whether the offence had taken place inside the penalty area. Despite strong protests from the Tottenham players, the referee decided that no foul had been committed and awarded a corner. Television replays suggested that Anderton had been fouled, but it was almost impossible to conclude whether it should have been a penalty or not. Either way, Arsenal had been fortunate, while Tottenham felt aggrieved. Some of their players were incensed – particularly Paul Allen who was booked for dissent – and their sense of injustice was clear as they took control of the game up until the interval.

Having looked so comfortable for so long, Arsenal now found themselves struggling as Tottenham piled forward, and on 37 minutes Spurs had the best chance of the game so far. Ironically, after his heroics for England, it was a mistake from Tony Adams that nearly put Arsenal behind. As the Arsenal captain received the ball just inside his own half, he stumbled as he attempted to pass the ball back to David Seaman and was robbed by the onrushing Vinny Samways. As Samways bore down on goal with just the goalkeeper to beat he shot low towards goal. Fortunately for Arsenal, Seaman managed to half save the shot before gathering the ball at the second attempt.

The pressure on the Arsenal goal continued as Austin, Anderton and Sedgeley all had shots charged down in the penalty area, while Seaman had to race out of his goal to deny Sheringham after the ball was played through by Anderton. As the pressure increased tempers frayed, Linighan was booked for a foul on Sheringham and both Dixon and Nayim were shown the yellow card as they squared up to each other. As the half drew to a close Arsenal were hanging on but, finally, after three minutes of injury time the referee blew the half-time whistle.

While Andy Linighan received medical treatment for a head wound that he had picked up earlier in the game, George Graham spent the interval trying to calm his team down. They had to get back to the play that they had shown earlier in the half. If they could do that, he told them, he was sure that the chances would come.

The second half began with the game becoming much less frantic and much more even than it had been before the break and, just as George Graham had forecast, Arsenal slowly began to resume control. As the Arsenal pressure grew, so they began to threaten the Spurs goal and after almost an hour had been played, they created their best chance so far. Kevin Campbell rolled the ball across the face of the penalty area where Ian Selley found himself unmarked. The young midfielder's first touch was not as good as he might have hoped as he knocked the ball in the air, but his second touch was a crashing goalbound volley which Erik Thorsvedt did well to palm away and even better to dive on the ball before the advancing Ian Wright could pounce on the rebound.

The Arsenal supporters now found their voices and they urged the team on as they attacked the Spurs goal. Moments after Selley had come so close, Paul Merson surged down the left-wing and crossed low to Ian Wright just ten yards out. So many times during the season Wright had slotted home chances such as these, but this time he missed the target and sent the ball wide of Thorsvedt's goal. Almost immediately Wright had a chance to redeem himself with a powerful shot from 18 yards, but this time the Tottenham goalkeeper managed to push the ball over the bar.

The Arsenal players knew that they had to achieve what Tottenham had failed to do – score while they were on top – and on 77 minutes they got the chance to do so. Arsenal won a free-kick after Ray Parlour's run towards the penalty area was stopped by a Justin Edinburgh foul just outside the box. As Parlour received treatment following Edinburgh's challenge and Ian Wright attempted to replace a damaged boot, Merson and Hillier stood over the ball and waited to take the kick. When the referee finally restarted play after a two-minute stoppage it was Merson who curled the ball towards the far post where Tony Adams was making a late run towards the goal. As Neil Ruddock belatedly spotted Adams's approach he attempted to get back but it was too late and the ball sailed over him and, just as he had done in the previous round at Ipswich, the Arsenal captain was able to head it back across the goal past Thorsvedt's despairing hand and into the goal.

Adams wheeled away in delight and was submerged by a crowd of delighted Arsenal players. They were a goal up and only 11 minutes of normal time remained. If any team could defend a lead in these circumstances it was Arsenal.

For the next five minutes, Arsenal looked as if they would hold on comfortably. Sheringham showed his frustration by pushing Lee Dixon and getting booked, while Tottenham manager Terry Venables tried to conjure something up by replacing Sedgeley and Samways with Barmby and Bergsson. Then, after 85 minutes, Spurs were thrown a lifeline. Lee Dixon, who had already been booked, brought down Justin Edinburgh and was shown his second yellow card. Arsenal were down to ten men.

George Graham immediately replaced Kevin Campbell with Alan Smith and moments later brought on Stephen Morrow for Ian Wright in order to shore up the defence, now the players had to work hard in the Arsenal penalty area. As the clock ticked towards, and past, 90 minutes, Tottenham piled on the pressure. Nayim found himself in space in the box but curled his shot straight into David Seaman's arms, Bergsson had a header saved and Seaman had to dive spectacularly to stop a deflected cross from Anderton. As each minute of injury time went by the whistling from the desperate Arsenal fans increased and as the second half entered its 50th minute they were begging the referee to blow the whistle. Yet still the game went on and still the Arsenal goal was bombarded.

Finally, after seven minutes of injury time, Philip Don blew the final whistle and the red-and-white half of the stadium began to celebrate. As Tottenham players sank to the ground in tears the Gunners embraced and acknowledged the cheers of their supporters. After two years Arsenal had finally gained revenge for one of the most depressing days in their history and the fans were not going to let their rivals forget it. They had been goaded by the Spurs fans for two years, but now it was their turn as they turned towards the opposite end of the stadium and sang, 'We Beat the Scum 1–0'.

The plaudits all went to the goalscorer and inspiring captain Tony Adams. George Graham was happy to pay his own tribute: 'Tony won me over a long time ago but it's taken a long time to win over the media and fans all over the country. All of a sudden I am reading in the papers that he is a hero and it amazes me. He's been a hero for me for six years . . . He's been held in very high esteem by Arsenal fans since he first came into the team and if you speak to the best managers in the game, they'll tell you the same thing about him.' As for himself, Adams admitted that it was one of the best moments of his life: 'That has to be the most important goal of my career. My biggest hurt was losing in the semi-final two years ago and this means such a lot. It's special because it was so heartbreaking then.' The atmosphere in the Tottenham camp was very different as Darren Anderton confirmed: 'The dressing-room is like a morgue. There's been tears and no one is talking. We are very upset.'

It was a great day for Arsenal and their supporters, but even more was to come. Two weeks later they returned to Wembley where they beat Sheffield Wednesday 2–1 to win the Coca-Cola Cup courtesy of goals from Merson and Morrow. And on 20 May, following a 1–1 draw, they won the FA Cup final replay, again by two goals to one against the same Sheffield Wednesday team, courtesy of a last-minute goal from Andy Linighan. This made George Graham the first man ever to have won all three domestic trophies both as a player and manager and also saw Arsenal qualify for European football the following season.

Both Cup final victories were celebrated with delight in the red-and-white part of north London and at the end of the season they were able to reflect on a unique Cup double. Above all else, however, the win that meant the most to the Arsenal supporters was the victory over Tottenham. The two wins over Sheffield Wednesday had been fantastic, but beating Spurs had put an end to all the taunts that they had had to endure over the last two years. It may not have been the most entertaining game of all time, it may not have had a sackful of goals, it may have been too tense to enjoy at the time, but at the end of the day it had given Gunners fans everywhere the thing that they most wanted – revenge.

FINAL SCORE

| Arsenal | 1 | Tottenham Hotspur | 0 |

Adams   79 mins
Attendance: 76,263

Arsenal: Seaman, Dixon, Winterburn, Linighan, Adams, Selley, Hillier, Parlour, Merson, Campbell (Smith), Wright (Morrow)

Tottenham Hotspur: Thorsvedt, Austin, Edinburgh, Mabbutt, Ruddock, Sedgeley (Bergsson), Allen, Nayim, Samways (Barmby), Anderton, Sheringham

Chapter 11

ONE–NIL TO THE ARSENAL

European Cup-Winners' Cup final
Arsenal v Parma
Wednesday, 4 May 1994

Following Arsenal's championship victory of 1991, hopes had been high amongst Gunners supporters that they would be able to mount a serious challenge in the following season's European Cup.

The campaign began promisingly with a 6–1 win in their first game against Austria Vienna. But, in order to reach the new league stage of the competition Arsenal then had to beat former European champions Benfica of Portugal. A 1–1 draw in the first leg in Lisbon put Arsenal in a strong position and an early goal at Highbury seemed to have put the Gunners on the road to victory, but a Portuguese equaliser followed by two more goals in extra-time saw the English champions crash out and so end any hopes of European glory for another season.

The Benfica defeat demoralised everyone at Highbury, but Alan Smith believes that the game had a great significance for future European campaigns. 'That was a milestone, not just for the players but for George Graham. He recognised that you can't be so gung-ho in European football . . . When it came to the next European competition I think we'd all learned.'

With this experience behind George Graham, the Arsenal manager believed that he and his team could beat the best in Europe and he was determined to prove it. The next opportunity that Graham had to take on Europe came as a result of Arsenal's dramatic FA Cup win in 1993, this meant that Arsenal qualified for the following season's Cup-Winners' Cup.

The Cup-Winners' Cup is traditionally the weakest of the three European competitions, but this year was to be an exception with teams such as Ajax, Paris St Germain, Parma, Real Madrid and Torino taking part, as well as the team that all at Highbury wanted to beat – Benfica.

The ban on English clubs playing in Europe which resulted following the Heysel disaster meant that Arsenal had played only five European ties since the Cup-Winners' Cup final in 1980. For a team with such little European experience it was going to be a very difficult task for them to progress far in a competition that contained so many of the continent's great teams. George Graham, however, was determined to show that he and his players could do it.

THE PLAYERS

The 1992–93 season had ended gloriously for Arsenal as they completed the Coca-Cola Cup and FA Cup double – the first time that any club had ever achieved such a feat. This could not mask the fact, however, that for most of the season the team's form had been very disappointing. Tenth position in the league is never satisfactory for a club of Arsenal's status – especially when they finished only seven points clear of relegation.

Most Gunners fans expected that George Graham would be busy in the transfer market during the summer. Not for the first or last time, however, the side that took the field at the start of the next season was very similar to that which had ended the previous one. With the exception of centre-back Martin Keown – who having been sold by George Graham in 1986 had been re-signed for £2 million during the previous season – the only notable addition to the squad was Irish international Eddie McGoldrick. Bought for £1 million from Crystal Palace, McGoldrick, while primarily a winger, was versatile enough to play at right-back if necessary and, as such, was a valuable squad member, but he was not the big-name signing that Highbury fans had been hoping for.

THE BACKGROUND

Despite a shock 3–0 home defeat by Coventry on the opening day of the season, Arsenal had a relatively successful league campaign which saw them finish in a respectable fourth place, yet they never threatened to mount a serious title challenge. From the very start it seemed that all sights were set on Europe.

The players were amazed at how the manager would chop and change the team to make sure his strongest team was available for European games and many of them were under the impression that league games were considered to be of secondary importance. In his book *The Glory and the Grief* George Graham admitted that, 'It was the European Cup-Winners' Cup that took my undivided attention in the 1993–94 season. I saw it as a challenge to my tactical perception and I spent hours studying videos and scouting reports and making secret trips to watch the opposition. I felt like a field-marshal making battle plans and for me this was the most satisfying part of my job.'

The European campaign began in Denmark against the Danish Cup winners Odense. With only three full-time players in their ranks the Danes were expected to be easily overcome, but as the game began they threatened to bring the Gunners' European tour to an early end.

Only two minutes were on the clock when Andy Linighan's foul gave the Danes a penalty, but fortunately for Arsenal Thorup's spot-kick came back off the post to safety. During the next 15 minutes Odense had further scoring opportunities before taking the lead after 18 minutes when Martin Keown tried to clear from a corner and the ball went into his own net.

If Arsenal had continued to play so poorly they would almost certainly have suffered an embarrassingly early exit, but luckily they managed to find their form and a scrambled first-half goal from Ian Wright and a brilliant solo run and shot from Merson after the interval gave the Gunners a valuable away win. The second leg was quite an anti-climax with Campbell increasing the aggregate lead early in the second half. Nielsen pulled one back for the Danes in the dying seconds, but Arsenal were safely through.

In the second round Arsenal had what appeared to be a tricky tie against Standard Liege of Belgium. Coached by Arie Haan, one of the great Dutch players of the 1970s, Standard had finished second in the Belgian league and won the Cup in the previous season, and had already put eight goals past Cardiff City in the first round of the competition. This suggested that they were likely to pose a much stronger test for Arsenal than Odense had.

The first leg at Highbury went very much to plan after Ian Wright gave the Gunners the lead late in the first half. Then a stunning run and lob from Wright and an inch-perfect 25-yard free-kick from Merson gave the home side a three-goal lead, Arsenal seemed to be firmly in control of the tie. Nothing, however, had prepared anyone for what would happen in the return leg.

With Ian Wright having been booked in the first leg George Graham decided not to play his star striker in Liege so as not to run the risk of him picking up a second booking and being unavailable for the quarter-final. With their top scorer not playing it was assumed that Arsenal would play a defensive game and try to keep their three-goal lead. Nothing could have been further from the truth.

A goal from Alan Smith in the second minute effectively put the tie beyond Standard's reach, but the Gunners had no intention of relaxing; by half-time it was 4–0 and another three in the second half, culminating in a fantastic shot into the top corner from Eddie McGoldrick, gave the FA Cup winners a 10–0 aggregate win.

When Arsenal's 1994 European campaign is remembered by critics, it is as a series of great defensive displays and 1–0 wins, the 10–0 victory over Standard Liege conveniently forgotten. Indeed, the Belgians were dismissed by many as being a second-rate team, yet they finished the season in sixth place in the Belgian league and were only a point away from the championship the following year. The second-leg performance in particular deserved more credit than it received. In *The Glory and the Grief* George Graham described it as 'one of the greatest attacking displays I have ever seen on an away ground . . . a mind-blowing performance, one of the best since I took over as manager'.

There was then a gap of four months before Arsenal took on Torino of Italy in the quarter-finals. In the intervening months,

Arsenal had gone out of both domestic cup competitions. If the team had not been concentrating 100 per cent on Europe before, they certainly were now.

There was no doubt that Torino represented Arsenal's most difficult challenge of the competition so far. In recent years Italian teams had dominated European club football – 14 Italian clubs had reached European finals in the previous five years – and beating any of them would be an achievement.

The Arsenal performance in the first leg in Turin was everything that the game in Liege was expected to be. Both teams were very wary of each other and goalscoring chances were extremely rare. Both teams had been determined not to give anything away, but at the end of the match it was Arsenal who were much the happier with the goalless draw.

The second leg at Highbury was an incredibly tense affair. The Italians were content to sit back and hope that they could hit the Gunners on the break. George Graham, however, had no intention of leaving his team open to such breakaway attacks and refused to pile forward in a cavalier fashion. As a result the second leg was almost as cagey as the first. Arsenal had most of the possession but made few goalscoring chances until the 66th minute of the game. Then Arsenal won a free-kick some 30 yards away from goal. The ball was curled across the penalty area by Paul Davis and Tony Adams ran in at the far post to head it home. Torino now had to score, but they rarely threatened to do so and Arsenal held on comfortably to win.

The Gunners' semi-final opponents were to be Paris St Germain who boasted world-class players like Ginola, Valdo, Rai and Weah and they were emphatic leaders of the French league.

The first leg was played in front of a packed Parc des Princes – the crowd included thousands of travelling Arsenal supporters. George Graham did his best to confuse his opposite number Artur Jorge by giving the impression that his team would go there to defend and that Ian Wright would not be playing. In fact, Wright played in a team that intended to attack from the start. Arsenal immediately took the game to their opponents and came close to scoring on several occasions, including a great save from the Paris St Germain goalkeeper that denied John Jensen his first goal for the club, before they took the lead in the 35th minute.

Arsenal were awarded a free-kick in almost exactly the same position as they were in the game with Torino. Again Paul Davis curled the ball across the area and this time it was Ian Wright who glanced the ball low into the far corner of the net to give Arsenal a crucial away goal. The score remained 1–0 as the two teams left the pitch at half-time to the roars of the travelling fans. At this point the song 'Go West' by the Pet Shop Boys was played over the tannoy. The jubilant Arsenal supporters began to sing '1–0 to the Arsenal' to the chorus and a football song was born.

Unfortunately the score-line did not remain '1–0 to the Arsenal' for long. With less than five minutes of the second half played, a Paris St Germain corner found Ginola at the near post and he headed the ball between Seaman and the post for the equalising goal. Arsenal, who were so good at set-pieces and particularly at corners to the near post, had been beaten at their own game.

Despite the disappointment of conceding such a goal, the Gunners continued to hold their own for the rest of the game, and they might have even won it if Alan Smith had done better when he found himself through on goal with only 15 minutes remaining. As the final whistle blew, however, it was the Arsenal fans who were the more optimistic. A win or a 0–0 draw in the second leg would see them through to the final in Copenhagen.

It was certainly a good result for Arsenal, but they were determined not to get over-confident, after all they had come away from the first leg against Benfica two years earlier with a 1–1 draw and still lost the tie. In his programme notes for the following game George Graham urged caution: 'I'm not getting carried away. Paris St Germain are a very good attacking team . . . we'll keep our feet on the ground and approach the second leg with the same professional attitude we showed against Torino.'

Arsenal's opponents had certainly not given up hope. First-leg goalscorer David Ginola recalled their 2–1 aggregate win in the previous round: 'We can still reach the final because we're a better team when we play away. We beat Real 1–0 in Madrid in the quarter-final and going to Highbury will hold no fear for us. We will give Arsenal the respect they deserve, but we will attack them.' Forward partner George Weah was also confident: 'Arsenal's defence is very strong, but I think we can beat them for pace. We have a lot of fast players in the team. We also have the players to defend in depth and not concede any more goals. I think we can win 1-0.' With so many good players in the French team Arsenal certainly had plenty to worry about, but they had one other man whose performance could have a major bearing on their chances of winning the cup – Danish referee Peter Mikkelsen. With eight players having picked up a yellow card during the competition, including the likes of Ian Wright and Tony Adams, most of the team knew that any indiscretion could cost them a place in the final. Before they took to the field George Graham reminded them to be careful as any silly challenge could see them booked and suspended.

The atmosphere on the night of the second leg was one of the best at Highbury for many years. As well as the cacophony of noise created by the supporters and an array of pounding drums, the club distributed red and white cards for spectators to hold up as the teams emerged on to the pitch. The result was a stunning array of red and white stripes around the stadium, which added to the great sense of occasion. There was no doubt that a truly memorable night lay ahead.

As the game kicked off the Arsenal players seemed slightly overawed by the atmosphere and their nerves were showing. Within minutes the normally dependable Seaman almost gave Paris St Germain the start they were looking for as he threw the ball straight to an opposing forward and was only saved by a desperate diving tackle from Tony Adams.

Arsenal nerves were soon settled when, after only five minutes, they took the lead. Lee Dixon took a throw-in on the right, mid-way inside the Paris half. He immediately received the ball back from Smith and sent a cross into the penalty area where Kevin Campbell, only in the team because Paul Merson was ill, headed towards goal. The ball hit the inside of the near post and went into the net. The roar from the crowd was deafening as they celebrated a crucial goal. The players, however, were determined not to get carried away – after all they had taken the lead in the second leg against Benfica as well but had still lost.

As the first half continued everything was going well for Arsenal as they held on to their lead but, with just four minutes to go before the interval, disaster struck. Once again the ball was cleared by the Arsenal defence and as the ball crossed the halfway line, Ian Wright and Paris defender Alain Roche chased after it. As Roche got in front of the Arsenal striker and attempted to shepherd the ball out of play, Wright lunged from behind in an attempt to hook the ball away. Unfortunately, all Wright succeeded in doing was to take away Roche's legs from under him and send the Frenchman crashing to the ground. The crowd hushed and Wright held his head in his hands as the referee advanced towards him and his hand moved towards his pocket. As the yellow card was produced a great groan rang out from the crowd and Wright walked away in tears. Whatever happened now he would miss the final.

At half-time Wright was very emotional and could hardly control himself. George Graham considered taking him off, but along with Tony Adams he managed to calm Wright down sufficiently to take his place for the second half where he managed to keep going for the rest of the match.

Arsenal's rock-solid defence continued to hold out, except for one occasion when Ginola found himself clear just 12 yards from goal, but as the crowd watched in suspense the Frenchman put the ball wide of Seaman's goal. It was the last real scare for the home team and as the final whistle blew players and supporters alike embraced each other with delight. They were all off to Copenhagen.

There may have been some slight disappointment when Parma followed their 2–1 defeat in Lisbon with a 1–0 home win over Benfica to reach the final on away goals, as many Arsenal supporters had looked forward to beating Benfica in the final to gain sweet revenge for their last European exit, but no one was going to let that spoil the anticipation of a European final. What it did mean, however, was that they were in for a very difficult match. Not only were Parma one of the best teams in Italy, they were also the Cup-Winners' Cup holders having beaten Antwerp in the final at Wembley just 12 months earlier. With players like Brolin, Zola and Asprilla in their team, Arsenal knew that this was going to be a difficult challenge.

With just two weeks to go Ian Wright was joined on the Copenhagen sidelines by John Jensen. Jensen had still to score his first goal for Arsenal but, with the final being played in his home town, it had seemed to many that this would inevitably be his day. Sadly, however, a scything tackle on him during an international friendly with Hungary left him on crutches and out of what would have been one of the biggest games of his career. Jensen said later, 'I knew it was bad. I knew at once the final was gone. It was a vicious tackle.'

On Tuesday, 3 May, the day before the final, the Arsenal team arrived at Stansted Airport to begin their journey to Copenhagen. The *Sunday Times* reported: 'On board the plane, Arsenal were nursing two dead legs attached to David Hillier and Kevin Campbell respectively, one suspected cracked rib [David Seaman], three sets of jangling nerves that would require sleeping pills that night and the unbreakable resolve of the manager George Graham that Arsenal, the underdogs, would hold the defensive line against the prodigiously talented principals of Parma.'

On arrival in Denmark's capital there were one or two complaints from the players about the standard of their hotel, but they were not about to allow such things to interfere with their preparation. That evening they took to the Parken Stadium pitch for the first time for a training session and they were pleased to note the resemblance that the high stands and the red seats bore to Highbury.

The day of the game began with the players having breakfast together in the hotel. Bob Wilson was amongst the diners and he recalled seeing Tony Adams enter the room: 'He strolled in like John Wayne. His face was fixed like a mask and it never broke again until the final whistle. You could see him thinking "This is the day of battle." He devotes himself to Arsenal and to winning a game of football. In the dressing-room he is extraordinary. It's the noise. He bellows at them. He is their rock.'

During the day Martin Keown failed a fitness test and with David Hillier also out injured it meant that Paul Davis would be accompanied by the two young midfielders Ian Selley and Stephen Morrow. With Paul Merson and Kevin Campbell supporting the midfield, Alan Smith would be alone up front in a 4-5-1 system.

The other major injury worry was David Seaman who had a cracked rib. If it had been a game of less importance he almost certainly would not have played, but this was a European final so he had a pain-killing injection before kick-off and hoped for the best.

Before the match, George Graham brought the team together for their final briefing. He then played videos of the Parma team in action and gave each player precise tactical instructions which left them in no doubt as to their role for the evening. Morrow was detailed to stay in front of the back four, while Paul Davis was told to track Thomas Brolin. There was no way that Arsenal could outplay Parma, but if they could get a goal, anything could happen.

THE MATCH

As the players took to the field to warm up before the game they immediately received a psychological boost. At least two-thirds of the crowd were clad in the red and white of Arsenal and the sound of '1–0 to the Arsenal' boomed out around the ground. As George Graham noted in *The Glory and the Grief*: 'It sounds more like Highbury than Copenhagen. We have won the support battle before a ball is kicked.' When the two teams entered the arena to start the game the noise level intensified.

The game kicked off with the Arsenal supporters in good heart and good voice, but the opening minutes of play showed what a difficult game the team was going to have. Almost immediately, the Colombian striker Faustino Asprilla was put through by Brolin. Asprilla stormed into the Arsenal penalty area and was about to shoot when a magnificent sliding tackle from Steve Bould took the ball off his foot and away from danger. The worst possible start for the Gunners had been narrowly avoided.

There was still more danger to come from Parma when, just three minutes later, a Benarrivo cross found Brolin unmarked at the far post, but he sent his header over the bar from 12 yards out. It looked like Arsenal were going to be in for a hard night. As Alan Smith recalls: 'For the first ten minutes they really came at us and we thought we might really be in for a drubbing.'

After these early scares Arsenal then seemed to calm themselves and the game down and for the next five minutes or so they managed to win possession of the ball and create chances. After six minutes, the Gunners won their first corner of the game and Merson's cross was headed across the goal by Campbell with the ball going just wide of the far post. A few moments later Campbell again had a chance to score as he found himself with just Bucci in the Italian goal to beat but, as a result of his poor first touch, the ball seemed to get stuck under his feet and was cleared. Almost immediately this led to danger at the other end of the field. The pace and accuracy of the Parma players saw Asprilla send the ball out to Zola on the left who crossed to Brolin on the right corner of the penalty area. Brolin measured his shot and powered the ball past Seaman, only to see the ball hit the inside of the far post and roll across the goal before going out for a goal-kick. Again Arsenal had had a narrow escape – perhaps it was going to be their night.

Once more Arsenal regained control of the game and began to create chances. First, a Lee Dixon free-kick was headed dangerously across the goal by Tony Adams, but was scrambled away before the waiting Campbell could get a touch. Then, with nearly 20 minutes on the clock, the vital breakthrough was made when Arsenal won a throw-in midway inside the Parma half. Dixon threw the ball to Smith and received it back before lobbing it towards Merson on the right-wing. Before the ball reached Merson, however, it was intercepted by Minotti who tried to clear it with an overhead kick but succeeded only in sending the ball to Alan Smith on the edge of the Parma area. The Arsenal centre-forward chested the ball down and volleyed it past the goalkeeper on to the inside of the near post and into the net for one of the most spectacular and important goals of his career. As Smith recalls: 'I chested it and players were closing in so I had to hit it fairly quickly or else they would have got a foot in. I jumped to volley it and didn't hit it that hard really, it was just the placement. The keeper dived so I couldn't actually see what had happened. Then I saw it go over the other side of the goal. I couldn't believe it had gone in on his near post. It was a brilliant feeling.'

The noise from the travelling Arsenal supporters was now intense, but so was the pressure on the Gunners defence as Parma put everyone forward in an attempt to find the equalising goal. The Italian team soon won a free-kick on the edge of the Arsenal penalty area. Zola's shot went high over the goal, but Adams was booked for encroachment and the kick was retaken. This time the ball just cleared the bar. Soon afterwards Zola beat Lee Dixon in the penalty area and Seaman was forced to palm the ball over the crossbar in spectacular style. Bearing in mind his cracked ribs, this was one of the best saves of his career.

For the rest of the first half there was almost constant pressure from Parma and Arsenal had virtually no possession, but the Gunners defence stood firm, and as half-time approached their opponents began to get increasingly frustrated. First Apolloni was booked for a body-check on Campbell and then Asprilla was yellow-carded for a foul on Adams. Arsenal were determined to reach the interval with their lead intact and, although they were not helped by the Czech referee who incredibly played almost seven minutes of injury time, they survived up to the break.

At half-time, while Seaman had another pain-killing injection, George Graham warned his team that they were defending too deep and allowing Parma too much space, but it had little effect as Parma proceeded to dominate proceedings in the second half as they had towards the end of the first. Despite the manager's warning the midfield and defence fell further and further back. 'It was the fear factor,' said Stephen Morrow. 'We just wanted to hang on to the lead.' And hang on they did.

Even though they exerted almost constant pressure, Parma rarely troubled David Seaman in the Arsenal goal. Up front Alan Smith won every ball and held on to it tenaciously. Campbell and Merson ably supported the midfield where Morrow and Selley were running all night harrying, hustling and denying their opponents in the middle of the park. At the back Dixon and Winterburn worked hard to deny the Parma forwards any width and send them inside where they would be met by the inspired Bould and Adams.

With 20 minutes to go the Italians sent on Melli, another forward in place of the midfielder Pin, but still they could not find a way through. Even when Arsenal were down to ten men for several minutes when Winterburn left the field after having the ball kicked into his face, the defence held firm.

With 86 minutes gone Eddie McGoldrick replaced Paul Merson to play out the game's final minutes, but Arsenal would have a couple of scares before the Cup was theirs. On 88 minutes the referee awarded Parma a free-kick for handball right on the edge of the Arsenal area. It would certainly have been a dangerous moment for the Gunners, but fortunately the linesman had spotted a Parma player who was offside and the danger was averted. Five minutes later, with the game in its third minute of injury time, it looked as though Arsenal had been denied the Cup when Seaman was finally beaten. Fortunately, however, the linesman came to the rescue once more as he flagged for offside.

With over four minutes of injury time played Alan Smith nearly scored his second of the night as he found himself in space just eight yards from goal, but his shot hit the heel of the approaching defender and went out for a corner. Just as the corner was taken the referee finally blew the whistle to end the game.

Arsenal had triumphed against the odds yet again and the players and supporters celebrated appropriately. Having gone to the end of the stadium where the majority of their supporters were, the Arsenal players lined up while Tony Adams lifted the Cup-Winners' Cup – the second time an Arsenal captain had lifted a European trophy – and as he passed the Cup along to his team-mates, the ghost of Benfica was finally banished. A European nightmare had been wiped out by a glorious triumph.

After 20 minutes of ecstatic celebrations with their supporters, the players finally left the pitch. As they had a league match to play on the following Saturday the team flew back to England that same night, which meant that the celebrations were not quite what they might have been, but the 20,000 Arsenal supporters that had travelled to Denmark more than made up for that as Copenhagen became a sea of red and white for the night. The exultant George Graham said afterwards:

> I'm very happy for myself, but most of all I'm just delighted for my team. This was their victory, their night. We had to put in players like Steve Morrow who has only played ten games this season and Ian Selley who is only 20. But it just showed the kind of character and commitment they have. Parma may have been more technically gifted but I must give tremendous credit to my team for battling the way they did.

The game was ultimately a tactical triumph for George Graham as Pat Rice recalls: 'Basically we went out there to stop them playing. The ploy came off because Alan Smith scored a great goal that night, but the defensive work of the midfield players was absolutely fantastic and I don't think David Seaman had a lot to do. It was a tremendous tactical victory.'

Graham's opposite number Nevio Scala was generous in defeat: 'My team were very nervous but Arsenal won the Cup with honesty and strength. They had one shot on goal and they scored from it, but they also played very well. They were the better side and showed that, despite all their injuries, they had the true English spirit.'

And that was what had won the day – spirit. Despite being up against a better team with better players, Arsenal's ten Englishmen and two Irishmen had won the game and taken the Cup back home. The following weekend's *Sunday Times* wrote that 'Arsenal in full spate remind you of Steffi Graf. Her belief in ultimate victory is so total that more gifted backhands falter and graceful shots wither in the face of her unremitting force. Parma, for all their exotica in attack and second-half possession, simply did not have as great a will to win.' Thanks to that spirit and will to win Arsenal had triumphed, and not only had they won the Cup-Winners' Cup, but they had also done it with the scoreline that every Arsenal fan had wanted. One–nil to the Arsenal.

FINAL SCORE

Arsenal	1	Parma	0

Smith	19 mins	
Attendance:	33,765	

Arsenal:	Seaman, Dixon, Winterburn, Adams, Bould, Campbell, Selley, Morrow, Davis, Merson (McGoldrick), Smith
Parma:	Bucci, Sensini, Apolloni, Minotti, Benarrivo, Pin (Melli), Crippa, di Chiara, Brolin, Asprilla, Zola

Chapter 12

JOY IN GENOA

European Cup-Winners' Cup semi-final (second leg)
Sampdoria v Arsenal
Thursday, 20 April 1995

That wonderful night in Copenhagen proved to be the pinnacle of George Graham's achievements at Highbury. For eight years Arsenal had enjoyed almost uninterrupted success, but the 1994–95 season saw a dramatic change in the club's fortunes. Whereas for the past eight years the talk around Highbury had been all about great victories and winning trophies, now bungs, sackings, drugs and even relegation were the main topics of conversation. On and off the pitch the club seemed to be falling apart as it endured one of its worst seasons for many years.

Yet amidst all the gloom and depression one game shone through like a beacon – even in this season from hell Arsenal managed to produce one of its greatest performances ever in one of the most dramatic matches of its history. It was a game of incredible tension, goals, controversy and comebacks where the fortunes of both teams ebbed and flowed throughout. The thousands of supporters who were there and the many more watching the match on television will always remember one incredible night in Genoa.

THE PLAYERS
The team that began the 1994–95 season was much the same as that which had finished the previous campaign. In fact, the back line of Dixon, Winterburn, Bould and Adams that had played in

the opening match against Manchester City was exactly the same as that which had played in the first game of the 1988–89 season six years earlier. Fellow Copenhagen heroes Seaman, Merson, Campbell and Smith also took to the field alongside the two players who had so unluckily missed out on the final, Jensen and Wright.

The only newcomer to the team was Swedish midfielder Stefan Schwarz. The left-footed international had been signed from Benfica in the summer for one and £1.75 million pounds in order to provide the sort of play-making skills that the Arsenal midfield had needed for some time. The Arsenal supporters and management hoped that his influence would be enough to see the team challenging for both domestic and European honours. As George Graham wrote in his opening day programme notes, 'I'm eyeing the title again. For all our cup success, it's time we had a good go at the championship.'

THE BACKGROUND

A 3–0 win against Manchester City on the opening day of the season promised much for the year ahead, but by the time Arsenal started the defence of the Cup-Winners' Cup on 15 September those were still the only goals they had scored following four games in which they had failed to find the net.

The Gunners' first game of the European season was in Cyprus against Omonia Nicosia. Despite a tricky first 20 minutes, the Cup holders ran out 3–1 winners to virtually book their place in the second round. A 3–0 win at Highbury – including a first Arsenal goal for Stefan Schwarz – completed the job.

The draw for the next round saw Arsenal on their way to Denmark for the third time in two years as they were paired with John Jensen's old team, Brondby. The Danes were not going to be easily overcome – George Graham felt they were stronger than the Odense side that Arsenal had squeezed past a year earlier – so a good first leg in Copenhagen was essential.

When goals from Ian Wright and Alan Smith gave Arsenal a 2–0 lead inside 20 minutes, it looked as though the Gunners would be able to coast to a comfortable victory, but that was not how things turned out. In the second half the home team bombarded David Seaman's goal and were rewarded with a goal from Mark Strudal. With a 2–1 lead from the away leg, however, it looked like the Gunners were safely through.

A crowd of 32,290 arrived at Highbury for the second leg against Brondby. The supporters were expecting Arsenal to cruise past their opponents, but right from the second minute, when Bo Hansen brought the aggregate scores level, it was clear that this was not going to be the case. A disputed penalty, which was awarded after Tony Adams went down in the penalty area, was safely dispatched by Ian Wright, while Ian Selley's goal just after half-time gave Arsenal a 4–2 aggregate lead and calmed the home fans' nerves. But when Dan Eggen scored for the Danes after 69 minutes the pressure was back on. One more goal for Brondby and they would be leading on away goals.

The last 20 minutes saw the Gunners defending frantically as the Danish forwards put them under a huge amount of pressure. The Arsenal defenders found themselves making increasingly desperate clearances – including one off the line from Lee Dixon – to keep their opponents at bay. The clock on the scoreboard seemed to be taking an age to count down but, as the game entered the final minute, it looked as though Arsenal had held on for a narrow victory.

Just then came the moment that could have led to an embarrassing exit for the Gunners: as Brondby launched one last attack on the Arsenal goal, Steve Bould threw himself at the ball and appeared to bring down the Danish forward inside the penalty area. The Brondby players, officials and supporters screamed for a penalty, but Russian referee Sergei Khusainov waved play on and moments later he blew the final whistle.

In his programme notes for the following game George Graham wrote: 'After Thursday's game, someone asked me if my blood pressure was up when Brondby had that penalty shout in the last minute. I replied that it had been high since the first minute! That was one of the closest Cup-Winners' Cup games we've had and I don't want too many of those.'

In fact it was to be George Graham's last major European match in charge of Arsenal.

By the time Arsenal's Cup-Winners' Cup campaign resumed in March, the club had gone through some of the most traumatic months in its long history. In November, Paul Merson confessed to drinking, gambling and drug-taking problems and checked himself into a rehabilitation centre to receive the help he required. Then, in December, the *Mail on Sunday* alleged that George Graham had taken transfer 'bungs' when signing John Jensen and Norwegian international Pal Lydersen. As well as – or possibly because of – all these problems the team's form hit rock-bottom. They won just two out of 17 league games, with no wins in eight matches at Highbury.

In mid-January, George Graham attempted to arrest the team's slide by signing two forwards – Chris Kiwomya from Ipswich and 19-year-old John Hartson from Luton – but the poor results kept coming as Arsenal went out of the Coca-Cola Cup away to Liverpool and the FA Cup at home to First Division Millwall. With the team only four points away from the relegation zone it seemed that the club had reached the lowest level possible. Then on 21 February, as the team prepared to take on Nottingham Forest at Highbury, George Graham was sacked.

George Graham's dismissal came as a huge shock to everyone involved with Arsenal. He had arrived eight-and-a-half years earlier and had presided over one of the most successful periods in the club's history. His character was stamped all over the club and his influence had been overwhelming; now, quite suddenly, he was gone. With league points desperately required and the team's next European game just over a week away, it was imperative that the team got on with playing as best they could.

George Graham's assistant, Stewart Houston, was installed as manager for the rest of the season and immediately presided over two crucial league wins.

On the night of George Graham's departure Arsenal beat Nottingham Forest 1–0, courtesy of a late winner from Chris Kiwomya, and on the following Saturday Crystal Palace were beaten 3–0 thanks to another two goals from Kiwomya and one from the recently returned Paul Merson.

After two wins morale was a little higher when Arsenal took on

Auxerre, the French team, in the first leg of their Cup-Winners' Cup quarter-final at Highbury. Despite this, however, the Gunners struggled to find a way past the French defence and it was not until the hour mark that they were awarded a penalty which Ian Wright scored, and so maintained his record of scoring in every European game so far that season. Even then it took Auxerre only three minutes to get back on level terms when Franck Verlaat headed home from a free-kick to score a vital away goal. With the game finishing at 1–1 Arsenal had a mountain to climb in the second leg.

Two weeks, and another two league defeats later, the Gunners travelled to Auxerre knowing that they had to score to have any chance of progressing to the semi-finals, and the man they were relying on to get their goals was Ian Wright. Fortunately, Wright was able to deliver after 16 minutes. Chasing a hopeful ball down the right-wing he beat the covering defender and, from the corner of the penalty box, curled a looping ball just over the despairing reach of Fabian Cool in the Auxerre goal and into the corner of the net. It was Wright's seventh goal of the campaign and almost certainly his best.

From then on Arsenal had to hang on as Auxerre piled forward in an attempt to draw level. Thanks to the heroics of Adams and Bould in defence and Seaman in goal, Arsenal kept the French attacks at bay and claimed a 2–1 aggregate win. Even without the circumstances of Arsenal's win being taken into account, it was a magnificent performance and one that matched even those of the previous season's European games. As Stewart Houston later wrote, 'that was one of our best-ever performances in Europe'.

Arsenal were now in the semi-finals, where they were joined by fellow Londoners Chelsea as well as Real Zaragoza of Spain and Sampdoria of Italy. The Italians were seen by most people as the team to avoid as they had players such as Zenga, Lombardo, Jugovic and Mancini in their side. But it was Sampdoria that were drawn out of the hat alongside Arsenal, with the first leg to be played at Highbury.

Matters were not helped by Arsenal's continued poor form in the league. After four successive defeats they sank to a precarious 14th place in the table, before a timely 5–1 win over Norwich five days before the European semi-final first leg restored some morale.

There was also good news for Arsenal when Sampdoria's David Platt was suspended from both legs after being sent off in the previous round, while Mijhailovic was suspended from the first leg. Also missing from the first game would be Ferri and Vierchowod, both being injured. Arsenal, too, were not without their problems. A cracked rib meant that David Seaman, who had only played against Auxerre in the previous five weeks, had to play with heavy strapping and pain-killing injections. While an injury to John Jensen and Martin Keown's suspension from the first game meant that David Hillier, who had only just returned from injury himself, had to bolster the midfield.

The first leg on 6 April was played on another balmy European night at Highbury. In his programme notes Stewart Houston wrote: 'I don't think there'll be many chances, and it's up to us to take a high percentage of them. We have to keep our back door tight too. No more conceding goals like we did against Auxerre.'

The game could hardly have turned out more differently.

Possibly the most significant moment of the match came after 30 minutes. An Arsenal corner was flicked on by Steve Bould at the near post and the Sampdoria goalkeeper, under pressure from Tony Adams, dropped the ball into his own net. The goal was disallowed by the referee, however, accusing Adams of 'intimidation'. The incident was immediately shown on the new giant television screens at Highbury and the injustice of the decision enraged the home crowd and made them urge their side forward even more passionately than before.

With the crowd roaring them on, the Gunners stormed upfield and within seven minutes were two goals ahead. On 34 minutes another Stefan Schwarz corner was struck into the penalty area. This time the ball fell to David Hillier whose shot was saved by Walter Zenga in the Sampdoria goal, but the rebound fell to Steve Bould who shot home from eight yards.

The crowd went wild as they celebrated Bould's first goal of the season, and they could hardly believe it when, three minutes later, he doubled his tally. Again Schwarz took the corner, this time to the near post, where Bould's flick on looped over everyone and fell into the far corner of the net. Steve Bould had scored two important goals in such a short space of time and Arsenal were now in control of the match.

Early in the second half, however, Arsenal received a setback when Sampdoria pressure forced Adams to make a desperate attempted clearance which fell only to the feet of Jugovic who stabbed the ball home. But 20 minutes later the home side's two-goal lead was restored when a beautiful through ball from Merson found Ian Wright ahead of his marker. As the ball entered the Italian penalty area, Wright was just able to lob the onrushing Zenga from 15 yards to make the score 3–1.

Arsenal would have been happy to finish the game there with a highly satisfactory 3–1 win but, unfortunately, there was still 20 minutes to go. Nine minutes later a clever back-heel by Mancini, who was near the edge of the Arsenal penalty area, found Jugovic who was unmarked once more and, once again, his shot found the net.

In the game's final moments both teams came close to scoring, but it finished with the score at 3–2, which left the Italians as slight favourites to reach the final. Goalscoring-hero Steve Bould was still confident, however: 'Sometimes we make life difficult for ourselves. The lads were disappointed afterwards because we twice threw away a two-goal lead. Credit to Sampdoria. They're a good side and I thought they did very well in the second half, but the fact that the second leg will be difficult will bring the best out of us. We've shown what we can do away from home. We were unbeaten last season and we've won on all our three trips this time.'

Arsenal were then required to play four games before the next leg two weeks later. Fortunately, a 4–1 win over Ipswich and a 4–0 victory at Aston Villa all but halted any relegation fears, and left the players to concentrate on reaching the Cup-Winners' Cup final for the second year running.

Despite all the evidence of their European performances over the previous two years, the pundits still doubted Arsenal's ability to triumph yet again. On the eve of the second leg, Rob Hughes at *The Times* wrote: 'Sampdoria at times mesmerised Arsenal with their quality on the ground; three times Roberto Mancini produced through-balls behind the static Tony Adams; twice Vladimir Jugovic, the Serb, scored. This time the Italians have a second Serb, the cunning Sinisa Mijhailovic, a wonderful free-kick exponent, back from suspension. Their defence not only benefits from the return of Vierchowod, but also the redoubtable skipper Riccardo Ferri. Add to those the splendid counter-attacker Attilio Lombardo and the suspicion is that Arsenal conceded at least one goal too many at Highbury.'

Others, however, were not so sure. Having seen his team beaten so often in the air during the first leg, Sampdoria manager Sven-Goran Eriksson said: 'The tie is 51 per cent in Arsenal's favour. After all, we cannot eat to be taller in one week.' According to assistant manager Pat Rice there was little doubt within the Arsenal camp: 'We always thought that we could beat them. There was a lot of talk about Mancini, but people that we had spoken to said that if you put Mancini out of the game, that was 50 per cent of their team gone.'

On the eve of the match, Ian Wright was certainly confident of becoming the first player to score in every game in a European competition: 'One chance, that's all I need the way I'm feeling at the moment. I want that record for the players and supporters who have been brilliant with me when, perhaps, I've let them down with my form and suspension. But I'm driven by people telling me I'm not an international footballer. I hate being told that.'

THE MATCH

The weather conditions in Genoa for the second leg were more British than Italian, as the fog lingered overhead and the rain came down. The grey weather matched the mood of the travelling Arsenal support who, having been promised a day out around the town before the game, had been herded into a car-park by the local police and kept there all afternoon with no entertainment or refreshment of any kind. By the time they reached the impressive Luis Ferraris stadium, the 2,000 Gunners fans were doubly determined to roar the team on to the final. Despite the slenderness of their lead, the Gunners were confident and determined to reach the final. After all, they had never lost a Cup-Winners' Cup game and a draw would see them through. Before they took to the field, Stewart Houston told them: 'This is "our" trophy. We still hold it. Tonight is about our ability and character and resilience.'

The game got under way with both teams mindful of the fact that conceding an early goal could have disastrous consequences. And while Sampdoria had Mijhailovic, Ferri and Vierchowod back in their side, Martin Keown had returned to the Arsenal line-up, in place of Ray Parlour, having served his suspension in the first leg. During the opening spell, therefore, only a Hartson header that was saved by Walter Zenga in the Sampdoria goal threatened to open the scoring. As the clock ticked past 13 minutes, however, it was Arsenal who saw themselves as the victims of bad luck as Sampdoria gained the upper hand.

The ball was cleared from defence by Ferri and as it flew over the halfway line, Lombardo was obviously in an offside position, but the referee ruled that he was not interfering with play. Mancini then raced past the Arsenal defenders as they stood with their arms aloft, and lobbed the ball from 20 yards out over the head of the onrushing David Seaman to give Sampdoria the crucial early goal that they had been looking for. The Arsenal players appealed to the Austrian referee in vain and the goal stood.

The goal shook Arsenal into action and for the rest of the first half they dominated the game in terms of possession and goalscoring chances. Having seen the way that the Sampdoria defence had struggled against the high ball in the first leg, they proceeded to launch the ball into the Italian's penalty area at every opportunity and, again, Sampdoria struggled to keep the ball away from their goal.

After half an hour a Winterburn free-kick was chested down by Steve Bould in the penalty area and Paul Merson had a clear sight on goal, but his shot was well saved by Zenga. Moments later a Dixon cross was headed goalwards by Hartson, only for Zenga to save again. On 40 minutes, another free-kick found Bould in the area and again his knock-down found Merson, but this time his shot was deflected behind the goal. From the resulting corner, Hartson headed narrowly wide.

Arsenal were playing well and dominating the game, but it was by no means one-way traffic. After the way that Sampdoria had taken the lead, the Italian team's players were sure that they could beat Arsenal's offside trap again, and they repeatedly sent testing balls over the Gunners defenders who had to scramble back on several occasions when the linesman's flag was not raised.

At half-time Stewart Houston told his team to just carry on playing as they had been. If they continued to have so much possession a goal would surely come. The only real worry was Sampdoria's ability to beat the offside trap.

As in the first half, the opening minutes of the second period saw little in the way of goalscoring opportunities. In an effort to brighten up Arsenal's attack, Eddie McGoldrick was brought on in place of David Hillier after 55 minutes. Sampdoria also made a change four minutes later when Invernizzi replaced Evani, but Sampdoria made the fatal mistake of making a substitution while defending a corner.

Just as Invernizzi had taken to the field, Merson took the corner on the left and swung the ball into the area. John Hartson rose to flick it on, and an off-balance Ian Wright was just able to shoot past Zenga into the corner of the goal. Wright turned away in delight. Not only were Arsenal back in front with only 30 minutes to play, but he had kept up his record of scoring in every game.

Wright's goal changed the whole course of the match as Sampdoria were forced to throw men forward. For the next ten minutes they pinned Arsenal back and created a succession of chances: Mancini headed just wide, Maspero shot wide when clean through on goal and Lombardo's shot was saved by Seaman. Arsenal hung on, however, and for the next ten minutes they regained their composure and even went close to scoring themselves when Ian Wright got behind the Italians defence, but his shot was well saved by Zenga.

After 75 minutes Sampdoria played their last card by bringing on 19-year-old midfielder Claudio Bellucci in place of centre-back Riccardo Ferri. Soon afterwards the hobbling Ian Wright was replaced by Chris Kiwomya.

As the game entered the final ten minutes, everything looked positive for Arsenal. If Sampdoria did not score the Gunners were through, and with the Arsenal defence looking solid once more the Italians looked unlikely to find a route to goal. On 82 minutes, however, Arsenal appeared to be the victims of another controversial refereeing decision. Tony Adams made another vital tackle just outside his penalty area, but as he did so, the ball bounced up off his foot and hit his arm. There was no way that Adams had handled intentionally, but the referee awarded a free-kick to the home team just 25 yards from goal.

When Mijhailovic's kick was blocked by the defensive wall the danger seemed to have been averted, but from the rebound Mancini took a shot at goal. Even now the ball seemed to be going wide of the target, but as the ball came towards Bellucci's head he deflected it past Seaman and into the net. Bellucci tore off his shirt and ran around the stadium to celebrate his crucial goal and so great were his celebrations that he was booked by referee Grabher.

Arsenal now had to throw men forward in a desperate attempt to score but, inevitably, this left gaps at the back which, just two minutes later, were exploited by the home side. An Arsenal attack was broken up and Lombardo was sent away down the right. As he approached the Arsenal penalty area he slipped the ball to Belucci who slid the ball under Seaman for his second goal of the night.

Surely Arsenal were now beaten. The Arsenal supporters in the ground looked on mournfully as the home fans celebrated their impending victory, while the thousands of Gunners fans watching back at home on television heard 'expert' summariser Ron Atkinson tell them: 'They're out now. With all the will in the world they're out now.'

All was not entirely lost – if Arsenal could get one goal back the teams would be level at 5–5 on aggregate and the game would go into extra-time. The only trouble was that they only had five minutes left in which to score and their principal marksman, Ian Wright, was off the field. But with three minutes to go they were thrown a lifeline when Bould was fouled 30 yards from the Sampdoria goal and the referee awarded a free-kick.

Unfortunately for Bould – who was still incensed about the decision that had led to Sampdoria's second goal – his protestations saw him receive a yellow card that would mean he would be suspended from the final, if Arsenal got there, but as they appeared to be going out anyway it hardly seemed to matter.

Stefan Schwarz, Arsenal's Swedish midfielder, hit a low, left-footed free-kick that beat the Italian wall and was on course for the corner of the net. Zenga dived to his left and got a hand to the ball, but only succeeded in palming it into the goal. Remarkably, Arsenal were back in the game.

Schwarz ran towards the Arsenal bench where he was embraced by Houston and Wright, while the previously sullen Arsenal supporters suddenly came to life as the majority of the crowd fell silent. Moments later the referee blew the final whistle and the teams prepared for extra-time.

Before extra-time began, both teams needed to compose themselves. Sampdoria had thought that they were safely through to the final, while Arsenal had appeared to be on their way out. Now the two teams were level again and had everything to play for. The extra 30 minutes saw numerous Sampdoria players being affected by cramp, while the Arsenal team were clearly suffering from the toll of a gruelling domestic programme. The Gunners failed to attack the Sampdoria goal, while the Italians only threatened towards the end when the prospect of a penalty shoot-out loomed, but the Arsenal defence stayed firm and held out until the referee's whistle. The game finished at 3–2 with an aggregate score of 5-5. After 210 minutes of football it would need a penalty shoot-out to separate the two teams.

Both teams had an international goalkeeper at their disposal, but with Arsenal's regular penalty-taker, Ian Wright, unavailable, the Italians had to be the favourites to win. In the lottery of a penalty shoot-out, however, anything could happen.

It was Arsenal who started the shoot-out, Lee Dixon taking the first penalty. The Gunners full-back shot high and to the goalkeeper's right and put Arsenal ahead. Sinisa Mijhailovic then stepped up to take Sampdoria's first spot-kick. He hit the ball to Seaman's left, but the Arsenal keeper dived and saved to the roars of the Arsenal fans. All Arsenal had to do now was convert their last four penalties and they were through. Unfortunately, they immediately lost their advantage as Eddie McGoldrick spooned his shot over the bar and walked back to the halfway line with his head in his hands.

Vladimir Jugovic then had the chance to bring Sampdoria level but, incredibly, Seaman saved again as he dived to his right and just stopped the ball before it sneaked underneath him. John Hartson then stepped up and confidently blasted the ball to Zenga's left to give Arsenal a 2–0 lead.

Seaman came close to saving a third penalty when he dived the right way for Maspero's shot, but the ball just eluded him and Sampdoria were off the mark. To the surprise of most Arsenal followers, the next man to step up was Tony Adams. Adams was not the kind of player that you would expect to take a penalty but, as always, he was leading by example. His supporters watched in trepidation and then elation as he struck his shot hard and straight past the goalkeeper to make the score 3–1. If Mannini failed to score, Arsenal were through.

Arsenal's celebrations were put on hold when Mannini sent Seaman the wrong way to score for the home side. This meant that if Paul Merson converted his kick, he would win the tie for the Gunners. It seemed as though Merson's season was about to turn full circle. After all the problems that he had come through, it seemed fitting that he would be the man to win the day. Unfortunately, Zenga did not follow the script and he dived to his right to keep out Merson's shot. If Lombardo scored his penalty the shoot-out would go to sudden death.

Seaman had done his job, but the failings of the goalscorers meant that he had to save three out of five penalties to see Arsenal through. If anyone could do it, however, it was David Seaman. The man who would take the kick was Attilio Lombardo who, four years earlier, had seen Seaman dive to his left and save his penalty in a pre-season tournament. Could the Englishman do it again? Lombardo ran up and again struck the ball well to the goalkeeper's left. Although he had gone the right way, Seaman looked as if he would dive underneath it, but he stuck up his right hand and palmed the ball away. He had done it, Arsenal were through.

The triumphant Seaman raised his arms aloft as he ran towards his team-mates. The first to reach him was the jubilant Wright who would play in a European final for the first time. The rest of the team soon followed and the goalkeeper was submerged underneath them. Seaman soon reappeared on the shoulders of the celebrating players as they paraded him towards their ecstatic supporters. Arsenal had pulled off a remarkable victory in the most dramatic way possible.

Despite his heroics, David Seaman was quick to pay tribute to the rest of the team: 'This must be remembered as one of the best performances ever by an Arsenal team. It swung to and fro. One moment we looked safe and then we were living dangerously, but I never felt we wouldn't get through, not really. When it came down to the penalties, my stomach wasn't churning. The pressure is not on the goalkeeper but the penalty-takers. You dive one way and if it hits you're a hero. I've got a formula about how to approach them, but I'm keeping that to myself.'

Stewart Houston, however, was quick to praise his goalkeeper: 'David's contribution was immense. His penalty saves were quite incredible, but that is why he is England's number one . . . We deserved what we've got. The players gave Arsenal Football Club everything they had.'

There was also praise for Arsenal's performance from the Italian camp. Sampdoria manager Sven-Goran Eriksson said: 'I think Arsenal played even better tonight than they did at Highbury. They made us play their way and they were better than us at what they do.'

This dramatic victory meant that Arsenal went on to play Real Zaragoza in the Cup-Winners' Cup final in Paris in May. The Gunners were favourites to become the first team ever to retain the trophy and, with the score at 1–1 in the last minute of extra-time, it looked as though Seaman would have the chance to show his heroics once more. With virtually the last kick of the game, however, a remarkable shot from Nayim won the day for the Spaniards and snatched the trophy away from Arsenal. And, so, Arsenal failed to be the first team to win the Cup-Winners' Cup two seasons in a row and Ian Wright failed to be the first player to score in every game. The season had ended in heartbreak.

Considering what Arsenal had been through that season, however, it had been a fantastic achievement to reach the final at all. Throughout their European campaign they had shown the same grit, determination and skill that had seen them lift the Cup-

Winners' Cup a year earlier. Nothing exemplified this more than the two games against Sampdoria. As the tie had twisted this way and that, Arsenal had never lost that determination to win – and even when they had seemed down and out they had kept going to the final whistle. They may not have won the Cup in the end, but the whole team deserved medals for the way they performed in Genoa that night.

Rob Hughes of *The Times*, who had been so pessimistic about Arsenal's chances beforehand, summed up the performance when he wrote the next day: 'The rest of Europe, never mind England, must now acknowledge that there is simply no side boasting greater depth of character, none with stronger nerve and will than Arsenal. Last night in Genoa, after a contest and a contrast that was sometimes brutal, often a test of heart and spirit, they trawled through extra-time before winning the Russian roulette of a penalty shoot-out.'

It went almost unnoticed that the 2–3 scoreline in the match represented Arsenal's first ever defeat in a Cup-Winners' Cup match. A proud Arsenal record had gone. Nobody was too bothered about that, however, for their first defeat had also been their finest hour.

FINAL SCORE

Arsenal	2	Sampdoria	3 (5-5 on aggregate)

Wright	60 mins	Mancini	13 mins
Schwarz	87 mins	Bellucci	82 mins
		Bellucci	84 mins

Penalties

Arsenal	3	Sampdoria	2
Dixon		Maspero	
Hartson		Mannini	
Adams			

Attendance: 34,353

Arsenal: Seaman, Dixon, Adams, Bould, Winterburn, Hillier (McGoldrick), Keown, Schwarz, Merson, Hartson, Wright (Kiwomya)

Sampdoria: Zenga, Mannini, Ferri (Bellucci), Vierchowod, Serena, Evani (Invernizzi), Jugovic, Maspero, Lombardo, Mijhailovic, Mancini

187

13

LE DOUBLE DOUBLE

FA Cup final
Arsenal v Newcastle United
Saturday, 16 May 1998

The start of the 1996–97 season saw Arsenal in disarray. Bruce Rioch, who had been manager for just one season, was sacked just days before the season began. And then, in mid-September, Stewart Houston resigned as caretaker manager and the club's inspirational captain, Tony Adams, admitted that he was an alcoholic. Spirits were not raised by the appointment of a little-known Frenchman as new manager.

Arsène Wenger had been successful in France and Japan but had never managed a club of Arsenal's size and stature and his arrival was greeted with scepticism by supporters and commentators alike. Over the rest of the season, however, Wenger impressed as, against the odds, Arsenal mounted a championship challenge that saw them finish in third place and start to play a more entertaining and expansive style of football.

Optimism abounded at the start of the following season but, despite a promising opening to the campaign, Arsenal found themselves trailing the reigning champions Manchester United by 13 points at the turn of the year. The pundits proclaimed the title race over; as far as they were concerned, the rest were now competing for second place for it would take something remarkable to dislodge United now. But something remarkable was about to happen at Highbury. Arsenal proceeded to put together a record-breaking run of form that would see them catch and pass United and open up the race for the Premiership once again.

The result was a thrilling and unforgettable championship climax. Not only was Arsène Wenger on the verge of becoming the first foreign manager to win an English league title, but the team had the chance to become the second Gunners side to do the elusive double. It was a lot to ask for a manager's first full season in a foreign country, but as the season drew to a close it was clear that his team were on the verge of greatness and that Arsène Wenger had an early opportunity to write his name into the club's long and glorious history. Now that they were so close they were determined not to waste the chance.

THE PLAYERS

Remarkably, the mainstays of the 1998 championship-challenging defence were the same as those that had won the title in 1989. Still there were Lee Dixon (now 34), Nigel Winterburn (34), Steve Bould (35) and Tony Adams (31). They were joined by David Seaman (34) – from the 1991 championship team – and Martin Keown (31). This Arsenal back-line was now one of the most enduring in football history and, despite having been written off as being past it for several seasons now, they were determined to prove their critics wrong. Their experience was to prove invaluable during the long season, but they were also helped by more youthful team-mates such as the reserve goalkeeper, 20-year-old Alex Manninger from Austria, £1 million teenage defender Matthew Upson and the French duo of Remi Garde and Gilles Grimandi.

In midfield the fans' favourite was another Frenchman, Patrick Vieira. Vieira was one of Arsène Wenger's first signings and had made an enormous impression ever since coming on as a substitute against Sheffield Wednesday at Highbury the previous season. With his long-legged tackles, driving runs through the middle of the pitch and accurate passing he soon established himself as one of the best players of his type in the country. Alongside him was his compatriot Emmanuel Petit who had been signed in the close season from Monaco. Other midfield players who would make major contributions throughout the season were 21-year-old

189

Stephen Hughes and former England captain David Platt. Platt had been signed by Bruce Rioch from Sampdoria in 1995 and, while no longer a first-choice player, he provided valuable experience and actually started or came on as substitute in the vast majority of games throughout the season. Hughes, on the other hand, had been brought in to the team by Wenger during the previous season and his appearances during the championship challenge emphasised his promise as an outstanding young player. On the flanks were the speedy winger Marc Overmars, signed for £5 million from Ajax in the summer, and Ray Parlour, now playing some of the best football of his career on the right-hand side of midfield.

Up front was potentially one of the most lethal partnerships in the country. One of the threats for the opposition came from Ian Wright who was still scoring goals on a prolific scale. At the start of the season he had been at Highbury for less than six years and yet he was poised to break Cliff Bastin's record goal tally for the club. It was inevitable that he would break the record during the early stages of the campaign but, during that time, he was to find himself being overshadowed by a man in the form of his life.

The biggest signing in Arsenal's history came in 1995 when they bought Dennis Bergkamp from Italian club Internazionale. As well as being the biggest transfer financially – the £7.5 million fee was a club record – it was arguably the most prestigious. Bergkamp was an internationally renowned forward who had burst on to the world stage at his first club, Ajax Amsterdam. His form for his club – and for Holland at international level – made him one of the most sought-after players in Europe, while his goals against England in the qualifying rounds for the 1994 World Cup boosted his reputation and recognition in this country. His time in Italy, however, was not happy with Bergkamp finding it difficult to come to terms with the style of play, although he did help his team win the UEFA Cup. His early days in England were also troubled as he took time to adjust to the unique demands of the Premier League. But once he found his feet, he soon showed the country and the rest of Europe what a world-class player he is, and he regularly scored some of the most spectacular goals seen throughout Arsenal's history. Bergkamp and Ian Wright were soon striking fear into the hearts of opposing defences.

While the two first-choice forwards were highly experienced in both club and international football, their understudies were the exact opposite. Nicolas Anelka was only 18 when he signed from Paris St Germain towards the end of the previous season and had made only four appearances for the club and was yet to score. While Christopher Wreh was a little-known Liberian signed from Monaco in the summer. With both Paul Merson and John Hartson having been sold only recently, it was generally feared that such inexperienced players would be unable to deputise effectively for either Bergkamp or Wright should the need arise.

THE BACKGROUND

The start of the season was a good one for Arsenal, but it was particularly good for Dennis Bergkamp – after eight league games he had scored eight goals. Arsenal were top of the table after an unbeaten run that had included victory at title-rivals Chelsea and a four-goal win against both Bolton (where Ian Wright finally broke the club's scoring record) and West Ham. Bergkamp was in such masterly form that he achieved the unprecedented feat of scoring the top three goals in the BBC's August competition of Goal of the Month, and he was being widely proclaimed as the best player in the world.

There was major disappointment when the Gunners were knocked out of the UEFA Cup in the first round by PAOK of Greece, but when Barnsley were dismissed 5–0 the following Saturday, with Bergkamp scoring two of the goals, it seemed like the European exit had been merely a blip in Arsenal's fortunes. Unfortunately, however, this was not the case. It was, in fact, the start of a slump. The main reason for this was the suspension of the mercurial Bergkamp. During his phenomenal run of form, the only downside had been his regular accumulation of bookings which climaxed with his fifth yellow card of the season against Crystal Palace, leading to an automatic three-match ban. Without the inspirational Dutchman the Gunners struggled desperately, and even when he returned it seemed that his form had been badly affected – after scoring ten goals in the first ten league games he failed to score in the next 11 – and the team won only two of their next eight games. The one bright spot amidst the gloom was the game against Manchester United at Highbury. If they had won, the reigning champions would have gone seven points clear at the top of the table, but they were soon behind. Nicolas Anelka scored his first goal for Arsenal and when Vieira scored a spectacular second United were in serious trouble. By half-time, however, the game was level thanks to two goals from Teddy Sheringham. But Arsenal showed the sort of spirit that would be so vital later in the season and won the game with a towering header by David Platt. United's lead was now down to a point, but Arsenal failed to capitalise and proceeded to lose their next two games, the first against Sheffield Wednesday and then at home to Liverpool.

The defeat against Liverpool prompted the players to meet and thrash out where they thought that they were going wrong. Views were frankly exchanged and everyone was made to realise what their team-mates expected of them. This seemed to have made an immediate impact when the Gunners won 1–0 at Newcastle – thanks to Ian Wright's first goal in seven games – but when Blackburn won 3–1 at Highbury the following week it appeared that any chance Arsenal had of winning the Premiership had gone for another season. The team had dropped from first to sixth in the table, and they were now seven points behind United who had a game in hand. The fans had rounded on Ian Wright, for a perceived lack of effort, and Tony Adams, who had been at least partially responsible for two of the goals conceded against Blackburn. Adams revealed that he had been carrying an injury and had decided not to play again until he was completely fit. Arsenal's season appeared to lie in ruins.

The defeat against Blackburn was undoubtedly the low point of the season. The players were desperate to come back in their next game at Wimbledon with a win, but with the game still goalless and the second half having just got under way the ground was plunged into darkness as the floodlights failed and the game had to be abandoned. With Manchester United now 13 points ahead of them, this seemed to sum up Arsenal's championship chances. From then on, however, the team slowly began to recover and results began to improve.

As the Gunners started to grind out wins and draws at the start of 1998, Manchester United unexpectedly began to drop points. Defeats against Coventry, Southampton and Leicester opened up the title race once more, and when Arsenal beat Chelsea 2–0 on 8 February following United's home draw with Bolton the previous afternoon, the Gunners were only six points adrift with a game in hand. Things were also looking up for Arsenal in their bid for cup silverware; a quarter-final victory over West Ham had put them into the semi-finals of the Coca-Cola Cup where they held a 2–1 first-leg lead over Chelsea, while wins at Port Vale (after a penalty shoot-out) and Middlesbrough saw them into the fifth round of the FA Cup. And all this without Ian Wright, who was out of the team with a long-term injury.

But in the space of four days Arsenal's chances of bringing home a trophy seemed to have receded once again. On 15 February they failed to beat lowly Crystal Palace at home in the FA Cup, and then on the following Wednesday they crashed to a 3–1 defeat at Chelsea to go out of the Coca-Cola Cup. On the same night Manchester United won 2–0 at Aston Villa to open up a nine-point lead. When Arsenal drew at West Ham on 2 March they were 11 points behind the leaders and, as far as all the experts and pundits were concerned, the championship race was over.

So convinced was everyone that United would retain the championship that one Manchester bookmaker even paid out on a United win before the season was over.

There were, however, plenty of twists and turns still to come.

After goals from Bergkamp and Anelka gave Arsenal a 2–1 victory against Crystal Palace in the FA Cup replay, the Gunners faced a home game against West Ham in the quarter-finals. The 1–1 draw meant that for the third time in the season Arsenal had failed to win an FA Cup tie at home, this meant that they would face a crucial replay just four days after the most important league game of their season.

As a result of Manchester United having taken just one point from their next two league games, coupled with Arsenal's 1–0 win in the rearranged game at Wimbledon, the Gunners were now nine points behind with three games in hand. This meant that the game between the two teams at Old Trafford took on enormous significance. If United were to win they would surely be uncatchable, but if the three points went back to Highbury the race would be wide open once again. The circumstances called for an impressive performance from Arsène Wenger's team, and that was exactly what they produced. With Alex Manninger, in for the injured Seaman, performing heroics in goal, Adams and Keown solid in defence, Vieira and Petit controlling the midfield and Marc Overmars at his brilliant best, the Gunners were always on top and when, after 79 minutes, Overmars found himself clear in the United penalty box and slid the ball under the goalkeeper to score the winning goal, Arsenal were right back in it. United manager Alex Ferguson had managed to psyche other managers out of title races in the past, and after the game he suggested that now Arsenal were under pressure they were bound to drop points. Would his mindgames succeed this time?

After such a magnificent win it would have been understandable if the players had suffered some sort of dip in form when, four days later, they took on West Ham in their FA Cup sixth-round replay at Upton Park. It soon became clear, however, that far from suffering the after-effects of their previous game, they were carrying on their form from Old Trafford. Arsenal soon took control of the game and a goal seemed inevitable before disaster struck: on 32 minutes their star striker, Dennis Bergkamp, was sent off for elbowing Hammers midfielder Steve Lomas, and the Gunners were forced to play the rest of the game with only ten men. Remarkably, however, just as half-time approached, a stunning shot from the edge of the penalty area by Nicolas Anelka found its way to the net and Arsenal had the lead. The second half predictably saw West Ham lay siege to Alex Manninger's goal, but up until the 84th minute it looked as though their efforts would be to no avail as Adams, Keown *et al* stood firm. But it was then that ex-Gunner John Hartson ran through the defence and beat Manninger at the near post to force extra-time. A West Ham victory now seemed inevitable, but the Arsenal defence held out and took the game to a penalty shoot-out. With Ian Wright out injured, Bergkamp sent off and Overmars, Anelka and Petit all substituted, the odds were still stacked in West Ham's favour, but anything could happen when it came to penalties.

What turned out to be an emotionally draining shoot-out began unremarkably enough with Stephen Hughes scoring for Arsenal and David Unsworth replying for the home team. When Christopher Wreh missed his kick the initiative was back with West Ham, but John Hartson was unable to repeat his earlier goalscoring as he put his shot wide to keep the score at 1–1. Luis Boa Morte and Frank Lampard made it 2–2, but when Remi Garde missed the target West Ham were favourites once more. Remarkably, West Ham immediately failed to take advantage once again as Manninger brilliantly saved Berkovic's shot and the teams were level again. Patrick Vieira's goal meant that Lomas had to score to keep the game alive, but he showed himself to be up to the task as he found the net to make it 3–3. Then Tony Adams stepped up, just as he had done three years earlier in Genoa, and once again, as the goalkeeper dived to his right, the Arsenal captain hit the ball straight and found the net. Abou had to score for West Ham, but his spot-kick struck Manninger's right-hand post and as he held his head in his hands, the Arsenal players and supporters danced with delight as they looked forward to a semi-final against opponents from the First Division – Wolves – and, for the first time, realised that the double was a real possibility. Looking back, Martin Keown said later, 'I thought that night, when we came through, this team was good enough to win something.'

In his last game before beginning a three-match suspension, Dennis Bergkamp scored the only goal against Sheffield Wednesday before Arsenal achieved two more crucial 1–0 wins at Bolton and against Wolves in the FA Cup semi-final both courtesy of goals from Christopher Wreh. With so many 1–0 wins and 1–1 draws the Gunners seemed to be going back to the glory days of George Graham, but they were about to show that they could score goals as well.

Having secured their place at Wembley, the players could now completely concentrate on their league campaign, a campaign which was helped when Manchester United could only draw with Liverpool on Good Friday. The first obstacle to be overcome was

Newcastle – the team that they would face in the Cup final. Arsenal made it a joyous Easter Saturday with a thrilling 3–1 win, with two goals from an in-form Anelka and a stunning 25-yard strike by Patrick Vieira. Two days later Bergkamp returned for the tricky away game at Blackburn, the last team to beat them in the league. This time it was a very different story from their first game at Highbury as Blackburn were blown away by an awesome Gunners performance. Bergkamp and Parlour both struck in the opening minutes and, before a quarter of an hour had been played, Ray Parlour scored again to make it 3–0 and virtually ensure victory. When Nicolas Anelka broke from his own half, leaving defenders trailing in his wake, dummied the goalkeeper and stroked the ball into the net for the fourth goal it was all over. Blackburn scored a consolation goal in the second half, but the 4–1 scoreline and the manner of Arsenal's victory sent a clear message to Old Trafford: Arsenal, now only one point behind with two games in hand, were marching towards the championship.

On 18 April, Arsenal finally reached the top of the table. While they were thrashing Wimbledon (5–0), United were being held at home by the Newcastle team that had been so comprehensively dismissed at Highbury just a week earlier. Arsenal now needed only three more wins from their remaining five games for the Premiership trophy to go to London for the first time. With their final two games being difficult trips to Liverpool and Aston Villa, the pressure was on to win the next three matches – away to Barnsley and home games against Derby and Everton.

The first hurdle was cleared when Barnsley were defeated 2–0. A superb curling shot from the edge of the penalty area by Bergkamp gave Arsenal the lead and Overmars, with his thirteenth goal of the season, made sure of the points. Barnsley manager Danny Wilson could not hide his admiration: 'They are so controlling and play at their own pace and will. I've been trying for 20 years to get through that back five. They just get better and better.'

The scene then moved to Highbury on the following Wednesday when Derby were the visitors. With the title so close, there was real tension in the air for the first time as the home crowd urged the team on. When the Gunners were awarded a first-half penalty for a foul on Anelka it seemed as though the breakthrough was about to be made, but when Bergkamp's spot-kick was saved it looked like it would not be Arsenal's night after all. When Bergkamp hobbled off with a hamstring injury that would put him out of the rest of the Premiership campaign – and possibly the Cup final – it looked like the dream was about to turn into a nightmare. But Arsenal battled on and took the lead when Petit's drive found the net from 20 yards out. With just a one-goal lead, the second half was extremely tense, but the Gunners held on comfortably to set up the possibility of winning the championship when they played Everton at home just four days later.

Arsène Wenger was optimistic believing that 'if we play well on Sunday the title is ours. But it will still be difficult and we have to stay focused.' The great blot on the landscape, however, was the injury to Dennis Bergkamp and it posed two questions: would the team manage to win such crucial games without their Dutch maestro, and would the now-fit Ian Wright come back into the team for the final run-in?

Expectations were sky-high around Highbury before Arsenal took on Everton. The Gunners needed just three points to clinch the championship, and they were overwhelming favourites to win the game. But, following Bolton's win the previous day, Everton were now in the relegation zone and desperate for points; they would certainly not want to make it easy for their opponents.

The roads around the ground were full of supporters well before kick-off, and when the team coach arrived the players were greeted by a cheering mass of people who had waited there to greet them. The players and management had made much of the fact that they would treat this game like any other, but they must have seen what it meant to the fans as soon as they turned into Avenell Road.

As expected, Ian Wright was consigned to the bench while Christopher Wreh started the game alongside Nicolas Anelka. Behind them would be the increasingly outstanding pairing of Vieira and Petit, along with the power and pace on the wings of Parlour and Overmars. And at the back was a defence that had conceded only two goals in their last 13 league games. Surely such a powerful, skilful and in-form team could not fail to beat a team struggling against relegation?

The team took to the field to a roar befitting a crowd of 38,269 who had gathered to see their team win the championship at Highbury for the first time in 45 years. As the teams kicked off, the sun emerged from behind the clouds and Arsenal powered forward, determined to win the championship in style. In the opening moments Arsenal's intentions were clear as a sweeping move from the edge of David Seaman's penalty area ended in a Christopher Wreh shot being well saved by Myrhe in the Everton goal. And then, after just six minutes, the breakthrough was made. Following a push on Ray Parlour near the right-hand corner flag, Petit swung the free-kick towards the far post where Bilic, under pressure from Tony Adams, headed the ball into his own net. From that moment on the Gunners were in complete control and it was only a matter of time before they added to their lead. Winterburn fed Anelka on the left edge of the penalty box and his cross went just wide, then a Parlour header was well saved by Myrhe and only the goalkeeper's alertness in coming quickly off his line prevented Anelka, Wreh and Dixon from scoring.

As Arsenal's control grew greater, so Everton's frustration increased and in the twenty-eighth minute, Petit was floored by the elbow of O'Kane. The Frenchman lay prostrate on the ground, but play continued and Anelka took the ball from Beagrie and fed Overmars just inside his own half. The Dutch winger ran at the back-pedalling Dave Watson until he reached the edge of the Everton penalty area where his cross shot was only half stopped by the goalkeeper and the ball slowly rolled into the net. Within moments Arsenal nearly scored the third as Anelka took the ball to the right edge of the six-yard box and squared to Vieira who had the goal at his mercy. Unfortunately Vieira blazed the ball over the bar, but his smile showed how confident and relaxed the team were – nothing was going to stop them now. Before half-time, however, the game was marred when the barely recovered Petit found himself on the end of a two-footed challenge by Hutchinson which left him with a huge gash down his leg. Petit threw his shin pads off in anger as he left the field to be replaced by David Platt. As the Frenchman said afterwards: 'I thought he had broken my leg. I feared the worst . . . I was furious with the referee. He should have sent off John O'Kane in the first half for elbowing me. Then he did nothing when Hutchinson caught me.'

Fortunately X-rays showed that there was no damage to the bone.

Everton manager Howard Kendall desperately tried to change the game around at half-time as he introduced three substitutes, but after 12 minutes of the second half the game was all over. Again receiving the ball from Anelka, Overmars ran at Watson from the halfway line once more and again his cross shot found the net. It was 3–0, surely now the game was all over and the championship was returning to Highbury? Arsène Wenger took the chance to reward two of his senior players for their contributions as he brought on Ian Wright and Steve Bould to roars from the crowd as they replaced Anelka and Wreh. And so Arsenal looked to play out the remaining time against a side that had barely threatened to score at any time in the match. The final *coup de grâce*, however, was still to come. As the game entered its final minute, from just inside his opponent's half, Steve Bould lobbed the ball over the Everton defence to the on-rushing Tony Adams. The crowd held its breath as their captain and inspirational leader found himself through on goal. Could he crown this magnificent afternoon? They were not to be disappointed as Adams coolly chested the ball down and unleashed a crashing half-volley that gave the goalkeeper no chance as it rocketed into the net. Even Dennis Bergkamp would have been proud of such a finish. As the goalscorer held out his arms and milked the acclaim, the crowd cheered and danced as they realised that the championship was theirs. And as the final whistle was blown, the Arsenal players embraced each other and raised their fists in salute to their adoring fans. Moments later, Tony Adams lifted the Premiership trophy aloft.

There was no doubt that the captain was the hero of the day and Arsène Wenger was quick to pay tribute to him: 'Since January we have seen the real Tony Adams. It was the turning point of his season and he has led by example ever since. He has got stronger and stronger, better and better. The closer we got, the more determined Tony Adams became. How fantastic for him that he should get that last goal. It was a superb effort.'

The man himself was determined to savour every moment of his third championship triumph: 'I can't remember the last two because I was drinking then, so I'll savour every minute of this one.'

The celebrations around Highbury would go on long into the night for the championship was won. Contrary to what Alex Ferguson had predicted, the Gunners had won ten games on the trot to take the title and Arsenal were now only one game away from an historic second double.

THE MATCH

Having won the championship in such style, the players were bound to suffer some reaction when they played out the final two games of their league season. Three days after their title celebrations, a team mainly made up of squad players went to Anfield and were beaten 4–0. The following Sunday the first-team players returned but were also beaten, this time by the only goal at Villa Park.

As the league season finished and Cup final week began, the big question was: 'would Dennis Bergkamp be fit to play?'. Arsène Wenger had been playing down his chances ever since the Dutchman had been injured against Derby but, as the big day approached, the noises coming from Highbury became more and more optimistic. By Thursday night when Bergkamp picked up the Football Writers' Player of the Year award, it looked as though he would be fit after all. He was obviously delighted: 'Just to be in with a chance of playing in the final is a huge bonus for me after all the problems I've had with the hamstring.'

His manager was also very happy to see his top striker fit: 'It looks good for Dennis. I will leave the decision up to him but the only thing I can see which will stop him playing is if he is not free about it in his own mind.'

Just 24 hours later, however, the Dutchman's dream was over as he limped out of a training session and out of the Cup final. He was obviously heartbroken: 'On Thursday I was so happy while I still thought I had a chance of making the final, but I have to admit that I was always thinking about the injury during training . . . It's so hard to miss the most important match of the season.'

This gave Arsène Wenger the problem of whether or not to start the game with Ian Wright, who had played in the Gunners' last two league games. In the event he chose to keep faith with the team that had won the championship against Everton and kept Christopher Wreh in the team with Wright on the bench.

The Newcastle team that stood between Arsenal and their second double had had a disappointing season battling against relegation, but there was little doubt that they had the players who could cause Arsenal problems on their day. Most notably, they had Alan Shearer, England captain and almost certainly the top centre-forward in the country. Shearer had been involved in much controversy in the days before the final after appearing to have kicked an opposing player in the face, but there was little doubt that he posed the major threat to the Arsenal goal. There were top players throughout the Newcastle team, however, including England internationals such as Stuart Pearce, Robert Lee and David Batty, and big-money signings like Pistone, Dabizas, Speed and Andersson.

As the two teams walked out of the tunnel and onto the Wembley turf the pitchside temperature was over 90°F as the sun shone down on the twin towers. With red and white at one end and black and white at the other, the stadium was a sea of colour and noise as the players prepared for the kick-off. For the Newcastle players this was a chance to redeem themselves after a poor season, for the men in red it was a chance to win the double and make history.

It was Newcastle who got the game under way, but it was the pace of Overmars and Anelka that first caught the eye as they caused consternation in the opposing defence. It was not until the quarter of an hour mark, however, that the first real attempt on goal came after an Overmars corner found Anelka's head, but the young Frenchman could only glance the ball wide of the far post. This appeared to spur the Arsenal players on and they proceeded to take control of the game. Minutes later they created the best chance of the game so far. After playing the ball patiently around in defence, Vieira suddenly found himself in space. The tall Frenchman found

Parlour who played it out to Dixon on the right-wing. Dixon returned the ball and as Parlour ran into the penalty area he reached the goal-line and crossed the ball to Anelka who was standing in front of an almost empty goal. Unfortunately, Anelka headed over the bar and Arsenal had missed an easy chance to take the lead.

Having missed such a good chance, many teams might have let their heads drop, but Arsenal became even more determined and just three minutes later they took the lead. As the game reached the midway point of the first half, Petit, from just inside the Newcastle half, lobbed the ball over the Newcastle defence and Marc Overmars was quickly off the mark and just managed to get himself ahead of the floundering Pistone. As the ball bounced in front of him he managed to nod the ball forward and, as the goalkeeper ran towards him, put the ball through the advancing Given's legs and into the net. Overmars ran towards the Arsenal supporters massed behind the goal and sank to his knees in celebration. The double was drawing nearer.

While Newcastle struggled to make any impact on the game, with only long-range shots from Ketsbaia giving Seaman anything to do at all, the rest of the first half saw further evidence of how dangerous the pace of Overmars and Anelka was proving. On the half hour, Anelka showed tremendous speed as he beat the Newcastle defence to the ball before shooting over the bar from the corner of the penalty area, while Overmars, a minute before the break, caused panic in the opposing defence as he advanced into the penalty area with defenders back-pedalling frantically, before pulling the ball back to Parlour who should have done better than blast the ball over from the corner of the box.

After that, the only thing of note to happen in the first half came as the game entered injury time. A Newcastle free-kick was headed towards touch, but as Tony Adams cleared the ball, he was sent tumbling to the ground by a late challenge from Shearer. The yellow card that referee Paul Durkin showed to the England centre-forward seemed to sum up Newcastle's first-half display.

The second half began with a flurry of yellow cards as Nigel Winterburn joined Newcastle's Barton and Dabizas in the book. There was little doubt that Newcastle had come out in a more determined mood, but at the start of the second period they were still unable to trouble the Gunners defence. As the game entered the last 30 minutes, however, Newcastle enjoyed a spell of dominance that could have seen them right back in the game again. On 62 minutes, Newcastle's pressure saw Tony Adams concede a free-kick on the left edge of the penalty area, and when the ball was floated into the box by Lee, Dabizas rose at the far post and headed onto the top of the bar. Arsène Wenger responded by replacing the fading Wreh with David Platt, but within two minutes Newcastle should have grabbed an equaliser.

There seemed little danger when the ball was passed to Martin Keown on the edge of his own area, but the normally dependable defender slipped on the ball and left Alan Shearer through on goal. With the goal at his mercy, Shearer's shot beat David Seaman, but the ball rebounded off the inside of the post to safety. It was not to be Newcastle's day.

The close shave at the other end seemed to reinvigorate the champions as they surged forward once more. A strong run from Winterburn ended with his attempted chip clearing the crossbar before, on 68 minutes, Nicolas Anelka made his mark. When Ray Parlour played the ball through, the young Frenchman had appeared to be offside, but television replays showed that the linesman was correct to keep his flag down. Running on to the ball, Anelka still had much to do, but he chested the ball down, ran towards goal and beat the goalkeeper with a cross shot that rifled into the corner of the net. Just like Jack Lambert after he had given Arsenal a 2–0 lead in the Cup final 68 years earlier, Anelka turned to find that his team-mates were all in the other half of the field, unable to keep up with his lightning pace, but as he ran back he was soon embraced by his colleagues who now had the double firmly in their sights.

Almost immediately from the restart, Ray Parlour threatened to make it 3–0 as he seemed to run through the entire Newcastle defence before being brought down on the edge of the penalty area by Howey, who was fortunate to receive only a yellow card. From the resulting free-kick Petit curled the ball just wide of target.

Before the final whistle there would be further chances for both teams to score. Parlour hit the outside of the post and Overmars saw a brilliant half-volley from 50 yards saved by Given, while at the other end Speed flashed a shot narrowly wide and Shearer looked set to make up for his earlier miss until he was denied by a remarkable saving tackle by Winterburn. But Arsenal never looked likely to lose a two-goal lead. As the game entered injury time, Gilles Grimandi stood on the touchline, ready to come on, but he was to be disappointed as the referee blew the final whistle before he had the chance.

The double double had been achieved as Arsenal became the first club to have two double-winning teams from different eras. After the players had congratulated each other and saluted their ecstatic fans, Tony Adams went up to collect the Cup from the Duchess of Kent. As he received the trophy he seemed to pause for a moment, determined to let himself take everything in, before holding it triumphantly aloft to the cheers of the exultant Gunners fans. As the Cup was passed along the line for each player to raise, the supporters cheered each of their heroes, but they reserved the biggest roar for Dennis Bergkamp, the man who had done so much to help the team achieve their amazing feat, yet who had been cruelly forced to miss the two biggest games of the season. The fact that Arsenal had been without their most influential player for so many crucial games only reinforced the quality of the squad that Arsène Wenger had assembled.

For the two goalscorers it was a dream come true. Despite coming from Holland, Marc Overmars appreciated what an FA Cup win meant: 'This is all so amazing, especially to win so much in my first year. It's special to win the FA Cup because it has this tradition as the oldest knockout tournament in the world.'

While Nicolas Anelka was equally enthusiastic as he talked about his crucial goal, 'I was on the same line as the Newcastle defender for the goal. I saw Ray Parlour line up the pass and moved. I was worried about being offside but I'm delighted and very excited to get a goal at Wembley.'

And it wasn't just the newer members of the team that were excited by what they had achieved. Despite having already won two championships, an FA Cup, a League Cup and the Cup-Winners' Cup at Highbury, Lee Dixon still thought that this was their greatest achievement. 'This just surpasses anything that we've done in the past. Winning the league was brilliant but winning them both together is fantastic.'

Arsène Wenger admitted that not only had it been difficult to raise the players again after their championship triumph but the pressure had also been enormous: 'Our concentration was missing in the last week. I was afraid before the game that we would not get it back, but that didn't happen. I also knew that coming here as champions and not winning the Cup would be terrible because we might not achieve the double again.' But in the event his tactics had been spot on: 'I thought we could beat their offside trap and that is how we got the two goals.'

Wenger's opposite number, Kenny Dalglish, was gracious in defeat saying 'full credit to Arsenal. They are a very impressive side, full of good players. They deserved to win the double.'

And so ended a quite remarkable season. As 1998 began, Arsenal found themselves apparently out of the title race and with no form to suggest that they could mount a challenge in any of the other competitions. Rumours of discontent in the dressing-room were rife and disgruntled supporters were questioning the ability of the manager and the players. And yet, slowly and surely, it all started to come right and from the moment Marc Overmars scored his crucial goal at Old Trafford to open up the title race they never wavered. In 1971 the team had come from behind with nine wins in a row to win the league and had battled their way through in the FA Cup needing three replays to reach Wembley. In 1998 it had taken ten successive victories in the league and three Cup replays, including two penalty shoot-outs. In the end it had all climaxed in one glorious fortnight when Arsenal achieved what no other club had managed. Manchester United had won two doubles, but they were only two years apart with the same manager and much the same team. Arsenal, however, became the first club to have two completely different double-winning teams from two different eras. The likes of Mee, Wilson, McLintock, Graham, George and the rest of the first double-winning squad would now be joined in the Highbury Hall of Fame by Wenger, Seaman, Adams, Vieira, Bergkamp and the rest.

All this had been achieved less than two years after the club had been plunged into chaos with four managers in two months. Thanks to Arsène Wenger it had all been turned around again and the glory days had returned to Highbury. Older players that many thought had seen their best days had become rejuvenated, while the new players that the manager had brought in had added skill, pace and extra determination. The second double in Arsenal's history had been won, history had been made and Arsène Wenger's French Revolution was complete. *Le double double – c'est magnifique!*

FINAL SCORE

Arsenal	2	Newcastle United	0

Overmars	23 mins
Anelka	68 mins
Attendance:	79,183

Arsenal:	Seaman, Dixon, Keown, Adams, Winterburn, Vieira, Parlour, Petit, Overmars, Anelka, Wreh (Platt)
Newcastle:	Given, Pistone, Dabizas, Howey, Barton (Watson), Pearce (Andersson), Lee, Batty, Speed, Ketsbaia (Barnes), Shearer

14

THE PRETTIEST WIFE

FA Premiership
Manchester United v Arsenal
Wednesday, 8 May 2002

The 'Double' triumph of 1998 had been meant to herald a new era of Arsenal supremacy. Arsène Wenger had triumphed in only his first full season and it seemed as though the team that he had constructed could only get better. And yet, over the following three seasons, despite promising much, the Arsenal team failed to add a single piece of silverware to the Highbury trophy cabinet. The double was almost retained the following season, but the FA Cup was lost in an epic semi-final clash with Manchester United and the Premiership was conceded on the last day to the same team. The 2000 UEFA Cup final was lost on penalties, while the 2001 FA Cup final saw Wenger's team dominate for 80 minutes yet lose 2–1 as two late Michael Owen strikes won the cup for Liverpool.

Now questions were being asked of the manager and the players: Were they happy to be perennial runners-up, did they just lack the bottle to win, or were the foreign players in the side insufficiently motivated? During the summer of 2001 there were rumblings of discontent from within the club as the manager's new contract remained unsigned and stories linked some of Arsenal's top players with moves away. At this stage, success seemed further away than it had done at any stage since Tony Adams had lifted the Premiership trophy and the FA Cup back in 1998.

And yet, the 2001–02 season saw Arsenal rediscover the character and unity that had seen them triumph four years earlier. Despite many hurdles that were put in their way, Arsène Wenger's team slowly improved over the course of the campaign before hitting a run of form that would even eclipse their finish of 1998, and at the end of it all, they found themselves with the chance of clinching a third double at the home of the team that had dominated the Premiership for the previous three seasons. Having been humiliated at Old Trafford a year earlier, everyone at Arsenal was determined to win the title at the home of the reigning champions, but Manchester United were equally keen to avoid the prospect of their main challengers celebrating the championship on their own ground.

Manchester United v Arsenal was the clash of the titans that the whole country was waiting to see. Could United re-establish their superiority and create doubt in the Arsenal camp, or could the Gunners achieve a hugely symbolic victory that would not only bring the Premiership trophy back to Highbury, but also demonstrate to the rest of English football that they were now the team to be feared?

THE PLAYERS

Despite their advancing years, several members of George Graham's legendary defence still remained at Highbury. The likes of Tony Adams and Lee Dixon were now seeing their influence waning as injuries cut their appearances to a fraction of those that they had previously enjoyed, but Martin Keown and David Seaman were still regular members of the team. To complement these experienced defenders, manager Arsène Wenger had added talented players with pace and strength. At right-back was Lauren, a Cameroonian international who had been signed from Spanish side Real Mallorca in the summer of 2000. Lauren had spent his first season in England playing in midfield, but at the start of the 2001–02 season he was moved into the full-back role where he gradually added defensive strength to his ability to get forward and help his front men. On the left-hand side was the one player to have made the breakthrough from the Gunners' youth system during Arsène Wenger's time at the club. Ashley Cole had broken into the first team near the end of 2000 and had immediately looked at home in both the Premiership and the Champions League. Like Lauren he had initially been better going forward than in defending, but he was still good enough to quickly establish himself in the England side and soon became an integral part of the Arsenal defence.

After Arsenal's Cup final defeat at the end of the 2000–01 campaign, it became clear that new blood was needed in the heart of their defence. Adams and Keown were still fine players, but as a pairing they were increasingly susceptible to the pace of younger and quicker opponents like Michael Owen, while they were both experiencing injuries on a regular basis. A top-class international defender was needed and several names were bandied around the media, but in the end, the man that Arsène Wenger succeeded in signing came as a huge shock to the football world. Sol Campbell was captain of arch rivals Tottenham Hotspur and had been the rock at the heart of the Spurs defence for the previous eight seasons. But at the end of the 2000–01 season Campbell's contract ran out and he became available on a free transfer. The likes of Inter Milan and Barcelona courted the England defender, but in the end he opted bravely to make the short move across north London to Highbury. When Campbell was paraded by Arsène Wenger in front of the assembled media in the summer of 2001, the shockwaves reverberated throughout English football and Arsenal's new signing found himself subject to all kinds of threats and abuse from his former supporters. But Sol Campbell had gone to Highbury in order to win trophies and he would prove to be a vital member of the team as Arsenal strove to provide him with the silverware that he yearned for.

In 1998, Patrick Vieira had been a highly promising young player in his first full season at Highbury, but by 2001 he was a World Cup and European Championship winner who was rated as one of the best midfielders in the world. Having been outstanding during the club's cup run of the previous season, Vieira had been the subject of huge speculation concerning his future during the close season. However, as the new campaign began he not only remained at the club but found himself appointed as vice captain which, with the inevitable injuries that would be suffered by Tony

Adams, meant that he would find himself leading the team for much of the term.

Of the other members of the double-winning midfield quartet, only Ray Parlour remained. Manu Petit and Marc Overmars had left a year earlier, but Petit had yet to be properly replaced, leaving the likes of Parlour, Grimandi and Lauren taking turns to partner Vieira in the middle. It was hoped that new signing Giovanni Van Bronckhorst, a Dutch international from Glasgow Rangers, would prove to be a more permanent replacement. On the left-hand side, however, Overmars' absence was no longer being felt thanks to the quality of the man who had replaced him – Robert Pires. Pires had arrived in the summer of 2000 from Marseilles, but had initially struggled to cope with life in the Premiership, much as the likes of Overmars and Bergkamp had done before him, but as he came towards the end of his first season at Arsenal he began to show the skills and finishing power that he possessed and gave a taste of what he would produce in his second season. Completing the midfield was Freddie Ljungberg from Sweden who had joined the club in the autumn of 1998. The hard-running, strong-tackling Swede with the red stripe in his hair had also taken a year or so to settle in, but was beginning to show his worth with his trademark runs into the penalty area, and was about to make a huge impact on the Premiership.

The new goalscoring sensation at Highbury was Thierry Henry. Henry had arrived from Juventus at a cost of £10 million as a French international winger, but had been transformed by Arsène Wenger into a world-class centre-forward. His pace, movement and skill on the ball made Henry feared by Premiership defences throughout Europe. His 17 goals scored in his first two Premiership seasons made him an automatic choice in the Arsenal attack, but he now had three players vying to partner him in attack. At £11 million, Sylvain Wiltord was Arsenal's record signing. Another French international, he had arrived during the early stages of the previous season and had shown himself to be a hard-working and pacy forward and had scored several important goals en route to the Cup final against Liverpool. In addition, Dennis Bergkamp remained at the club and was still capable of showing breathtaking skill and scoring spectacular goals, but with only nine Premiership goals in his previous two seasons he appeared to have lost the ability to shine on a consistent basis. In this respect he was similar to Nigeria's Kanu who had arrived shortly after the double triumph and had initially thrilled the Highbury crowd with his outrageous ball skills and close control, but with only three league goals in 2000–01 had lost much of his original impact. With such a long season and with so many important games, however, all would have to make their mark if silverware was to return to the Highbury trophy cabinet.

THE BACKGROUND

The lack of a serious title challenge in the previous season had been mainly due to an appalling away record, so when Arsenal started their league campaign at Middlesbrough, it was seen as an indicator as to whether they would be able to keep up with Manchester United, who were now going for a fourth successive championship. When Middlesbrough were brushed aside 4–0, the tone was set for the rest of the season and when the Gunners travelled to Anfield two days before Christmas, they were still unbeaten on their travels. This did not mean, however, that things had gone entirely smoothly during the first half of the campaign. A home defeat to Leeds just three days after the win at the Riverside Stadium, points dropped against Bolton and Blackburn at Highbury, and a catastrophic 4–2 loss at home to Charlton meant that Arsenal were back in fifth position in the middle of November. However, a 3–1 win over Manchester United and an amazing comeback from two goals down to beat Aston Villa, coupled with an impressive demolition of Juventus in the Champions League raised Highbury spirits and saw Arsenal apparently poised to challenge both at home and in Europe.

Then there was a setback as Newcastle visited north London. The Tynesiders had been in good form and the winners of the match were set to go to the top of the table, but Arsenal expected to pick up all three points nonetheless. An early goal from Robert Pires was just reward for their early domination, and seemed to set Arsenal on the road to victory, but the sending off of Ray Parlour changed the course of the game as Newcastle grabbed an equaliser in the second half before taking the lead with a controversial penalty and then making it 3–1 in injury time. The sense of injustice around Highbury at some of referee Graham Poll's decisions was exemplified by Thierry Henry's castigation of the referee at the end. Newcastle were now top of the table but their manager Bobby Robson was not happy at the Gunners' reaction and famously complained that 'some people around here have to learn how to lose'. Fortunately, they never did.

Five days later came the trip to second-placed Liverpool where Arsenal had not won since 1992. With the Gunners needing to bounce back with a win after the Newcastle defeat, their hopes received an early setback with yet another controversial sending off as Van Bronckhorst was shown a second yellow card for alleged diving. At this point, however, Arsenal showed the sort of spirit that had been missing on their travels in previous years and clawed their way back into the game. A penalty from Henry and a goal from Ljungberg after brilliant work by Pires early in the second half put the ten men into a two-goal lead which was enough to see them hold out for a 2–1 win. Such a triumph of determination over adversity sent spirits soaring in the Arsenal camp and Arsène Wenger later described it as a crucial moment in the season: 'That was the turning point for us – winning there with ten men convinced me we would win the championship.'

By mid February, Arsenal were in the middle of an injury crisis that would have broken most teams. Third-choice goalkeeper Stuart Taylor had been called up to play a dozen games in place of the injured Wright and Seaman; defenders Adams, Keown, Upson, Dixon and Cole were all out; Freddie Ljungberg had been missing for several weeks; and both Lauren and Kanu were away in the African Nations Championship. And yet, despite this, they not only maintained their unbeaten run since December, but they began to run into irresistible form. On 23 February, Fulham were thrashed 4–1, a win that was marred only by yet another injury as Giovanni Van Bronckhorst was sidelined for the rest of the season, and four days later in the Champions League, the Germans of Bayer Leverkusen were beaten by the same scoreline after an Arsenal performance that was simply irresistible. With Bergkamp and Pires pulling the strings and Henry and Wiltord combining pace with finishing power it would have been hard for any team to live with them.

It was just as well that the Gunners were hitting form because their next game was a trip away to the last team to beat them. Newcastle and Arsenal were just tucked in behind Manchester United in the Premiership table and the team that came out on top in their meeting would be well placed for the final championship run-in. Arsène Wenger was once again without key players as Ray Parlour and Thierry Henry joined the injury list, but he was still confident, saying, 'although I would say that our squad is reduced, I will not say that we are weakened because we have a big squad here at Arsenal and we will need it. The spirit in the squad is so strong and they are so determined that I believe that these guys can achieve anything.' In the previous few games, Dennis Bergkamp had shown glimpses of a return to his best form, but at St James' Park he blew Newcastle away with a goal that possibly surpassed any that he had scored before. Receiving the ball on the edge of the Newcastle penalty area with his back to goal, Bergkamp flicked it to the right of the defender standing behind him while running around the defenders left, before stroking the ball past the goalkeeper and into the corner of the net. Just before half-time the lead was doubled as Bergkamp curled a free-kick onto the head of Sol Campbell who powered the ball into the goal. Newcastle were completely unable to come back from that and Arsenal gained a crucial three points on the back of a championship-winning performance.

With the team now into the FA Cup quarter-finals following wins over Watford, Liverpool and Gillingham, well placed in their second-round Champions League group and winning consistently in the Premiership, there was now the very real possibility of an amazing treble, but such hopes were about to be dashed. Defeat at home to Deportivo La Coruna and a lacklustre loss in Turin to Juventus put Arsenal out of the Champions League and put doubt into Highbury minds for the first time since Christmas. It was reported that Manchester United's players had drawn encouragement from Arsenal's European exit, believing that it would affect their morale and damage their title chances. The Gunners, however, had little time to dwell on their defeat as their next game was an FA Cup replay with Newcastle that could result in them going out of two competitions in the space of four days.

Fortunately Arsenal showed the sort of determination that had propelled them to the upper reaches of the Premiership as they simply blew Newcastle away with early Pires and Bergkamp goals. A Sol Campbell header made it 3–0 at the start of the second half and a semi-final place was safely in the bag. Later that afternoon came more good news as Manchester United were beaten at home by Middlesbrough. The loss of three vital points left United manager Alex Ferguson conceding that 'we need Arsenal and Liverpool to make mistakes now, it's out of our hands and I would say that Arsenal are big strong favourites.' It was only March, and there were many more games to be played, but Arsène Wenger responded with complete confidence as he spoke of a '100 per cent guarantee' that the title would go to Highbury. And yet, amidst all this good news came a crushing blow as Robert Pires, whose performances had illuminated the English season to such an extent that he would go on to be named Footballer of the Year, was ruled out for the rest of the season with a knee injury picked up against Newcastle. With such vital games to come, would Arsenal survive without their most influential player? What they needed now was another player to fill the gap that Pires had left, and fortunately they had just that man coming back into the team after his own injury.

As the championship race entered its final stages there were still three teams in the running. Arsenal knew that if they won all their games they would be champions, but any slip-ups would let in Manchester United and Liverpool who were close behind, and as each of the three teams continued to win they all knew that any dropped points could prove crucial. Wenger, however, had no doubt that the Premiership was headed back to Highbury: 'What makes me so confident about winning the title is we have the spirit and mental strength. No matter who comes in plays with the same determination, and we have the talent and pace.'

From 1–24 April, Arsenal played four vital Premiership matches and they won them all, mainly due to the form of Freddie Ljungberg. The home games against Tottenham, Ipswich and West Ham were particularly tight and nervous affairs, but each time it was Freddie who popped up in the penalty box to break the deadlock and earn another vital three points. With five goals in those four games, the Swede became the new hero in the Highbury stands and he moved Arsenal to within touching distance of the 'Double'.

After a scrappy and slightly fortunate semi-final win over Middlesbrough, Arsenal now had an FA Cup final to look forward to, followed by another two league games, but on the Monday night before their trip to Cardiff they had an important Premiership match at Bolton to contend with. Having received unlikely assistance from White Hart Lane two days earlier when Tottenham beat title rivals Liverpool, the Gunners now knew that the championship was a two-horse race. The first of the two games that they would play after the Cup final was away to Manchester United so although they were two points clear of United with a game in hand, any slip-ups at the Reebok Stadium would mean they had to gain a result at Old Trafford to stay in charge of their own destiny.

With the Cup final just five days away, Sol Campbell and Thierry Henry were not risked, but the likes of Adams, Cole and Parlour were now back into the team so Arsène Wenger was still able to field a strong side. Also taking to the field was Brazilian midfielder Edu. Edu had arrived at Highbury in the summer of 2000 but had made little impact until scoring at Newcastle in the Cup in March. Since then he had played regularly and had used his cultured left foot to such good effect that he appeared to be solving the problem of who to partner Patrick Vieira in midfield.

First-half goals from Ljungberg (again) and Sylvain Wiltord gave Arsenal a crucial three points at Bolton that not only meant that a draw at Old Trafford would give them the title, but also gave the team and the supporters a huge boost before their trip to the Cup final at the weekend.

Arsenal's Cup final opponents were Chelsea, a strong but inconsistent side which included former Gunners Double winner Emmanuel Petit and a potent strike force in Jimmy Floyd Hasselbaink and Eidur Gudjohnsen. The Gunners had a very good recent record over Chelsea, but at the back of every Arsenal supporter's mind was the doubt that came from having finished second five times in the previous three seasons and the memory of a crushing defeat at the same venue a year earlier when victory had been just minutes away. The only changes from the team that won at Bolton were Sol Campbell and Thierry Henry returning to replace Edu and Keown.

For the second year in a row, with Wembley waiting to be rebuilt, the final was played at the Millennium Stadium in Cardiff, and although it was much cooler than the baking heat of twelve months earlier, the game again kicked off with the stadium bathed in sunlight. As so often happens on the big occasion, the first half was something of an anti-climax as each side weighed up their opponents, and there were only half chances to excite the capacity crowd. But early in the second half, Thierry Henry forced Cudicini in the Chelsea goal to save and the game seemed to open up from then on. For the next 15 minutes it was Chelsea who held the upper hand as Gudjohnsen brought a good save from Seaman and Le Saux shot wide, but with 70 minutes on the clock it was Arsenal who broke the deadlock.

Receiving the ball from Sylvain Wiltord, Ray Parlour surged towards the Chelsea penalty area. As he did so he was surrounded by a swarm of blue shirts and he looked around for support from his teammates. Realising that he was on his own, Parlour decided to go for goal himself from 25 yards out. He hit a shot that appeared to be just clearing the corner of the crossbar to the goalkeeper's left, but at the last moment the ball dipped below the woodwork and into the net for one of the best Cup final goals to have been scored for many years. Parlour clenched his fists and ran to the Gunners' fans behind the goal to celebrate. Afterwards he said, 'no one was up in support so I thought why not? Usually they go into the crowd, but today it went into the top corner.'

Arsenal were ahead as they had been at almost exactly the same time a year earlier, but this time they were not to be denied. On 79 minutes, Freddie Ljungberg picked the ball up just inside his own half and ran at the Chelsea defence. As he got to the left-hand edge of the penalty box he shrugged off the challenge of defender John Terry before curling the ball past Cudicini and into almost the same spot that Parlour had found minutes before. That made it seven goals in seven games for the Swede, and it almost certainly meant that Arsenal finally had a trophy to take back to Highbury. The new 'We love you Freddie' song rang out in celebration.

When the final whistle went, the Arsenal players needed no excuse to celebrate. Having been branded perennial losers and having suffered heart-breaking defeat at the same stadium a year earlier, victory had been achieved at last and a trophy was theirs once again. As captain Tony Adams and the man who had worn the skipper's armband for most of the season, Patrick Vieira, approached the podium together and held the FA Cup aloft, the players and supporters who had travelled to Wales from north London celebrated wildly, but they knew that the job was still only half done and it was not long before thoughts turned to Old Trafford just four days later with 'We'll win the league in Manchester' being the most loudly heard chant to emanate from the red and white end of the stadium. 'We beat Liverpool, Chelsea and Newcastle, so we deserved to win the cup,' reflected Arsène Wenger. 'Every game has been a Cup final for us but it is another final on Wednesday. We will have dinner with the family tonight but we will finish by midnight.' Goalscorer Freddie Ljungberg was also looking forward to the next game. 'We will now focus on Manchester United – we are already thinking about it. The Cup final is over for us now. You usually celebrate when you win but we can't yet.' Half of the double was now won, but the half that they yearned for most of all would have to wait another four days until Arsenal travelled to Old Trafford and attempted to take the Premiership crown away from the reigning champions.

THE MATCH

As the season had drawn to a close and Manchester United manager Alex Ferguson had realised that Arsenal were going to pose a considerable threat to his team's title chances, he had increasingly attempted to unsettle the Highbury camp by using his famous 'mind games'. Ferguson's attempts to out psyche his opponents had memorably led to Kevin Keegan losing his cool on live television as his Newcastle team surrendered a commanding lead to an ultimately successful United side in the mid-1990s, and he had continued to use this method over the years in order to get one over his rivals. Having apparently conceded the title to Arsenal in March, Ferguson then accused the Highbury camp of being 'cocky' before proclaiming, on the night that United were knocked out of Europe, that his side had been the best in the Premiership since Christmas (during that time United had been beaten twice at home in the league and been knocked out of the FA Cup while Arsenal had remained undefeated). If there was one manager who was not to be deviated by Ferguson's feeble attempts it was Arsène Wenger. When told about Ferguson's latest claim he responded by saying that 'everyone thinks they have the prettiest wife at home'. And yet still the Manchester United boss persisted as he tried to hype up the Old Trafford clash by saying that it would be the 'biggest match for ten years'. Wenger, however, would remain unmoved by such amateur psychology, as he continued to proclaim his confidence. 'A draw is enough to win it, but that isn't the best way to play at United. I want to win, and we will do it, of course, believe me.' In the end, it seemed that it was Ferguson who had come off second best when he launched an expletive-ridden tirade at a journalist on the eve of the match – it appeared that the pressure that had been exerted by Wenger and his side was beginning to tell.

All was not well in the Arsenal camp, however, as skipper Tony Adams, and first-choice forward pairing of Dennis Bergkamp and Thierry Henry all failed to recover from their Cup final exertions in time to be in the starting line up. This meant that Martin Keown partnered Sol Campbell in defence, Edu came in to the midfield and Kanu played up front with Sylvain Wiltord. But there was also some interesting team news from the home dressing-room where it emerged that midfielder Nicky Butt was injured and that their top goalscorer, Ruud van Nistelrooy, had been left on the bench, to be replaced by new signing Diego Forlan.

The two teams took to the field in front of a packed and expectant Old Trafford crowd. The home fans were hoping for a repeat of the previous seasons 6–1 mauling of the Gunners that would show that they were still the better team and ensure that the title race went down to the final weekend. The visitors, however, had the sort of confidence that comes from seeing your team win their last eleven Premiership games in a row. Such confidence was perfectly exemplified by the banner unfurled by Arsenal supporters which read 'Old Trafford Champions' Section'. The next 90 minutes would decide whether that confidence was misplaced or justified.

With less than two minutes on the clock, it was Arsenal in their changed kit of gold shirts, who came close to making the perfect start. The ball was won in the air by Kanu and found its way to Ray Parlour on the right wing. Parlour crossed the ball first time into the penalty area where Wiltord turned and hit a shot that was headed to the top corner of the net before it deflected off United defender Laurent Blanc and out for a corner.

The home side responded with a Paul Scholes shot being deflected away for a corner and a Wes Brown header just clearing the bar, but despite having the majority of the play, United failed to create any clear chances. They soon became frustrated by the strength of the Arsenal defence and began to resort to a different tactic. First Keane and Scholes lunged at Parlour as he waltzed through the midfield. Scholes was then booked for a repeat performance on Edu, while Phil Neville received a yellow card for a challenge on Wiltord that was ferocious enough to have the Arsenal manager leaping from the bench to protest. Roy Keane then made it three United cautions in six minutes when he went in on Vieira with his boot dangerously high. And yet the Arsenal defence remained undaunted by their opponents' aggression. Campbell and Keown were resolute in the middle while Ashley Cole was showing that he was as good defending as he was going forward. And in front of the defenders, the midfield of Parlour, Edu, Vieira and Ljungberg worked tirelessly to keep the ball away from David Seaman and the Arsenal goal. Just before the interval, Edu became the first Arsenal man in referee Paul Durkin's book after one foul too many, but as the half-time whistle blew, Arsenal knew that the job was nearly done and that 45 minutes of the same would see the Premiership trophy won once more.

United's possession of the ball increased as the second half began, but their goalscoring chances were still few and far between. Veron steered a Forlan cross straight into the arms of David Seaman, but that was the only threat to the Arsenal goal in those early stages. At the other end, meanwhile, the visitors were starting to threaten a goal of their own. The warning came when goalkeeper Barthez cleared straight to Wiltord near the edge of the penalty area. Fortunately for Barthez, he was saved by a crucial

Wes Brown tackle as the Arsenal forward bore down on goal. Next time, however, he would not be so lucky.

With 57 minutes on the clock, United tried once more to build an attack against the massed ranks of gold shirts that were arrayed in front of them. The home defenders passed the ball between themselves as they waited for an elusive chink to appear in the Gunners' armour. And yet they had to be wary of the Arsenal counter attack that would pounce on any error that they might make. All of a sudden that mistake was made as Mikael Silvestre lost the ball to Parlour with his team-mates all in front of him. Before he could react, the ball found Wiltord who played the ball into the path of yet another penetrating Ljungberg run that saw him heading for the edge of the penalty area. With Laurent Blanc at his shoulder, it seemed that the Swede would have to run away from the goal, but he turned and muscled his way past his aging opponent to suddenly find himself with a clear view of the target. Ljungberg, in sight of yet another crucial goal, quickly shot low towards the far post, but this time he was denied by the diving Barthez who plunged to his right and clawed the ball away. The goalkeeper's efforts were in vain, however, as Wiltord followed up the rebound and fired the ball home with his left foot.

In the Old Trafford visitors' section and all across north London, pandemonium broke out. Wiltord sank to his knees as Kanu leapt over his head in delight. It was Sylvain Wiltord's 100th appearance in an Arsenal shirt and what a way to mark that anniversary as he scored one of the most memorable goals in the club's history. Freddie Ljungberg, who just days earlier had spoken of his desperation to win trophies at Highbury, clenched his fists in celebration in front of the Arsenal fans, for they now had one hand on the Premiership trophy.

Alex Ferguson's immediate response was to bring on his top goalscorer Ruud van Nistelrooy in place of the ineffectual Veron, but he was to have no greater impact than the departed Argentinian. Both he and Giggs threw themselves over as they attempted to gain the sort of penalty decision that they were used to getting in their favour at Old Trafford, but referee Durkin remained unmoved and waved play on. On 68 minutes, the misfiring Forlan made way for Quinton Fortune, but still the

United attacks came to nothing. Indeed, as the game drew to a close it was Arsenal who threatened to score the second goal as Kanu struck narrowly wide from twenty yards out.

With the game in its final minute, Arsène Wenger made a poignant substitution as he brought on Lee Dixon for Kanu. Having been born in Manchester and been a childhood City fan, the moment must have been extra special for the veteran of the 1989 Anfield triumph as well as many others, who was set to announce his retirement from the game just days later – what better way to go out than by clinching the Premiership at Old Trafford?

And moments later that was exactly what Dixon and his Arsenal team-mates did as the referee blew time on the match and on Manchester United's three-year-long reign as champions. The title was now Arsenal's and the players ran towards what really was now the Old Trafford Champions' Section to celebrate with their supporters. They sang and they danced as they produced a banner proclaiming that they were the 2002 Premiership champions and showed it off to all those jubilant fans that were so glad that they had made the journey.

Arsène Wenger was justifiably buoyant. 'Once again tonight, we had to show great character. We were solid as a rock in the first half and they never really threatened us. We kept our discipline and our nerve on the night – there was a lot of provocation, but we kept our nerve. To win the championship at United and bring the title back home to Highbury is fantastic. We wanted tonight to be a shift in power.' Freddie Ljungberg, who had done so much to keep Arsenal in the title race over the previous month was delighted. 'I've been waiting three years for this – it's a sweet moment.' Lee Dixon concluded that the team surpassed all the others that he had played with over the years. 'It's been an outstanding season. It's brilliant to be a part of this squad – it's the best I've played with, with depth in every position.'

The only thing missing on such an incredible evening was the Premiership trophy itself. Unlike that night at Anfield thirteen years earlier, Tony Adams would not lift the championship trophy in front of its former holders – that would have to wait until three days later in front of 38,000 Arsenal fans at Highbury following the Gunners 4–3 last-day victory over Everton. That subsequent win meant that Arsenal had scored in every game over the season and set a new Premiership record of 13 consecutive victories. The win at Old Trafford had seen Arsenal become the first team since 1889 to go through an entire league season without an away defeat and equalled the top division record of eight consecutive away league wins. Added to that, Tony Adams became the first man to captain championship-winning teams in three different decades, and Arsenal became the first club to win the double in two different centuries.

As Tony Adams lifted the Premiership trophy above his head in front of the North Bank, the whole of Highbury roared in appreciation of a remarkable season where so many records had been broken and so many obstacles had been overcome. Battling wins against the likes of Liverpool, Newcastle and Chelsea had seen the FA Cup head back to Highbury, while victories at places like Anfield, Villa Park and St James' Park had contributed to a victorious league campaign. In all, 60 games had been played in a season that had culminated in such success, but in the end it had all come down to one game at Old Trafford where, exactly 31 years to the day that Arsenal's first double had been won, the club's third double was achieved. Up against a team that had humiliated them 6–1 just over a year earlier, a team that had pushed them into second place over the previous three seasons, a team that had spent nearly £50 million on two new players at the start of the campaign, and knowing that defeat would put them under almost intolerable pressure going into their final game, the Arsenal team had shown the spirit and the character that had served them so well over the entire season and had not only won the Premiership but had sent out a statement. There is no doubt that the Manchester United management and players were desperate to beat what they saw as the cocky upstart pretenders from London, but in the end there was nothing that they could do in the face of a supremely slick, solid and professional performance. Arsenal had shown that their league triumph had been no fluke, they had gone to the home of the reigning champions and beaten them fair and square, just as they had at Highbury earlier in the season.

The defeat of Manchester United not only sealed a glorious

double. Having won the 1971 championship at White Hart Lane and the 1989 title at Anfield, Arsenal had completed an amazing trio of championship-winning games at the homes of their three greatest rivals, an achievement that made them unique amongst English clubs. The win at Old Trafford was certainly an occasion to rank with those previous triumphs and, coming as it did after so many near misses and with so many questions being asked about the character of those within the club, it may even have surpassed them. Having outplayed Manchester United and the rest of the Premiership over the course of the season they had added the proof of their superiority in a one-off match to dispel any doubts as to where the power in the English game now resided. Arsenal were the champions and Arsène Wenger had his second double in five years. There was now no doubt which manager had the prettiest wife at home.

FINAL SCORE

Manchester United	0	Arsenal	1
		Wiltord 57	
Attendance:	67,580		

Manchester United: Barthez, P. Neville, Brown, Blanc, Silvestre, Veron (Van Nistelrooy), Keane, Scholes, Giggs, Forlan, Solksjaer

Arsenal: Seaman, Lauren, Keown, Campbell, Cole, Parlour, Edu, Vieira, Ljungberg, Wiltord, Kanu (Dixon)